THE *BBC'S* GENERAL ELECTION GUIDE

Edited by Richard Bailey

HarperCollins*Publishers*

HarperCollins Publishers
P.O. Box, Glasgow G4 0NB

First published 1997

Reprint 10 9 8 7 6 5 4 3 2 1 0

© 1997 British Broadcasting Corporation

ISBN 0 00 472040 7

A catalogue record for this book is available from the British Library.

Typeset by Davidson Pre-Press, Glasgow

Printed and bound in Great Britain by
Caledonian International Book Manufacturing Ltd, Glasgow G64

PREFACE

In the next few weeks, up to polling day, voters will face a blizzard of persuasive, conflicting rhetoric – party election broadcasts, soundbites, partial newspaper 'stories' – 'facts and figures' through their letterboxes, over the airwaves, on billboards and in person. Through all of this contradiction, prejudice and persuasion, each will have to decide where to place their cross in deciding who should govern Britain.

To these arguments, the BBC's top correspondents bring two key qualities in these individually authored guides to the campaign issues, to the factors which will decide the results and to polling night itself. First and foremost, there is one priority in which all BBC journalists take fierce pride – their impartiality: reading their comments, interpretations and judgements – often strongly stated – viewers and listeners know, or should know, that there is never party favour. Secondly, nowhere else can that impartiality be matched with such a range and depth of specialist knowledge from correspondents who know their subjects well enough to offer an authoritative, trustworthy account of where the parties stand and what is really happening beneath the surface of political activity.

This book has brought together many of the Corporation's best journalists – the people who will be reporting on the progress of the election – in an attempt to steer a course through the blizzard. Reference book, stimulating read, at-a-glance guide, its aim is to be an indispensible companion for the coming campaign.

Richard Bailey
Editor,
Network News
BBC Political Programmes

ACKNOWLEDGEMENTS

Pinning down a couple of dozen of the busiest people in Britain, who are seldom more than an hour from a really pressing deadline, is a monumental task no sane editor would have contemplated. I am grateful to all the contributors, not simply for their work – a considerable burden beyond the call of duty – but also for their patience and goodwill, especially when, after being neglected for long periods they have then been expected to produce expert copy by yesterday.

The task would have been impossible without the calm and persistent efforts of Karen Charnock. From her initial enthusiasm for the project, through the search for the right publisher and on to the painstaking job of pulling together so much material in as ordered a way as was feasible, she has kept everything on the rails. Several authors also donated rather more than their own chapters – Robin Oakley, Bill Bush and Niall Dickson have all been generous with their experience, knowledge and wisdom. But without Huw Edwards it is quite likely the book would barely have been ready for the election after next. His sure political grasp and strong editorial judgement were complemented by unexpected skills on a PC and, despite the many calls on his time, he never complained once at the appalling way I abused his friendship in hours of direst need. Thanks are due too to a number of people who helped to keep the project manageable, particularly Martin Leeburn and Craig Braheny of the BBC's Economics Unit. The three Nicks from the Political Research Unit – Sutton, Toon and Banner – all made invaluable contributions, usually under considerable pressure, as did Nick Robinson. Enormous thanks too, to all those at HarperCollins, especially Elizabeth McLachlan and Edwin Moore, and above all to Christopher Riches, who displayed such consistent patience and confidence dealing with a first timer. Authors and editors traditionally acknowledge the supportive role spouses and children have played through their forbearance ... I now know why and gladly subscribe to the tradition – but gratitude to my wife, Joni Lloyd, goes much further. I trust her journalistic instincts completely – so her fresh eye, sensitive antennae and constant encouragement were priceless, and really appreciated.

Richard Bailey

CONTENTS

FOREWORD
David Dimbleby

David Dimbleby will be presenting the BBC's General Election night programme, as he has since 1979. He joined the BBC as a news reporter and has appeared on network television since 1962. He has presented many programmes including 'Panorama' and '24 Hours' and has written and presented documentaries. In addition he has been a commentator for a wide range of outside broadcast events and has presented many Budget Specials and BBC Election programmes.
Since 1994 he has been Chairman of 'Question Time'. In 1995 he presented the five-part series 'The disunited Kingdom' for Radio 4.

The coming election will promise no miracles. There have been elections in the past where the distinction between the main parties on great issues has led to a change in political direction which has lasted for a generation. 1945 brought the promise of a welfare state offering support from the cradle to the grave. 1979 offered the rolling back of the frontiers of the corporate state and the unleashing of the pent-up energy of capitalism. But this time no party is making grand promises, and it would be ridiculed if it did. The mood of the country is dour. The sobering constraints of struggling for a place in a competitive world have become generally accepted.

We voters do not get much of a say in the way we are governed. Even 70-year-olds at this election will only have had 14 opportunities in their lifetime to change their rulers. And even such power as they have will have been diminished over the years as the influence of Westminster has waned, circumscribed by legislation from Europe, by the power of global currency markets reacting in an instant to changing circumstances, and by an economy subject more than ever before to the vicissitudes of world trade.

Their influence will be further diminished because at this election the two major parties will agree on so much. Both will elevate the control of inflation to be the principle indicator of economic success.

Both will commit themselves to delivering government borrowing at the 3 per cent Maastricht limit without increasing taxation, which means both will be committed to containing government spending rather than expanding it. Both will therefore be cutting back on the scope of the welfare state, cutting back on what many believe to be their entitlement. Neither party will claim that it can provide full employment or jobs for life. Neither believes there is any longer a serious choice to be made between nationalisation and privatisation. The argument is rather about ways of regulating the key monopolies. Not since the days of Butskellism have we seen such political conformity on the key issues facing the country.

But this does not mean the election will be dull. On the contrary, with so much common ground the political territory left to fight over will be contested vigorously, with each party trying to highlight what distinguishes it, hoping to present the voter with a vivid choice. Politicians always campaign as though the issues were matters of life or death, even though privately they may concede that their rhetoric bears little resemblance to reality.

Some issues, such as our relationship with Europe, and arguments over constitutional change, will offer a genuine if somewhat confusing choice. Others will be about style as much as about substance, with 'New Labour' presenting itself as a refreshing change after 18 years of Conservative government.

An election campaign is a drama in which we can all play a part. There is humour and human foible in the intense battle for the voter's ear. After three weeks of interviews and debates, phone-ins and opinion polls, everyone, voters, journalists and politicians, are left in a state of exhausted stupefaction. There will be distractions and irrelevancies, spurious conflicts, ill-judged comments that will be batted backwards and forwards between the parties, misunder- standings, sudden insights and revelations, and many slips of the tongue. And through the fog a sceptical electorate will be gradually making up its mind about which party and which party leader should be offered the key to Number 10 for the next five years.

Election Day, with its 659 separate constituency races, is a fine spectator sport. The outcome is rarely predictable, as even the exit pollsters at last ruefully admit. In the BBC's election studio, we will have rehearsed every likely outcome: the probable, the improbable and some so quirky that they can make the psephologists bridle. In the 1979 rehearsals, one of the team brought the studio to a halt, his sense of outrage spurred on by hubris: 'That result is so absurd that I refuse to waste my time commenting on it.'

Only killjoys go to bed early on election night. Most of us enjoy the
spectacle of victory and defeat, the first recriminations between those
for whom the campaign has gone wrong, and the sight of the victors
swiftly abandoning the hyperbole of their campaign for the more
sober and cautious stance of government. I used to think election
nights were like an archaeological dig: the first few results were the
tops of walls or towers of a great city emerging from the sand, inviting
speculation but requiring more evidence before the truth could be
known. Modern computer technology seems to be speeding the
process up, so that it is now more like the techniques of carbon
dating. But we have not yet reached the point when we can give a
psephologist the first result and he will offer the complete picture.
There is still the ebb and flow of forces on the battleground to be
described, different results coming in from different regions, and
in some places, with luck, duels which will prove decisive.

I hope this book will serve you as a useful and enjoyable guide
to the battles ahead.

POLITICAL LANDMARKS
Political Research Unit

April 1992

9   General election. The Conservatives return to power with a majority of 21.

10   IRA bomb explodes outside the Baltic Exchange killing 3.

11   Cabinet reshuffle – John Patten, Virginia Bottomley, Gillian Shephard, Michael Portillo and Sir Patrick Mayhew enter the cabinet for the first time.

13   Neil Kinnock and Roy Hattersley resign as the Labour leader and deputy.

27   Betty Boothroyd elected as Speaker of the House of Commons.

May 1992

6   The State Opening of Parliament.

7   Local government elections in England (except London), Wales and Scotland. The Conservatives gain 300 seats.

21   The Bill to ratify the Maastricht Treaty is given a second reading in the House of Commons by 336 votes to 92.

July 1992

18   John Smith and Margaret Beckett elected as the Labour leadership team.

September 1992

16   UK withdraws from the ERM after Black Wednesday. Interest rates increase from 10 per cent to 12 per cent. An increase to 15 per cent is later revoked.

24   David Mellor resigns following revelations about his private life

October 1992

13   British Coal announces that 31 pits will close within six months, with the loss of up to 30,000 jobs, including a large number of compulsory redundancies.

November 1992

4   Maastricht 'paving' debate – Government wins by 3 votes.

10   The Prime Minister appoints Lord Justice Scott to investigate allegations that ministers lied about government policy on arms exports to Iraq.

March 1993

16   The Budget. Norman Lamont announces the introduction of VAT on fuel.

April 1993

1   Queen starts paying tax. Council tax comes into effect.

May 1993

6   Newbury by-election. Liberal Democrat win from Conservatives with a swing of 28.4 per cent.
County council elections – the Conservatives lose control of 15 counties.

27   Cabinet reshuffle. Norman Lamont is replaced by Kenneth Clarke as Chancellor, Michael Howard is moved to the Home Office, and John Redwood joins as Secretary of State for Wales.

June 1993

9   In his resignation speech to the House of Commons, the former Chancellor Norman Lamont, accuses the government of giving the 'impression of being in office but not in power'.

July 1993

23   The government wins a confidence vote after its defeat on Maastricht 24 hours earlier.

25   John Major reported to have described some of his cabinet as 'bastards'.

29   Christchurch by-election – Liberal Democrat gain from Conservatives with a record victory.

August 1993

2   The UK ratifies the Maastricht Treaty.

September 1993
27   Labour party approves the one member, one vote system for electing prospective parliamentary candidates, at the party conference.

October 1993
5   John Major launches 'Back to Basics'.

23   IRA kill 9 in a bomb blast in Belfast.

November 1993
30   First unified Budget, including two-stage VAT on fuel.

May 1994
5   Local government elections – large number of government losses.

12   John Smith dies after a heart attack.

June 1994
9   Government loses 14 seats in the European elections, winning less than 28 per cent of the vote.
Liberal Democrats win Eastleigh by-election, and Labour hold onto the safe seats of Bradford South, Newham North East, Dagenham and Barking.

July 1994
20   John Major reshuffles his cabinet with Jeremy Hanley becoming the new Chairman.

21   Tony Blair and John Prescott elected as Labour leader and deputy.

August 1994
31   IRA announces complete cessation of military operations.

October 1994
4   Tony Blair announces his plans to update Clause IV of the Labour Party constitution.

25   Corporate Affairs Minister, Neil Hamilton, resigns following allegations about his links with Mohammed Al Fayed.

November 1994
3   The government forced to abandon Post Office privatisation plans after failing to get support from its own back-benchers.

27 Sir James Goldsmith announces his intention to establish the Referendum party.

29 Government withdraws party whip from eight Euro-rebels. Sir Richard Body resigns the whip in protest.

December 1994

6 Government loses vote on increasing VAT on fuel from 8 per cent to 17.5 per cent.

9 First talks between government officials and Sinn Fein at Stormont in 20 years.

15 Labour gains Dudley West from the Conservatives in a by-election.

April 1995

20 Commons votes to suspend Graham Riddick and David Tredinnick from the House following *The Sunday Times* 'Cash for Questions' investigation.

25 Eight of the nine whipless Tory rebels agree to rejoin parliamentary party.

29 Labour party votes for Clause IV reform at special conference.

May 1995

4 Local government elections (England and Wales). Conservatives lose over 2,000 seats (almost half of their councillors).

24 The former prime minister, Lord Wilson of Rievaulx, dies.

25 SNP gain the Perth and Kinross seat from the Conservatives.

26 Liberal Democrats release a position document dropping 'equidistance'. They will not support the Conservatives in the event of a hung parliament, but promise 'no let up on Labour'.

28 Lady Thatcher praises Tony Blair, describing him as Labour's best leader since Hugh Gaitskill.

June 1995

12 Lady Thatcher criticises government policy urging the Prime Minister to 'return to Conservative policies' – particularly on taxation, Europe and home ownership.

15 North Down by-election is won by UK Unionist party from the Ulster Populist Unionist party.

22   John Major resigns as leader of the Conservative party.

26   John Redwood resigns from the cabinet to stand against
       John Major.

July 1995
4   John Major wins the Conservative party leadership ballot
       with 218 votes, against 89 for Redwood; 12 papers were spoilt,
       8 MPs abstained and 2 did not vote.

5   Cabinet reshuffle. Michael Heseltine is made deputy PM,
       and Malcolm Rifkind moves to Foreign Office.

27   Liberal Democrat, Chris Davies, wins the Littleborough and
       Saddleworth by-election after a bitter fight with Labour.

October 1995
7   Conservative MP Alan Howarth defects to Labour.

December 1995
29   Emma Nicholson defects to Liberal Democrats.

January 1996
8   Labour's 'all-women' shortlists are branded illegal by an
       industrial tribunal.

17   Sir Richard Body MP provisionally takes back the Conservative
       whip.

19   Harriet Harman discloses that she sends her child to a selective
       grant-maintained school.

February 1996
9   IRA bomb in London Docklands kills two and marks the end
       of the ceasefire.

22   Peter Thurnham resigns the Conservative party whip.

March 1996
11   Referendum party advertisements published setting out their
       political position.

13   Dunblane primary school massacre.

20   BSE crisis begins, with the government admitting for the first
       time that there may be a link between BSE in cows and

Creutzfeld-Jakob disease in humans. Douglas Hogg says: 'We believe beef can be eaten with confidence.'

April 1996
11   Labour wins the Staffordshire South East by-election with a 22 per cent swing from the Conservatives.

May 1996
1   Arthur Scargill launches new Socialist party.

2   Conservatives lose 578 council seats in the local elections in England.

14   Conservatives launch a major poster campaign – 'Yes it hurt. Yes it worked.'

June 1996
10   Northern Ireland talks begin. Sinn Fein not allowed into the talks.

14   Lady Thatcher donates money to Bill Cash and his European Foundation.

15   IRA bomb explodes in Manchester.

21   First day of Florence summit sees government secure a beef deal.

27   Labour announces its plans to hold referendums on devolution in Wales and Scotland.

July 1996
2   Conservatives begin 'New Labour, New Danger' campaign.

4   Labour launches Road to Manifesto document.

10   MPs vote to increase their pay by 26 per cent.

22   Treasury Minister David Heathcoat-Amory resigns to fight against EMU.

24   Final pre-election Shadow Cabinet elections (brought forward from autumn).

August 1996
9   Tories launch poster showing Tony Blair with 'demonic eyes'.

October 1996

12   Peter Thurnham MP joins the Liberal Democrats.

November 1996

12   European Court of Justice rules UK must implement Working Time Directive.

26   Kenneth Clarke cuts the basic rate of tax by a penny in the final budget before the election.

December 1996

2   Conservative MP Sir Nicholas Scott loses vote of confidence in his constituency and is deselected as election candidate.

11   David Willetts resigns as Paymaster General after being criticised for 'dissembling' by the Standards and Privileges Committee.

12   Barnsley East by-election wipes out Conservative overall majority.

January 1997

5   John Major appears on *Breakfast With Frost;* attacks Lib-Lab talks on constitution.

7   Tony Blair interview in *Big Issue* promoting 'zero tolerance' of petty crime.

12   Tony Blair appears on *Breakfast With Frost*; says he is not persuaded of the need to change to a proportional voting system.

16   Conservative MP Iain Mills found dead. Government slips into minority.

20   Labour announces it will not raise income tax rates and will stick to Conservative public spending pledges.

30   Sir George Gardiner deselected as Conservative candidate for Reigate.

February 1997

5   Militant Labour relaunches as the Socialist Party.

6   The anti-abortion Pro-Life Alliance Party launches its manifesto for the General Election.

17   House of Commons debates a censure motion against the Government for its handling of the BSE crisis.

20   Liberal Democrats launch their pre-election manifesto,
      Priorities for Britain – Making the Difference.

27   Conservatives lose Wirral South by-election with swing of
      17% from Conservative to Labour.

March 1997

5   The report of the Labour and Liberal Democrat Joint
      Consultative Committee on Constitutional Reform is published.
      The Government announced 'Basic Pensions Plus' calling for the
      abolition of SERPS and reform of the state pension.

8   The defection of the Conservative MP, Sir George Gardiner, to
      the Referendum Party announced.

15   John Major, at his party's Central Council meeting in Bath
      launches the campaign slogan 'You can only be sure with the
      Conservatives'.

17   John Major declares Election Day will be May 1st.

PICKING A
PRIME MINISTER

JOHN MAJOR

Robin Oakley

*Robin Oakley is Political Editor for BBC News.
He joined the* Liverpool Daily Post and Echo *in
1964 and in 1967 became political correspondent.
He has been a lobby correspondent ever since, moving
to Fleet Street in 1970, working on the* Sunday
Express, Now! *magazine, the* Daily Mail *and,
from 1986 to 1992, as Political Editor of* The Times.
*During this time he contributed to many TV and
radio programmes and was a regular presenter of
Radio 4's 'The Week in Westminster'. He succeeded
John Cole as the BBC's Political Editor in October 1992.*

Few have had bumpier rides on the roller coaster of politics than
John Major. On 9 April 1992, Mr Major, already the youngest prime
minister this century, led the Conservative party to victory with
14.1 million votes, the highest total ever recorded for one party at a
British general election. Within two years, he and the Conservatives
were measured by opinion pollsters as the most unpopular prime
minister and party since polling began. No Conservative prime
minister has been so reviled by the so-called 'Tory Press' and
Mr Major has been subjected to constant sniping from within his
own party, most notably by right wing Eurosceptics. The combination
several times seemed likely to bring about his imminent downfall.
When he won the leadership in 1990, some fashionable commentators
predicted he would be no more than an 'interlude' in British politics.
And yet he goes into this election having spent longer as prime
minister than anyone this century except Herbert Asquith,
Harold Wilson and Margaret Thatcher.

Few prime ministers have made the job less glamorous. John Major
has taken no obvious pleasure in the trappings of power. The man
who opened his first cabinet after he won the contest to succeed
Mrs Thatcher with the exclamation 'Well, who would have thought it'

and who bade the nation 'God Bless' at the end of his famous Gulf War broadcast has delighted in the ordinariness of his Brixton background and his Middle England tastes for warm beer, village cricket and 'Happy Eater' fry-ups. In an age of processed politics he has resolutely resisted attempts to graft on charisma or to coach him in image-making, while remaining painfully sensitive at times to his treatment by the media.

He has not been the kind of party leader or prime minister who 'makes the weather', nor one who inspires with the music of words or who triumphs by sheer force of personality. As was shown when MPs contemptuously rejected his call to settle for a 3 per cent pay rise rather than taking the 26 per cent recommended by the Senior Salaries Review Board, few in his party have feared this prime minister.

Critics insist that he has also lacked what his American ally, George Bush, called 'the vision thing'. Indeed, he made a Tory conference speech celebrating his lack of it. His essentially pragmatic approach has offered no 'Big Idea', no definable 'Majorism' to follow 'Thatcherism'. And yet he has, after a fashion, kept together a party which has been riven from the moment he took over on the greatest political issue of the day: Europe. He made significant progress on the most intractable political issue of our times: Northern Ireland. He has won many of the battles he has taken on, if only on points. And he has eventually presided over an economic recovery which offers the winner of this election the prospect of a significant period of sustainable, export-led growth accompanied by the low inflation which has been John Major's political Holy Grail. If there is one quality which explains this, say his friends and colleagues, it is sheer political doggedness.

THE THATCHER FACTOR

From the start of his party leadership, when he succeeded Margaret Thatcher in the autumn of 1990, John Major's premiership has been haunted by her legacy. When she gave him her backing as the candidate most likely to beat Michael Heseltine, many of the party's Thatcherites, forgetting that he had been a member of the 'Blue Chip' dining group along with Chris Patten, Ian Lang and William Waldegrave, assumed they would get a 'Thatcher Mark II' by voting for him. When he emerged in his own light as a more middle-of-the-road Conservative determined to keep Britain, as he soon put it 'at the heart of Europe', they and their vociferous supporters in

Fleet Street made no secret of their disappointment. His predecessor herself, first in private gatherings, then in her published memoirs, and finally in interviews and speeches, became steadily more critical of his conduct, especially on Europe, taxation and housing, eventually accusing him of failing the middle classes.

When Mr Major emerged victorious from the 1992 election, which many Tories believed they could not have won under Mrs Thatcher, it was with a majority of only 21, compared to the majorities she had enjoyed of 44, 144 and 101. A party which had become steadily more ideological under her vigorous leadership then proved hard to handle. The old Tory pragmatism, concerned chiefly with the getting and holding of power, had given way to a more issue-based 'conviction' politics which had diminished the coherence of the party, especially on the dominant issue of Europe.

The rebellions over Maastricht bred new group loyalties and demonstrated the power of determined minorities, but Mr Major seemed uncertain of the best tactics for handling this phenomenon. He acknowledged there would be a need to tack and weave and compromise to keep the party and its programme intact, a course which offered little chance of appearing heroic. But sometimes he chose to indulge in bouts of macho leadership too. One example was when he gambled on a Maastricht 'paving' debate in November 1992 and survived by only 3 votes. Another was when he withdrew the party whip from eight rebels who failed to support the government in what he had made a confidence vote on European Union finances in November 1994, a move which served only to advertise the party's divisions and which ended in ignominy: they were readmitted to the party some months later without any assurances as to their future conduct. And he was similarly forced to climb down and concede a debate on the single currency last December after vowing it would not happen.

On Europe, it can certainly be argued that Mr Major, a pragmatic rather than a romantic European, has steadily been forced to adopt more 'sceptical' views as his majority has declined and as the Tory party's centre of gravity has shifted in that direction.

His adoption of a policy of non co-operation with Europe over the ban on British beef in the BSE crisis signalled both his own deep frustration with the way in which he believed European partners were 'playing politics' with the issue and his growing readiness as an election approached to play the Eurosceptic card in the hope of wrong-footing Labour, a tactic which misfired as polls showed the public blaming the government rather than Europe for mishandling the issue. On the single European currency he was forced to stick with a 'wait and see' policy for fear of provoking his chancellor's resignation.

But it has not been all retreat. Mr Major can claim in some areas to have proved a better Thatcherite than his predecessor, tackling privatisations like British Rail and the nuclear industry which she had ducked, and proving more consistent to market principles by allowing his chancellors to cut back on mortgage tax relief. His government too has done more to trim Welfare State spending. But in general, the man who talked on becoming premier of creating a 'nation at ease with itself' has acted more in the 'One Nation' tradition of Conservatism. His tensions, both within the cabinet and within the party, have been more with the Right, notably with the cabinet Eurosceptics whom he described famously in an off-camera leak as 'bastards'.

His style of running what initially became known as a 'cabinet of chums' has been less autocratic than hers. There has been more discussion and debate at the top, although cabinet colleagues say that Mr Major, who had no lengthy cabinet experience before becoming prime minister, has 'learned on the job' and become more dominant. But because his has been a pragmatic approach, he has always in times of trouble lacked the strength of a Praetorian Guard of true believers around him, prepared to die in the last political ditch for their shared convictions. It was this style which enabled his former chancellor, Norman Lamont to say woundingly in his resignation speech to the Commons that the government gave the appearance of being 'in office but not in power'.

Mr Major's strengths also contrast with those of his predecessor. He has proved a highly effective conciliator and negotiator. For all his party's later traumas over Europe, the Maastricht negotiations were seen at the time as a triumph for the Prime Minister. He won concessions, like the Social Chapter opt-out, which others had simply not believed possible, thanks to his readiness to master complicated briefs better than some of his fellow European heads of government, and to what colleagues call his 'ability to say no without giving offence'. The same qualities enabled him to overcome one setback after another in the slow and painful search for a peaceful political settlement in Northern Ireland, although the prize of a lasting peace has eluded him.

LEADER OR MANAGER?

Despite the bank manager's manner, John Major has always been prepared to gamble on his own instincts, and to fight. His roughing-up by Socialist Workers' party supporters in Bolton at the last election led him to bring out his soap box, Brixton market style. His sophisticated handlers were alarmed, but the public warmed to such a demonstration of his political street-fighting qualities. In the same contest, he amazed commentators by choosing off his own bat to make devolution and constitutional reform a central issue. But instead of benefiting the Nationalists and Liberal Democrats as they had predicted, it wrong-footed Neil Kinnock and gained the Tories seats in Scotland.

At times in the 1994 European Parliament elections, John Major seemed to be the only senior Tory involved in the contest at all. When in the 1992 General Election aides brought him opinion polls with bad news, he would scarcely look up from his papers before remarking that it would make victory all the sweeter when it came. And the sheer resilience of a man who saw his government's whole economic strategy wiped out by the humiliating exit from the Exchange Rate Mechanism of the European Monetary System in September 1992 should not be underestimated. After all, he, as Chancellor, had persuaded Mrs Thatcher to enter the ERM. And if Mr Major's old idea of the 'hard ecu' nowadays looks to have been a wise contribution to the single currency debate it is also a measure of his and his chancellor's misjudgement then that only weeks before the ERM debacle which destroyed confidence in Tory economic competence, Mr Major had been suggesting that sterling could become an even harder European currency than the deutschmark.

His boldest and most significant gamble of all came when he resigned his party leadership in a challenge to the party snipers in June 1995. Although his cabinet colleague, John Redwood, unexpectedly entered the contest Mr Major emerged victorious by 218 votes to his challenger's 89. Characteristically, it was a sufficient victory rather than a glorious one, and friends as well as critics have accused him of failing to exploit it effectively. Management of a splintering party and coping with crisis have so dominated John Major's time in Downing Street that he has sometimes seemed to make less than effective use of such patches of clear water as he has enjoyed.

Typical of such crisis management have been the Nolan committee inquiry into standards in public life and the Scott inquiry into whether the government had connived in the evasion of its own guidelines on arms sales to Iraq. Opposition critics say that both were classic examples of time-buying by a hard-pressed government reeling under the ever-mounting accusations of 'sleaze'. The Prime Minister insists vehemently that he embarked upon both in a simple desire to get at

the truth and to ensure that proper standards were maintained.
But the cabinet appeared ill-prepared to cope with Nolan when the
report was published, and the conclusions alienated large numbers
of Tory MPs while the Scott Inquiry saw at least two ministerial
careers hang in the balance, to the government's prolonged and
evident discomfort.

Mr Major is accused of lacking ruthlessness. His attempts to
maintain David Mellor and others in office after Fleet Street had
wounded them beyond saving, and his public remarks about Chris
Patten after the Governor of Hong Kong intimated that he might be
willing to return to British politics in 1997, were typical of a man who
remains truer than most to his personal friends. But he paid a political
price each time for his lack of detachment. As a leader he has not
always been consistent. Thus, in March 1994 he was declaring in the
starkest terms that Britain would not weaken on any extension of
qualified majority voting in Europe as new partners entered. In the
event, there was an abject climbdown which saw Mr Major at his
lowest ebb with Tory MPs amid open talk of a leadership challenge.
But then came Mr Major's sterling effort in the European Parliament
elections, and his vetoing of Jean-Luc Dehaene as the European
Commission president, the start of a new period of progressive
Euroscepticism.

John Major has survived partly because he has read the changing
mood of his party, partly because he has genuine admirers of his
integrity and straight-dealing style, and partly because he has always
been what one of his ministers called 'the least worst option' as leader.
Any of the alternatives whenever his leadership has been under threat
– Michael Heseltine, Michael Portillo, Kenneth Clarke, John Redwood
– have been perceived by many MPs as people who would inevitably
split the party further. But the penalty that he has paid for being a
reconciler and bridge-builder, a 'split the difference' lowest common
denominator man, is to be dismissed as a politician without
a vision or a grand strategy.

The Citizen's Charter, instead of being seen as a reaffirmation of
quality public services, has led him to be mocked as a 'traffic cones'
prime minister. His 'Back to Basics' programme was designed as a
return to higher school standards, better law and order measures and
commonsense economics. Seized upon by the Right as a way of
hooking the party into moral majoritarianism, it became instead a
hunting licence for Fleet Street to probe the lives of Tory politicians.

John Major has proved an effective performer at Question Time,
the twice-weekly ordeal for Britain's political leaders. He has shown

political skills in extricating his party from the nightmare of the poll tax, in winning the last election against the odds, in the Northern Ireland peace process and as a practised and effective summiteer at European Councils, G7s and the like. Less hog-tied by his party, he would probably prove a very effective Continental-style politician, scratching backs, winning concessions and cutting deals in a way his predecessor's absolutist approach did not permit. But as he has watched a small majority chipped away to a minority, he has been a prisoner of events and prey to determined minorities within his own ranks. Tony Blair's stinging assertion one Parliamentary Question Time that 'I lead my party, he follows his' is not demonstrable on all subjects. But political realities have ensured that it was near enough the mark to hurt.

Ironically, it is John Major himself, despite the way his own party has treated him, who may yet prove to be the Tories' most significant asset in this election. His lack of artifice helped him to remain comparatively untainted by the 'sleaze factor' haze which has clung around his government. He has consistently polled ahead of his party. And while he may have been criticised for his mistakes he has never engendered the degree of personal hostility which accompanied his predecessor's more glamorous style. Few actively dislike John Major.

In its more forgiving moments the tabloid press has called him 'the Comeback Kid'. He now faces the task of making the biggest political comeback of them all.

TONY BLAIR
Jon Sopel

*Jon Sopel is a Political Correspondent for BBC
News. He was a freelance writer and broadcaster
before joining the BBC as a reporter and producer
on Radio Solent. He moved to Radio 4 as a
reporter for the 'World at One' before becoming
Political Correspondent and a regular presenter
of 'PM'. His biography* Tony Blair – the
Modernizer, *was published in 1995.*

When Tony Blair rose to make his first speech as Labour party leader
in Blackpool in 1994, he did so against a strangely coloured pistachio
backdrop (no hint of red to be seen), with the slogan *New Labour,
New Britain*. In politics slogans come and go with such regularity
– and even monotony – that they pass through the mind of even the
most avid student of domestic politics with barely a subliminal glance.
But Blair and those around him had ambitions for the phrase 'New
Labour'. The new leader of only a few months' standing wanted to
give the impression that he had a new party too. His acolytes would
ceaselessly refer to 'New Labour' as though anything that went before
was of a different era. Mr Blair was petitioning for divorce from what
had gone before.

Repackaging old goods with a shiny new wrapper is the oldest trick
in marketing – and politics, and Tony Blair recognised that 'New
Labour' would need substance as well as gloss. In the course of that
first speech as leader, full of exhortation and ringing phrases, came
a curious passage. It read:

> *It is time we had a clear up-to-date statement of the objects and
> objectives of our party. John Prescott and I, as Leader and Deputy
> Leader will propose such a statement to the NEC ... And if it is accepted*

*then let it become the objects of our Party for the next election and take
its place in our constitution for the next century.*

Although not everyone twigged immediately what he meant, it soon
became clear. Mr Blair wanted to rip up Labour's most sacred article
of faith – Clause IV, Part 4 of the Labour constitution – and start over
again. At the time, many older, wiser heads were saying it was a
reckless gamble; an unnecessary distraction, they argued, from
Labour's main job of fighting the Conservatives. These were people
who remembered what happened to Hugh Gaitskell, the last person
who tried to rewrite Clause IV, 35 years earlier. His efforts to move
Labour away from its traditional commitment to nationalisation – or
as the 1917 formulation put it:

*to secure for the workers by hand or by brain the full fruits of their
industry and the most equitable distribution thereof that may be
possible upon the basis of the common ownership of the means of
production, distribution and exchange*

– ended in humiliation. And such was the scale of his defeat that
no other Labour leader had thought it worth the inevitable fight.

Tony Blair had come to see Clause IV as a millstone. Out of date,
but never out of fashion for the activists, it was used by them as a
benchmark against which any betrayal by a Labour government could
be measured. Since no Labour administration after Attlee's post-war
government thought that nationalisation was a panacea, there was
an awful lot of betrayal for the Left to find. More than that though,
Clause IV was a propaganda weapon beyond price for the
Conservatives. They were able to ridicule all suggestions that Labour
had become a modern political party with a faith in the market
economy while it was still wedded to massive state ownership.

Two days after Mr Blair's first conference speech, the same
delegates who had cheered him to the rafters, showed that 'old'
Labour was alive and well. The conference voted to retain Labour's
commitment to public ownership. If Blair was to secure support for
a new clause, he would have to appeal over the heads of the activists
to ordinary members. When Tony Blair was elected leader, and John
Prescott his deputy earlier that year, the two men promised to mount
a membership drive to reverse what had been a long, steady and –
apparently – irreversible decline. Within a year Labour had recruited
an extra 100,000 members: these were the people to whom Blair
would turn for support for his new clause.

THE NEW CONSTITUTION

In all but one of the constituencies where ordinary members were balloted on the new clause, it was passed. The new statement of aims and values was passed easily when it was put before a special one-day Labour conference at the end of April, 1995. In terms of what it said, the antecedents of the new clause could be traced back to a communitarian Christianity that Mr Blair had discovered when he was an Oxford undergraduate. Just as the new clause discussed rights, it spoke too of responsibility. Individuals would only be able to achieve their potential when they worked through their communities. On the economy, resonant phrases about state ownership were gone, and instead the emphasis was on 'the enterprise of the market', where the 'rigours of competition are joined with the forces of partnership and co-operation.' To achieve these objectives it was made clear that the unions – the organisations that had given birth to the Labour party as their political wing – would have no special place over traditional enemies like employers' groups.

Whatever the shortcomings of the new clause in terms of its lack of poetry or fiery rhetoric, Tony Blair was anxious that it should set Labour an ideological 'compass', a direction in which the party should travel. He took as his model what Margaret Thatcher achieved for the Conservatives prior to the 1979 general election. Her enticing, populist themes under the general heading of rolling back the frontier of the state, had three main policy ambitions: curbing the power of the unions, cutting direct taxation and allowing tenants to buy their council houses. This clear ideological agenda would later become known as Thatcherism. Indeed Mr Blair likes to think that what he is offering via 'New Labour' is the intellectual successor to Thatcherism, believing that whatever John Major had intended, his policies lacked any ideological coherence. But where Mrs Thatcher was radical in her policy ambitions, Mr Blair – although he would dispute this vigorously – has been extremely cautious. And where Mrs Thatcher was tentative in her dealings with her party – it would be some time before she would purge the 'wets' from her cabinet – Mr Blair has been fearless, almost cavalier, in the way he has handled the Labour party.

PARTY MANAGEMENT

The campaign to rewrite Clause IV had taught Tony Blair a way of reaching out beyond the entrenched power bases within the party the constituency activists and the union barons. He would deploy the same tactics a year later when it came to framing Labour's election manifesto. By promising to consult the membership over what should go in the manifesto, Mr Blair was effectively rendering meaningless any policies passed by the party conference whose motions – if passed by a sufficient majority – are supposed to form the basis of the party's election platform.

In matters of party management, Tony Blair showed himself to be ruthless. 'New Labour' would be marked by discipline. The same self-belief about what Labour needed to do to make itself electable again that had propelled Mr Blair to the leadership, transferred into an almost authoritarian style of leadership. Power was concentrated around the leader's office. The National Executive was peripheral, the party headquarters at Walworth Road became a servant to Blair's office, the shadow cabinet was held on a tight rein, and even the Parliamentary Labour party was cowed. After 17 years of unbroken opposition, dissent, when it surfaced, found only a muffled voice.

There were some notable exceptions to this which some saw as a portent of the stresses and strains that might come if Labour were to win power. The first was when it was disclosed that the Blairs were sending their eldest son to an 'opted-out', grant-maintained school, the Oratory. What was interesting about this episode was that the most violent reactions came neither from the Conservative party nor what is commonly described as the Tory press – they were rather muted. It was the membership of the Labour party itself that was seething. For years it had been Labour policy to campaign against schools moving out of local authority control, believing that the government was using grant-maintained status as a Trojan Horse for reintroducing selection at the age of 11. A significant proportion of Labour members are either teachers, lecturers, students or school governors, and they were incredulous that the party leader had chosen such a school. The Blairs, in mitigation, were able to point out that the Oratory did not operate by selection, it was still a comprehensive school, and perhaps most important (at least for the Blairs themselves) it was a Catholic school. Tony Blair is a devout church-going high Anglican; his wife Cherie a Catholic, with the children brought up as practising Catholics.

On the second occasion when the party bared its 'old' Labour teeth, there were no such mitigating circumstances. Harriet Harman – seen by the party at large as a Blairite – had not only chosen to send her son to an opted-out school, but to a grammar school where entrance was determined by examination. It seemed to make a mockery of David Blunkett's speech to the party conference a year earlier when he stated in absolute terms Labour's opposition to selectivity by examination.

This time there was no reticence from either the press or the Tory party. It was Blair's worst period as party leader. The Conservatives were at last on the attack, and John Major worsted Tony Blair in a series of bruising encounters at Prime Minister's Questions. Even if these twice weekly exchanges are of limited importance to the wider public, they had the important psychological effect of making the Conservatives at Westminster believe firstly, that Blair was not invincible, and secondly that they were back in the fight. Tony Blair's 'New Labour' said one thing, but did another, was the repeated rejoinder from Conservatives, reinvigorated by the Harman affair.

ERADICATING THE NEGATIVES

In polling terms, the damage caused was short term. But it did seem to mark a change in attitude towards Tony Blair and his party. The questions asked of what a Blair-led government would do in power became more searching. To put it another way: while detractors and supporters knew what Blair meant by 'New Labour', there was ambiguity about what his 'New Britain' would look like.

Labour's traditional problem has not been a lack of policy, but a veritable surfeit of it. But on the grittiest questions of detail there was a haziness. Shadow cabinet members not wedded entirely to Mr Blair's project to modernise the party complained bitterly in private of 'policy paralysis' and stifling caution. Before Mr Blair became party leader, he warned the then leadership of the late John Smith that simply hoping that the Conservatives would self-destruct and that Labour would win a general election by default was complacent.

But Tony Blair's dilemma has been that while he wants to set a firm intellectual route and enthuse people with his vision of Britain in the next millennium, the very voters he most needs to attract to win power are conservative with a small 'c', cautious, and those who still harbour doubts about what a Labour government would do. They are the aspirant middle classes Mrs Thatcher so effectively won over with her brand of popular capitalism. Much energy has been expended by senior Labour politicians in the run up to the election telling this group that their taxes would not rise under Labour; there would be no return to the tax and spend policies of previous years; there would be no re-nationalisation of the privatised utilities like gas and water; Labour would not reverse the Tories' firm trade union laws, nor would they overturn all sorts of other reforms introduced by successive Conservative governments. Indeed it became a common criticism that while everyone was very clear about what a Labour government would *not* do, it was far more difficult to discern the distinctive agenda which would guide Labour in government. In essence, how was Tony Blair to appear both reassuring and radical, surely two mutually exclusive ambitions?

STAKEHOLDING

At the beginning of 1996, Tony Blair flew to the Far East to visit Tokyo and Singapore. The keynote speech was to have been in Japan to their equivalent of the CBI, but it was during an address to businessmen in Singapore that Blair tried to square the circle of being both bold and reassuring. He spoke of a new kind of politics, and a new kind of economics; his vision was of a 'stakeholder society'. At the time, Tony Blair and his aides said they had found the unifying theme that would give policies a guiding principle. The principle was one that was easy to articulate: the route to economic success rested in giving everyone a 'stake' in the enterprise for which they worked. And expressed in those simple terms it could be applied to more or less anything at all. The goal of policy-making must be to include. Everyone must have opportunity, no one should be excluded. It required partnership: partnership between the public sector and private; between government and industry; between worker and individual.

Some argued this was no more than a return to the 'corporatism' of the 1960s and 1970s, but that was decisively rejected. In Peter Mandelson and Roger Liddle's book *The Blair Revolution* (Mandelson, the Labour MP for Hartlepool, is one of Tony Blair's most trusted confidantes), it is argued that 'stakeholding' is following the egalitarian model of the companies of the Far East, and will not herald a return to old-style union power.

The Singapore speech contained nothing new in terms of policy pledges, and that again brought criticism from commentators that stakeholding was long on aspiration, but short on detail. To counter this, soon after Tony Blair returned from the Far East, he announced that he and his front-bench colleagues would start to sketch out a manifesto for government. The 'Road to the Manifesto' project would then be voted upon by the entire membership. Although they would be asked to endorse the package, there would be no question of them amending it, inserting their own favourite policy, deleting this or that. It was take it or leave it, and with the election just over the horizon, there was little or no chance of the latter happening. This was top-down democracy.

ROAD TO THE MANIFESTO

In July 1996 the draft manifesto was launched, under the slogan 'New Labour, New Life for Britain'. The negatives of what Labour would not do in government were again out in force: no scrapping of grammar schools, no running down of the armed forces, no stifling of industry with controls and regulations, etc. But at the end of the 10,000 word document, there were five specific pledges of what a Blair government would do:

- First, cut class sizes to 30 or under for 5, 6 and 7 year olds. This would be achieved by scrapping a scheme which the Tories had introduced of allowing some of the brightest children from poor homes to go into private education.

- Second, introduce fast-track punishment for persistent young offenders by halving the time from arrest to sentencing.

- Third, cut NHS waiting lists by treating an extra 100,000 patients through cutting down on the cost of managing the health service.

- Fourth, take 250,000 young people off benefit and into work by using money from a windfall tax on the privatised utilities.

- Fifth, to set tough rules for government spending and borrowing so that interest rates are as low as possible.

- A sixth pledge was later added, to legislate for a Scottish parliament and a Welsh assembly in the first year of government by holding a referendum on devolution and campaigning for a 'yes' vote.

This of course is a draft manifesto, not the real thing, but as a guide to where Tony Blair is setting Labour's sights, there is likely to be little deviation. Journalists who questioned Mr Blair about its contents persisted with the line that this was hardly a radical bill of fare, and certainly had precious little to do with socialism as understood by many in his party. But the Labour leader was insistent that what the manifesto offered was a new route map for Britain, a new kind of politics that was neither 'Old Labour', nor 'New Right'.

By polling day, Labour will have been out of office for 18 years. There is no doubt that Tony Blair has created something called 'New Labour' – even the Conservatives now recognise that Labour has changed, although they stress there are new dangers as well: whether it be on Labour's devolution plans, or Britain's relations with Europe, the focus of the Tory attack is that just because Labour has changed does not mean it is any more acceptable. It is certainly a more coherent line of attack than many which the Tories have mounted. The 'newness' which Labour strategists hope will be one of the party's biggest selling points, the Tories want to turn into a source of unease and fear for voters.

But for all the talk of 'New Labour, New Danger', perhaps the greatest challenge for Blair is to persuade voters that his 'New Labour' is offering a new kind of politics as well. He has set a broad macro-economic framework which is not very different from that of the Conservatives. It is unapologetically in support of free trade, free markets and fiscal and monetary stability. Labour has not fought an election in the last thirty years without finding itself in a tangle over tax and spending. It is the single issue that Blair has spent most time agonising over. It is the area where Tories have always brilliantly exploited Labour vacillation. The results of the Labour leader's agonising became clear at the beginning of 1997 when the Shadow Chancellor, Gordon Brown, stunned politicians by announcing that Labour would accept the government's spending plans for the first two years of a Labour administration, and would not alter the standard or top rate of tax during the lifetime of the parliament. Labour will campaign hard on the theme 'Time for a change', but the Blair project is all about reassuring voters, and so the advertising copywriters could easily add in small letters underneath 'but not too much, nor too quickly'.

PADDY ASHDOWN

Carolyn Quinn

Carolyn Quinn is a Political Correspondent for BBC News. She started with the BBC in local radio and then moved to BBC Westminster, where she has been a general reporter, Southeast Correspondent and Parliamentary Correspondent before being appointed to her current position in 1994.

Entering this election campaign, Paddy Ashdown faces a dilemma. The drive at the top of his party is for closer co-operation with Labour if Tony Blair wins power – either through coalition or more informal arrangements. The belief is that a Liberal Democrat government is not a realistic prospect, but wielding influence and sharing power is. Many grassroots Liberal Democrats, though, abhor the idea of realignment and continue to view Labour as the enemy. Paddy Ashdown insists he is 'keeping his options open' and has ruled out the prospect of playing 'bridesmaid' to Tony Blair. However, few observers of this election believe that the fate of the Liberal Democrats is not inextricably linked with that of Labour. The question is whether this provides Paddy Ashdown with his big moment or causes untold damage to the party he has weaned so skilfully from its turbulent post-Alliance birth in 1988. No election has been so crucial for him.

In 1988, the Liberal Democrat coffers were virtually empty and morale was at an all-time low. The modern Liberal Democrats are undoubtedly more professional, better strategists and more disciplined. But they know that to have any credibility, they have to build on the 1992 election, and increase their number of MPs. On the new boundaries, they are defending 18 seats. In 1992, they received 18 per cent of the vote. Their minimum hope is to increase the number of their MPs to at least 30 or 35. They know they will not form a government, but their abiding hope is to have at least the force of numbers to be able to influence policy or win a share of power.

RELATIONS WITH LABOUR

During the past year, some Labour and Liberal Democrat politicians have spoken of a realignment in British politics with the aim of creating one Centre-Left alliance, marginalising the Labour Left-wing and shutting the Conservatives out for a generation. In reality, a great many Labour and Liberal Democrat members still need convincing. The bitterness of the campaign in Littleborough and Saddleworth hardened the attitude of Liberal Democrats like Liz Lynne who have remained opposed to closer links with the Labour party. She and her predecessor as MP for Rochdale, Sir Cyril Smith, are among the key agitators in the anti-Labour camp, Sir Cyril being among those calling for a special Liberal Democrat conference after the election to approve or reject any proposed deals with Labour.

In January of this year David Alton, who is standing down as an MP at the election, added his own withering assessment to the debate. In a newspaper article he accused Paddy Ashdown of risking the party's election prospects and independence by encouraging closer links with Labour and holding out for a cabinet seat. He said it was no coincidence that the party's poll ratings had slipped, as talks continued. And he said he feared Paddy Ashdown's judgement had been clouded by his frustration at never being in the centre of power. 'It is time he put the interests of his country and party first and those of personal ambition second.' It is clear, too, that on the Labour front and back-benches, there are numerous politicians who view the Liberal Democrats as insignificant and reject any notion of teaming up with them.

In some Labour quarters there is also unhappiness at the suggestion that, even if he achieved a majority in the Commons, Tony Blair might still want to use the Liberal Democrats as a bulwark against MPs on his own Left wing if he ever felt they were trying to hold him to ransom.

Many grassroots Liberal Democrats feel a coalition would simply destroy the hard work the party has done to build up its identity and establish a clear set of distinct policies – like its belief in Euro-federalism, a hard-hitting environmental policy and its commitment to put a penny on income tax to fund a £2 billion investment in education. They continue to feel that 'New Labour' is still concerned only with getting power at any price. One senior Liberal Democrat MP argues that if they propped up Labour in government and contributed to the legislative programme, they would get none of the credit but all the blame if it went wrong: 'We go down with them', he says. He and many others in the party, particularly at grassroots level, prefer to retain their independence until such time as constitutional reform has been delivered. Then, with PR in place, and no party forming a clear majority, that is the time to form a coalition and seek influence.

Paddy Ashdown continually denies that any formal deal with Labour has been mapped out. And in the run-up to this election there have been moments when the channels of communication have run dry. However, since Ashdown ruled out the prospect of propping up a Conservative government by ditching the policy of 'equidistance' – the concept of staying equally aloof from both Tories and Labour – the question has remained about the price he might exact from Labour for his support. In a speech in January 1995 Ashdown introduced the concept of 'Partnership Politics' – of how to repair the damage of the past 17 years of Conservative rule and restore trust in government. He spoke of a culture in British politics in which 'parties which are different, distinctive and independent, offer separate choices at the ballot box but are prepared to work together where they agree and they believe it is in the nation's interest to do so'. He insisted that he was not talking of pacts or coalitions, but the underlying impression was that he would be prepared to support a Labour government for at least two parliaments. For the Liberal Democrats, the price of support has traditionally been conditional on the delivery of electoral reform, in this case, a commitment by Tony Blair to campaign for a 'yes' vote in his promised referendum on proportional representation.

However, after the four-month long talks on the constitution between the two parties, headed by Robert Maclennan and Robin Cook, the Liberal Democrats do appear to have had to make some pragmatic compromises. They have agreed to the setting up of an advisory commission on voting systems which would report within 12 months on which alternative electoral system for the Commons should be proposed in Labour's promised referendum. But the Labour leader Tony Blair still says he is unpersuaded of the benefits of PR. Many of his senior colleagues agree, and it remains unclear how a Labour cabinet would campaign during the referendum (a date for which, incidentally, is also left hanging in the air). Paddy Ashdown hailed the agreement as 'the foundation stone for a modern system of Government'. But critics say Labour have actually achieved far more from the deal than their 'partners'. Tony Blair has effectively secured the promise of Liberal Democrat support for his constitutional programme – including devolution, House of Lords reform, the introduction of the European Convention on Human Rights into British law and a Freedom of Information act – but has retained his own room for maneouvre on PR.

PROPORTIONAL REPRESENTATION – THE HOLY GRAIL?

Proportional representation provides a glimmer of hope for a party like the Liberal Democrats which traditionally suffers under the first-past-the-post system. They feel they are constantly punished for having a more even spread of support. This means they can come a close second, they can increase their share of the vote and the number of votes, but they cannot increase their number of Parliamentary seats.

The preferred option of the Liberal Democrats is the Single Transferable Vote (STV) system which is based on multi-member constituencies and takes into account voters' second choices. The Labour leader's close ally, Peter Mandelson, has explored the prospect of another form of PR – the Alternative Vote system (AV) (*The Blair Revolution – Can New Labour Deliver?* by Peter Mandelson and Roger Liddle). Many Liberal Democrats view AV as a halfway house which may allow Labour to grab more votes but would do little to improve Liberal Democrat hopes.

Some Liberal Democrats are starting to dissent from the party line, and warn against holding PR up as the Holy Grail. One senior MP said he was concerned that the Liberal Democrats would appear 'obsessive' if they rejected a deal on a plate with a weak Labour government and sacrificed the chance for power because they were blinkered into saying 'PR or nothing'. Officially the Liberal Democrat leadership is insistent that if Labour only gets a small majority – say below 20 – or if there is a hung Parliament, there would be no formal coalition without a Labour commitment to PR. But that does not rule out regular detailed informal talks with, or informal support for, a Blair government during its first years in office, with agreement bit-by-bit on individual pieces of legislation. Some Liberal Democrats hope that if that government remains weak numerically or troubled by Left-wing dissent, this could open the door to greater influence two or three years down the road or even herald cabinet seats for some in the smaller party. Paddy Ashdown denies he is obsessed 'with getting my backside on to the leather seat of a government Daimler', but some anti-coalitionists fear he and other senior members like Menzies Campbell are allowing themselves to become hypnotised by thoughts of ministerial power into compromising their true Liberal Democrat beliefs.

As if to prove he is still his own man, from time to time Paddy Ashdown has lobbed missiles into Labour's camp. At the party's 1996 spring conference in Nottingham he criticised what he called 'new Labour's 'state-sponsored morality' and its desire to reshape Britain in the image of Singapore:

> *It starts with community based projects, residents helping older neighbours, the promotion of social cohesion. But it ends by telling people how to live their lives. By limiting freedom of speech. By spot fines for chewing gum and neglecting to pull the lavatory chain. It ends in policies which punish the sinner, but ignore the sin. Policies which have more to say about driving beggars from the streets than housing the homeless and helping the poor.*

At times Liberal Democrats have claimed to be the only real opposition to the Conservatives: – voting against tax cuts in the last two budgets and stating clearly their intention to buy back Railtrack after privatisation. The truth is that, despite such side-swipes, it will be difficult for the Liberal Democrats to play hard to get or try hard bargaining if, as expected, a new Blair government were to produce a Queen's Speech in favour of devolution, improved education and was comparatively pro-European. Many Liberal Democrats realise their potential powerlessness – that Tony Blair would simply defy them to vote against the Queen's Speech, stand back and watch them squirm.

Despite the continued suspicion between the two camps, Liberal Democrats and Labour have shown they can work together successfully in certain areas, the most recent example being the constitutional talks. Early in 1996, they employed a joint strategy to attack the government over the controversial Scott report on arms to Iraq. Outside Westminster, they work together in 19 local councils with joint administrations, and joined forces on the Scottish Constitutional Convention (though Mr Blair's sudden decision on a referendum on devolution did not involve consultation with Mr Ashdown). Besides all this, there is the ever closer relationship between the two leaders, which is said now to extend to invitations to each other's family homes. The two men apparently have a 'chemistry' between them. The elements seem to be there for a potential working relationship.

CAMPAIGN THEMES

The Liberal Democrats' attractiveness as an alternative home for disgruntled Tory voters has obviously been deeply challenged by the onset of moderate 'New Labour'. Some party members fear that Ashdown's troops will be branded the new Left after Blair's shift to the centre and so frighten off those voters who may have turned to them in the past, simply as a conduit for protest votes. The Liberal democrats deny they are 'Left-wing', but readily accept being labelled 'radical'. Throughout the campaign they will be depicting theirs as a bold and candid party which has demonstrated clarity of thought and honesty in policy presentation. Labour, on the other hand, they will say, are cautious and evasive.

Campaigners will be outlining what they view as their major achievements:

- Liberal Democrats have won four by-elections since 1992 (Newbury, Christchurch, Eastleigh, and Littleborough and Saddleworth) and will fight hard to keep them, though the Conservatives are confident of wresting back Christchurch.

- They have broken through to the European Parliament for the first time, taking two seats, Cornwall and West Plymouth, and Somerset and North Devon in 1994.

- The 1996 local elections sealed their position as the second largest party in local government, having beaten the Conservatives into third place. The Liberal Democrats control 59 councils, and have over 5,000 councillors. Their people on the ground control £13 billion of expenditure. They calculate that this not only proves that Liberal Democrats can take the responsibility for important financial and social decisions, but also helps draw into the party an increasing number of higher-calibre candidates who, for the first time, may see the prospect of real power.

- There was welcome attention for the party with the high-profile defections from the Conservative party of Emma Nicholson and Peter Thurnham and regular rumours about other potential Tory defectors.

TARGETING SEATS

More crucial than ever for the Liberal Democrats will be their targeting policy. They realise that instead of taking solace in their percentage share of the national vote, they need to concentrate on getting as many parliamentary seats as possible. They are focusing hard on 50 key marginals. These include those where the party already holds the seat and those where they came a close second last time. 80 per cent of the top 20 targets are now held by the Tories, who are, in the main, their chief opponents. Liberal Democrats hope to benefit from any tendency in the British electorate to vote tactically to get the Tories out. Both Labour and the Liberal Democrats deny there is any deal between them not to fight a seat too hard when the other has a better chance of squeezing out the Conservative. But the conclusion after the Staffordshire South East by-election in April 1996, where the Liberal Democrats lost their deposit while Labour stormed to victory, was that that was exactly what happened. More covert, informal deals could be employed during the general election. However, another reading of the Staffordshire result is that disillusioned Tories, sensing the presence of a new-style Labour party, jumped straight over the party boundaries to vote for them, rather than stopping off at the Liberal Democrats as the more cautious may have done in the past. If so, that is a worrying trend for Ashdown and his team to contemplate.

The Liberal Democrats traditionally do well in the South and Southwest. Outside this area there is a scattering of targets. Elsewhere expect little or no high profile campaigning.

- In the South and Southwest: Devon, Cornwall, Somerset, Hampshire, Wiltshire, Oxfordshire.

- In the Northwest: Southport; Liverpool Broad Green; Hazel Grove.

- In the Midlands: Birmingham Yardley.

- In Yorkshire: Sheffield Hallam; Harrogate (watch the fight against the former chancellor, Norman Lamont).

- In Scotland: Inverness Nairn and Lochaber.

- In Wales: Conwy; Brecon and Radnor.

Of these targets, Liverpool Broad Green and Birmingham Yardley provide a head-to-head contest with Labour – notably city areas, where Liberal Democrats are improving in council terms but have yet to prove their parliamentary ability. In Oldham East and Saddleworth (formerly Littleborough and Saddleworth) there will also be a clash with Labour after the two parties locked horns in the July 1995 by-election. And in Rochdale, site of many a bitter battle between Labour and Liberal Democrat councillors, Labour will be doing their best to oust the high profile anti-labour MP, Liz Lynne.

LIBERAL DEMOCRATS – THE NEW LEFT?

The Liberal Democrats know they have to tread carefully. They want to sell themselves as a party with relevant policies, more radical on taxation, education and Europe than Labour, but also as a party which is trustworthy, which tells it as it is, the 'what you see is what you get' approach to policy. But in many areas where they have achieved electoral success it has been purely because they are an alternative to Labour or the Conservatives. The fear for some now is that their close association with Labour may impede that source of votes and deter disillusioned Tories from voting for them if they suspect a vote for Ashdown equals a vote for Blair in the long run. Conversely, the other concern is that they may be perceived as being more Left-wing than Labour, particularly on taxation and social policy and thus equally lose votes. Many of the voters they need are opposed to high taxes and are socially authoritarian. Liberal Democrats are in favour of hypothecated (or earmarked) higher taxation and are socially libertarian.

Liberal Democrat success has always been difficult to quantify, since they seem to operate in a permanent conundrum. They are a relatively Left-wing party with a higher profile in areas where voters tend to be more Right-wing. They are strong in the Southwest which has suffered from EU fishing regulations, yet the Liberal Democrats are thoroughly Euro-federalist. Nationally, they are opposed to blood sports, yet in many of the seats they hold or are targeting, hunting and game sports are large employers. In the Newbury by-election, their candidate David Rendel supported the building of a controversial bypass, yet the party nationally credits itself on its 'greenness' and proposes to limit or penalise the use of cars. The fact is that the Liberal Democrats can get away with it because, as a smaller, third party, they are not subject to anything like the scrutiny forced on Labour and the Conservatives. The irony is that their popularity in certain areas could be due to voters simply not knowing or not caring about their national politics.

THE CAMPAIGN STYLE

In 1992, the Liberal Democrat election campaign was a one-man band, centred around their 'action-man' leader. Paddy Ashdown dashed from one end of the country to the other – he even made a trip to

Northern France. Dick Newby, his press officer at the time, now acknowledges that the political message was often sacrificed for the sake of a good photo-opportunity: Paddy Ashdown at a seal sanctuary in Cornwall was one of the highlights. This time, Newby says, there will be regional tours, but fewer photo-stops per day and the politics will be king. There will, of course, be limits on the campaign: while Labour and the Conservatives have between £15 and £20 million to spend, the Liberal Democrats are restricted to around £3 million.

Paddy Ashdown says his party will attract attention and converts because it is the only one which indulges in plain speaking. There will be a fully costed manifesto spelling out bluntly what people will get for their vote and how it will be used. And selling Ashdown's blunt message on the doorstep will be a new, more professional pavement army. No sandals and pullovers this time – like Labour, the Liberal Democrats have recognised the advantage in smartening up. The party's Director of Campaigns, Chris Renard, says the assault on the 50 target seats is being run with military precision and voters will be told not just the benefits of supporting the Liberal Democrat candidate but also about the tactical ramifications of their vote.

'CLEANING UP THE MESS' IN BRITISH POLITICS

A popular theme for Paddy Ashdown since the last election has been the concept of 'cleaning up the mess in British politics'. He speaks in his book, *Beyond Westminster,* about the distrust of politicians expressed by many of the people he met on his weekly travels. As a political pitch it may well be timely – Westminster has been waking up to the idea that its inhabitants have slid so deep into the relegation zone of public esteem that there is some benefit in being perceived as distanced from it. After polling day, that may well prove to be the Liberal Democrats' greatest dilemma – whether really to join the political establishment with all the risks that entails or stick to being one of the 'voices off' – a spur or irritant to a new government. It is a dilemma the Liberal Democrats would be happy to face rather than the alternative: the questions over the party's future, and particularly over the leader himself, would be far greater if the Conservatives were once again in power.

ISSUES WHICH WILL HELP DECIDE THE ELECTION

WEALTH
THE PARTIES' POLICIES

YES IT HURT
TAXING AND SPENDING
Evan Davis

Evan Davis is Economics Correspondent for BBC2's 'Newsnight'. Prior to joining the BBC in 1993, he worked at the Institute for Fiscal Studies and at the London Business School. He is the author of the Penguin Dictionary of Economics *and is writing a book entitled* Public Spending *to be published in 1997.*

A NIGHTMARE ON DOWNING STREET – THE PUBLIC SPENDING STORY

Remember 92? The election campaign was launched with a tax-cutting budget. Norman Lamont, then Chancellor, suggested more would follow. He offered a scenario in which there would be £2 billion of tax cuts, and around now, the government's debt – the PSBR – would be a mere £6 billion!

Within a year of the Conservative election victory, the picture being painted of 1996/97 was rather less attractive. There were tax increases that aimed to raise about an extra £11 billion in 1996/97; the spending plans for 1996/97 were trimmed by £5 billion, and yet the PSBR for 1996/97 was now set to be £34 billion!

By now, it is clear that the underlying state of the public finances has worsened further. Although borrowing is expected to be lower than 34 billion pounds, taxes have gone up and spending plans cut substantially to pay for that.

In effect, the Conservatives made a £56 billion error in their PSBR projection for 1996/97 – an error that was in their favour at the time of the last election and most of which became apparent very soon after it. Dealing with the actual state of the public finances – rather

TABLE 1: GOVERNMENT PROJECTIONS OF 1996/97

	What they said about 1996/97 before the last election	What they said about 1996/97 one year after the last election	What they say about 1996/97 now
Extra revenues to be raised from higher tax rates than there were in 1992	£2 billion of tax cuts	£11 billion of tax increases	£14 billion of tax increases
Cuts in projected spending for 1996/97 from the levels expected in 1992	None	£5 billion of cuts in spending plans	£20 billion of cuts in spending plans
The PSBR projected to occur in 1996/97	£6 billion	£34 billion	£26 billion
Overall deterioration in 1996/97 public finances from 1992 projection	n/a	£46 billion	£56 billion

Source: Author's calculations based on HM Treasury's *Financial Statement* and *Budget Reports*.
Notes: Figures adjusted for actual inflation and government inflation projections. Spending changes based on control total not total general government expenditure.

than the imagined state of them – has dominated much of this government's term of office and promises to dominate much of the election campaign.

In all, then, this year the tax system is set to collect £14 billion more from us than it would have if all the budgets of this Parliament had been neutral. That is the equivalent of £12 or £13 pounds a week for every household in the country. At the same time, spending plans have been trimmed by £20 billion. A nightmare indeed.

THE CASE OF THE MISSING REVENUES

Much of the error was down to mistakes in forecasting the size of the economy. The economy was smaller (in real terms, after taking inflation into account) than Norman Lamont had supposed. If he and Kenneth Clarke had not put tax rates up, tax revenues would have been dismally low – some £42 billion less than expected at the time of the last election. Even after all the tax rises of the current Parliament, tax revenues are still lower than Norman Lamont predicted in 1992. And if discretionary spending plans had not been curtailed, overall spending (on things like unemployment benefits etc.) would have been some £10 billion higher.

TABLE 2: THE BUDGETS OF THE CURRENT PARLIAMENT

Date	Chancellor	Impact on tax revenues in 1996/97	Impact on spending plans for 1996/97	Some key measures announced
March 1993	Norman Lamont	£11 billion extra	£5 billion less	National insurance to 10 per cent. VAT on domestic fuel. MIRAS and the married couples allowance (MCA) restricted
Nov 1993	Kenneth Clarke	£7 billion extra	£3 billion less	Insurance and airline taxes. Further restriction of MIRAS and MCA. Petrol and tobacco tax rises
Nov 1994	Kenneth Clarke	£1 billion less	£9 billion less	VAT implementation defeated; VAT remains at 8 per cent on domestic fuel
Nov 1995	Kenneth Clarke	£3 billion less	£3 billion less	Basic income tax rate to 24p. Savings income taxed at 20p. Income tax allowances raised. Income tax 20p band widening
Nov 1996	Kenneth Clarke	n/a	n/a	Basic income tax rate to 23p. Further steps against tax evasion

But while the length and depth of the recession at the start of the government's period in office created a public finance nightmare, it is not alone responsible for the problem: the deterioration of the financial position is larger than the deterioration of the economy. Only about half the financial mess can be attributed to the disappointing performance of the economy generally.

It is quite clear that in its 1992 budget 'Red Book', the government was being optimistic in its assessment of how far it could harvest tax revenues from the British economy. One of Norman Lamont's special advisors at the Treasury has subsequently written a paper arguing that the government underestimated the loss of revenues from North Sea Oil, the loss of profits from nationalised industries that moved into the private sector, and the loss of revenue that occurred in the change from old style rates to the council tax, via the poll tax.

TABLE 3: WHAT WENT WRONG: THE DETERIORATING PICTURE OF 1996/97 (£BILLIONS)

	What they said before the 1992 election	What they say today	The difference
Projected size of the economy (GDP) in 1996/97	795	746	49 smaller
Projected tax revenues in 1996/97 if tax rates had not been raised	312	267	45 smaller
Projected public spending in 1996/97 if there had been no change in real spending plans	317	329	12 larger

Source: Author's calculations based on HM Treasury's *Financial Statement* and *Budget Reports.*

Whatever the explanation for the loss of revenues since 1992, in the last 12 months, the 'mystery of the missing revenues' has deepened even further. VAT has not been contributing as much as expected. Some suggest that the black economy has grown disproportionally; others that legal tax avoidance has grown; and others say that the structure of the economy has changed towards the kinds of spending (and saving) that is not subject to VAT. At the same time, increasing numbers of part-time and low-paying jobs do not yield as much in income tax as would the equivalent well paid full time jobs.

In all, therefore, the public finance backdrop to the economy has been far worse than the government, or indeed anyone, imagined at the time of the last election. In effect, the UK has had to run fast, in order to stay still.

And although the public finances are no longer in a state of crisis, it is still not clear that the current projections for borrowing are acceptable. The main parties are committed to meeting the Maastricht criteria that the government should not borrow more than 3 per cent of the country's total output – the GDP. The Conservatives are additionally committed to 'balancing the budget in the medium term'. Although this is not a very precise policy formulation, it could mean a zero PSBR in a 'normal' year for the economy. At the moment, it appears that we will have to be in an overheated economy for budget balance.

Labour, meanwhile, is committed to the so-called 'Golden Rule' that borrowing should not, on average, exceed the level of capital spending by government. As Labour believes we are currently in an average year in the economic cycle, that can only imply we should be obeying the Golden Rule now. We are not.

So if the politicians from any party are to meet their objectives and are to keep the economics profession happy, taxes may still have to rise, or spending plans be curtailed in the new Parliament. That *should* be high on the minds of those who participate in the election argument about who will tax or spend the most.

THE PUBLIC'S VIEW: THE SEARCH FOR THE GRAIL OF PUBLIC OPINION

For parties to campaign on this issue effectively, they need to understand what it is the public wants. When it comes to taxes and spending, both Labour and the Conservatives appear to be clear: the public want lower taxes and lower spending. Only the Liberal Democrats have differentiated themselves with a pledge to tax and spend more.

However, it is one of the great challenges of opinion research to explain what the public really want the balance between taxes and spending to be. Table 4 documents the results of opinion polls. These overwhelmingly – and increasingly – portray a public keen for better services, and apparently willing to pay for them. More detailed results show that health and education come top of the public's shopping list.

TABLE 4: WHAT THE PUBLIC SAYS IT WANTS

If the government had to choose it should...	All voters 1983	All voters 1994	Tory supporters 1994	Labour supporters 1994	Lib Dem supporters 1994
...reduce taxes and spend less on health, education and social benefits	9%	4%	4%	4%	2%
...keep taxes and spending at the same level as now	54%	33%	47%	24%	30%
...increase taxes and spend more on health, education and social benefits	32%	58%	46%	69%	65%

Source: British Social Attitudes, the Twelfth Report, 1995.

The problem with this finding is, that by electing four Conservative governments in the last two decades, the public are thought to have been revealing a deep scepticism about the role of the state. Even Labour appears to accept this view.

There are several possible explanations to the dilemma. It maybe that the public in fact dislike higher taxes, but think that it is more socially acceptable to say otherwise in answer to pollsters' questions. Alternatively, it maybe that the public do want better services – but only if they think someone else will pay for them. They may not have voted Labour in the past, for fear that under Labour, a higher tax bill would come their way personally.

This might well account for Gordon Brown's promise earlier this year that income tax rates would remain unchanged under a Labour government. There is some evidence that the public now believe the rich pay too little tax (indeed, the richest third of the population themselves believe they pay too little tax!). It would thus be quite consistent for a population to vote for a more progressive tax system – in which a rich minority are expected to find extra money for everyone else's benefit – but not to vote for a party which may increase taxes generally. But this hypothesis, that the public want the rich to pay more, is hardly satisfactory at explaining successive Conservative election victories.

The hypothesis that is perhaps most likely – and difficult to test – is the idea that the public *would* like more of the services taxes buy as the polls suggest; that the public *would* be willing to pay for them; but that they doubt the ability of the public sector in its current form to deliver them. In other words, we would love to pay higher taxes and have better services, but we're darned if we are going to pay higher taxes to Whitehall, because we will not actually get better services.

Under this interpretation, the party which will score well on the tax and spending issue need not be the one promising the lowest tax and spending; it could be the one promising the most effective use of the money raised. This has not in fact been the focus of election debate in the past, nor does it promise to be this time round. It is the decisions over level and complexion of spending that have dominated and will continue to dominate.

PARTY PLATFORMS: THE CASE OF THE MISSING DIFFERENCES

Given the state of public opinion and the backdrop of the public finances, one might think all parties would like to avoid the issues of taxes and spending. In fact, the parties if anything have tended to highlight the issues and exaggerate their differences on them.

Labour has attempted to neutralise its historically poor performance on tax with attacks on the Conservatives' record, and by the unprecedented promise to leave current rates unchanged. They have also pledged to follow Conservative spending plans for the first two years of the next parliament, with the exception of a windfall tax on utilities, to be dedicated to spending on welfare-to-work programmes.

This raises several (unanswered) questions. Has Labour devised sufficient income-raising tools to fund its (modest) spending plans? The consensus seems to be that they have not. And precisely which utilities will be hit by the windfall tax? Gordon Brown is sticking to a 'category' – namely 'privatised utilities'. Behind the scenes, what Labour aides talk of is 'price-controlled utilities'. This clearly means Gas, and perhaps BT, Electricity and Water, but not British Airways, Associated British Ports – or the privatised buses. Tony Blair, though, speaks of 'monopolies', a slightly different categorisation again. For their part, the Conservatives, with a somewhat embarrassing record more recently, have argued that it would have been even worse under Labour. The Liberal Democrats believe that they scored well arguing for higher income tax and more education spending – but their voters never believed they would end up being in office to impose higher taxes.

In practice, the differences between the actual expressed policies of the larger parties are smaller than the rhetoric would imply.

There are a number of specific disagreements on the direction of the tax system. The Conservatives have tended to favour cuts in income tax, even at the expense of increases in other taxes. The party is committed to a 20 per cent basic rate, and as a signal of its seriousness of intent, it has left us with a slightly bunched tax schedule with both a 20 and a 23 per cent rate band.

Labour in its past has attached less importance to the basic rate of tax, and more importance to the rates paid by those on low incomes, though it has proposed to introduce new lower rates when resources allow. Unfortunately, the poor would find any gain in disposable income taken away by reductions in benefits, so that expensive compensating changes in the benefit systems would have to be made.

But other differences on taxation are less clear cut. The Tories used to be the party of VAT, for example. Now, though, the party's stomach for increasing it, or widening the tax base, is limited after the domestic fuel debacle. Labour meanwhile portrayed VAT on fuel as an evil tax measure – oddly, agreeing with the Tory Right, and disagreeing with environmentalists and economists. Labour now suggests VAT on fuel should stand at 5 per cent, and discuss the idea of more general energy tax on top. Labour's more recent campaign suggesting that the Tories will put VAT on food seems to have had little effect, not least because ministers have been unusually bullish in denying the claims.

In terms of structural tax reforms, both Labour and the Conservatives continue to favour beneficial treatment for the income from savings. Both are committed to maintaining incentives for high earners to work. Neither is presently proposing the full integration of National Insurance and income tax.

Even in terms of their general philosophies, the parties are more divided within than between. Kenneth Clarke, for example, has declared himself a 40 per cent man: he believes government should not spend more than 40 per cent of GDP. With help from some statistical re-definitions, he is now on course to get Britain back to that level. William Waldegrave, Clarke's deputy at the Treasury, has mentioned 35 per cent. Many Tories – including Chris Patten – talk favourably of the Asian Tigers, where spending is more like 15 to 20 per cent of GDP. As for Labour, the leadership is clearly in practice fairly close to Mr Clarke, even if it would not choose to express agreement in any recognisable form.

TABLE 5: TAXING YOUR PATIENCE – AT-A-GLANCE

CONSERVATIVE	LABOUR	LIB-DEM
Tend to favour cuts in income tax, with greater burden on indirect taxes (VAT).	Trying to assert new low-tax philosophy.	Support keeping a low tax burden, consistent with priorities for public spending.
Committed to a 20 per cent basic rate.	Set long-term goal of 15p or even 10p basic rate.	Propose raising the basic rate of tax by a penny, to fund education spending.
Committed to maintaining incentives for high earners.	Promise not to raise current income tax rates in first term of Labour government.	Propose 50% tax rate for those earning over £100,000 the revenue from which would be used to remove 750,000 people from the tax system altogether.

We have moved on a great deal since the last election. 1992 was a Tory–Labour battle involving two clearly distinct tax and spending packages. John Smith opened the door to a massive Conservative advertising bombshell, and tax was the defining policy issue. 1997 will be very different. The two main parties will, no doubt, claim to be offering vastly differing proposals. The reality of the promises – if not the outcome – is that Labour and the Conservatives have never been closer on tax and spending policies.

THE ENGINE ROOM

INDUSTRY AND THE UNIONS

Stephen Evans

Stephen Evans is the Industry Correspondent for BBC News. Prior to joining the BBC, he has worked on newspapers and was a reporter for HTV.

How the parties would help or hinder industry is one of the crucial questions of the election campaign. The answer affects the pay of individuals and the taxes to government. It determines how much is spent on everything from health and education to the National Lottery. How much goes on foreign aid and how much on foreign holidays is set by how much employees and employers produce in the first place.

Working out what difference the parties would actually make is more difficult than it used to be. In the 1980s, the divisions seemed clearer: on one side were the Conservatives, broadly believing that the state meddled in markets at the economy's peril; on the other, Labour, dominated by people calling themselves Socialists and emphasising 'planning' and 'intervention' in markets they believed might occasionally deliver the goods but rarely fairness.

But Labour's revolution has made the choice in this election more difficult. Political dividing lines are more blurred than they have been for more than two decades. There is a spectrum running from a Labour Left that still mistrusts capitalism, to the Conservative Right which mistrusts nearly all state intervention. And in the middle, there is an overlap between the two big parties where the primacy of private ownership and markets is accepted. Here, the disagreements are over how much and when the state should get involved.

A FLEXIBLE LABOUR MARKET

The Conservatives believe that too much regulation of the relationship between employers and employees hampers the ability of firms to generate wealth and jobs. This, according to one leading Conservative policy-maker, is a crucial difference in this election: 'We face a choice between two models of capitalism. One option is the free market model which prizes mobility, flexibility, enterprise and individualism: this is the basis for the policies we have been pursuing since 1979. The second option is the Continental model, espoused by 'New' Labour, which stresses 'social partnership' with stakeholders such as trade unions.'

It seems likely, therefore, that a Conservative government would continue 'deregulating the labour market'. It might remove the right of employees in smaller firms to go to Industrial Tribunals and claim unfair dismissal – such a proposal was shelved before the election but ministers said it had not been forgotten.

The Conservatives argue that the benefits of deregulation are now evident. Firms can hire and fire with greater ease, so unemployment falls faster when prospects improve. They say that other governments now accept this – the Organisation for Economic Co-operation and Development (made up of the world's most developed economies) recently reported that Britain had one of the 'least regulated labour markets' and this had resulted in a 'steady drop in structural unemployment and a relatively good unemployment record compared with many Continental European countries'. The independent and respected National Institute of Economic and Social Research echoed that view when it said: 'The more flexible labour market engendered by the reforms of the 1980s may mean that the UK economy can now enjoy a longer period of faster economic growth and lower levels of unemployment before inflationary pressures develop.'

This theme will be shouted from the rooftops during the campaign by Conservative politicians who see their best chance of re-election in the assertion that the painful climb out of recession is now reaching the sunny uplands – and opting for Labour would put that recovery in jeopardy.

INSECURITY

Labour believes the whole approach is flawed and threatens to take Britain in completely the wrong direction. It argues that the evidence shows that successful economies, like Germany's and Japan's, do not rely only on a flexible jobs market, but also on well-trained, better-paid workers: economies, it argues, that try to compete largely through lower wages ultimately do not become prosperous.

It is not clear, however, whether Labour would undo Conservative changes, though it seems unlikely that it would extend them. Rather, it puts its emphasis on a balance between flexibility and employment protection. Insecurity, it believes, leads to low morale and low productivity among current employees, not to mention pain among many former employees.

There has been some debate about what effect job insecurity will have on this election. The argument is that it could help Labour by inhibiting voters from 'feeling good' as their incomes rise.

The difficulty with that argument is that it is not clear that jobs are actually less secure now than they were, say, a decade ago when the Conservatives won a thumping general election victory: unemployment is now lower, and the time that the average worker holds onto a job has barely changed since 1987.

People who believe insecurity will influence this election result say it is because the overall figures conceal important changes: there is more contract work (voters may work for just as long with one employer but they cannot be sure that the work will continue). On top of that, the recession of the early 90s hit professional and white-collar workers, unused to unemployment and crucial to this election result. And those who retained jobs still feared for them – the so-called 'survivors' syndrome' in firms which have made managers redundant.

Of course, talk of insecurity may be louder than the figures warrant because the one area where it certainly has risen is in the media. All the same, people often vote on perceptions rather than objective truths. It is not clear, however, if insecure voters cling to what they know or opt for change.

UNION LAW

Labour would be unlikely to undo the changes that have transformed working habits. Since 1979, there have been seven major pieces of legislation, with the main effect of outlawing sympathy action and making ballots compulsory before strikes or other industrial action.

Mr Blair has toured the country's seaside resorts telling unions they would get 'fairness not favours'. His party is, however, pledged to make secondary picketing legal in limited circumstances – for example, where work normally done in a strike-bound factory has been switched to another plant of the company in dispute. It is also committed to granting 'the right to recognition' to unions, so that where most employees wanted a union to negotiate for them, the employer would have to deal with that union. It is not clear, though, what penalty there would be on employers who refused to cooperate, or exactly how the majority view of a workforce would be measured or defined.

The Conservatives argue that Labour would offer unions a back-door to Downing Street. They have proposed tougher laws, to allow the public to sue unions in some strikes, and to make unions give more notice before industrial action. These proposals have met a cool response from employers, not least the Confederation of British Industry which called them unnecessary.

There is no way of judging how unions would behave under Labour. Expectations would clearly be higher, but much has changed since 1979: tougher union laws, higher unemployment, more (mortgaged) home-ownership, fewer union members and more contract and part-time employment all tend to soften the ability to strike.

All the same, there is a view among Left-wing activists, particularly in Unison, the country's largest union, that a Blair government would have to be challenged early on pay. This feeling was stoked when, in February, the Pay Review Bodies for nurses, doctors and teachers recommended rises above the rate of inflation. The Shadow Chancellor, Gordon Brown, further fanned the flames when he sent a 'tough but fair' signal, saying he would freeze the pay of judges, military top brass and other senior public servants.

In the private sector, there is evidence that attitudes have changed since Labour was last in power. Union officials recognise that big global companies switch investments between countries.

It is hard to judge what the public now makes of unions. Are they viewed as essential defenders of the weak or as bogeymen waiting to return from the wilderness? Polling evidence indicates some popular feeling that unions should have a role as protectors against employers. There is no evidence, though, that the public wants them close to government.

THE MINIMUM WAGE

One of the Labour leadership's hardest battles with unions has been over the minimum wage. In 1992, the party was committed to setting it by formula at half the hourly earnings of the average male worker. This time, the commitment is simply to introduce a statutory minimum wage, and to have it determined later by a newly formed

Low Wage Commission made up of people from both sides of industry. It would be a national figure in contrast to the Liberal Democrats' proposals of a range of figures varying by regional conditions.

JOBS AND WORKING CONDITIONS – AT A GLANCE

CONSERVATIVE	LABOUR	LIB-DEM
Too much regulation hampers firms' competitive ability.	Workers often need protection from strong employers.	Want to increase flexibility in the labour market but also recognise employee rights and responsibilities.
Continued deregulation of labour market.	Would not undo Conservative trade union reforms, except to allow limited secondary picketing.	Support most of the government's trade union legislation.
Propose stripping unions of immunity from legal action where strikes 'disproportionate or excessive'.	Allow unions a greater voice without them dictating policy.	Believe unions should have an important role to play in many areas of employment.
Oppose minimum wage believing it would cost jobs.	Introduce a statutory national minimum wage determined by a Low Wage Commission representing both unions and employers.	Support a regionally-varied minimum wage set by a new Low Pay Commission. Believe the tax payer should not have to supplement wage bills through state benefits.
Support the British 'opt-out' of the Social Chapter.	Committed to end the 'opt-out' of the European Social Chapter.	Reject Britain's Social Chapter 'opt-out', arguing that Britain should be seeking to shape the legislation from the inside.

The Conservatives argue that a minimum rate would impede growth in general and harm some of the very people it was meant to help by putting them out of work – a garage manager might employ one less petrol-pump attendant, or working parents might find leaving their children with higher-paid child-minders uneconomic. Many of the low-paid are female, the argument runs, so the measure would deprive women of work and push them back into the home, exactly what many of Labour's loudest campaigners would not want.

Labour counters that there is a real problem of miserable pay, and addressing it through a minimum wage might relieve some of the financial burden currently borne by the state – a form of minimum wage was introduced by Winston Churchill in 1909 and survived through Wages Councils without obvious damaging effects until they were abolished just under five years ago. Labour also says that a minimum wage would be introduced carefully, looking at particular

circumstances in particular industries – some, where employers
dominate an area and an industry and squeeze wages, might be able
to raise wages without job losses; others, like textiles, which face
fierce Third World competition would present real difficulties.

Some employers, notably the Safeway supermarket chain and some
private contractors in catering, cleaning and security say they would
welcome a minimum wage – it would offer them protection against
competitors employing at lower rates ('cowboys', or fierce but fair
competition, depending on your point of view).

The academic evidence is not conclusive. Studies of the way
minimum wage laws work in France and the United States indicate
that the impact on jobs depends on where the minimum is pitched.
Union and employer representatives on Labour's Low Pay
Commission would struggle fiercely to pitch it so that poor people
were protected but firms and jobs were not harmed.

THE SOCIAL CHAPTER

Apart from the minimum wage, the Conservatives turn their fiercest
fire on Labour over the European Union's Social Chapter. Labour is
committed to end the British opt-out, so the provisions agreed so far
would come into force if the party won the election: employees in big
British companies that operated elsewhere in the European Union
would have to be consulted through Works Councils, and fathers
would get paternity leave.

One of the concerns of industrialists is that Labour would go along
with proposals to let more measures, like health and safety or
consulting workers, go through on a majority vote rather than
unanimity. Mr Blair has tried to reassure the CBI, telling it: 'I have no
intention whatever of agreeing to anything and everything that emerges.'

'STAKEHOLDING'

On a trip to Singapore a year ago, Mr Blair flagged 'stakeholding'
as one of his key tenets. The difficulty with this concept is that
it can mean many things to many people. In the United States,
it is associated with companies that take a broad view of their
responsibilities, widening beyond their shareholders to employees
and the community around factories. On the Continent, notably in
Germany, it echoes the idea of the 'social partners' – employers
and employed – both having a say in policy, in individual firms
and nationally.

In Labour's case, 'stakeholding' seems to indicate a consensual attitude where the 'social partners' recognise that the prosperity of each depends on the prosperity of the other – a 'we're all in the same boat' approach, rather than 'treat 'em mean to keep 'em keen'. Labour cites Marks and Spencer, or the way Rover negotiated widespread change, as good examples of 'stakeholding'.

The Conservatives retort that Labour is mouthing a warm, empty phrase. The employers' bodies share some reservations, though Adair Turner, the director-general of the Confederation of British Industry, appeared to endorse stakeholding when he said that employers could not go on assuming that employees would receive little of the benefits of growth.

The Conservatives also say that they intend to make practical changes to give employees a greater stake in companies. In particular, they say they will change Inland Revenue rules to encourage firms to offer free shares to employees.

PRIVATISATION

The Conservatives say that co-operation may be fine, but it cannot be imposed. Industry flourishes when managers have a free hand. Removing 'burdens on business' is their phrase – nowhere more so than when the burden of state-ownership is removed. They cite privatisation as the great triumph. Since 1979, more than forty publicly owned businesses have been sold, though it is a rarely appreciated irony that Labour actually set the ball rolling in 1977 when it sold part of BP, with Tony Benn the reluctant Energy Secretary. No one would doubt, though, that it was the Conservatives who took the policy, shook it up and pursued it with relentless vigour.

The early sell-offs were enterprises which faced competition. Privatised companies like British Steel and British Airways have thrived – though sceptics say that many of the most important managerial changes took place under state control. The later sales of monopolies, like the water, electricity and gas utilities have been much more contentious. None the less, the measure of the Conservative achievement is that Labour has no plans – and probably no broader intention either (or at least, not in the leadership) – of re-nationalising these industries.

The one exception is rail. Labour is committed to a 'publicly owned and accountable' railway. It has been divided over what exactly this should mean, with the rail unions wanting re-nationalisation. The indications are that Labour would not pursue that in government, but continue to operate a privatised system, seeking private finance to augment public funds for major projects. The main question would be what would happen to franchises granted to private companies to run train services once those franchises expired. Labour has indicated that they might then revert to the state-owned British Rail.

For the Conservatives, the sheer scale of past privatisation limits the scope for future sell-offs. A matter of weeks before the election was called, the Transport Secretary, Sir George Young, confirmed in a Commons statement that the London Underground would be privatised by a re-elected Conservative government. However, the main outstanding example is the Royal Mail, the part of the Post Office that delivers letters. Since its privatisation was blocked in June 1994 by Conservative backbenchers, ministers have reaffirmed that privatisation had not been ruled out for ever. Accordingly, there is little doubt that privatisation would resurface in some form if the Conservatives are returned to power.

REGULATION

While Labour would be unlikely to put privatisation in reverse, it would shake-up, and probably toughen, the regulation of the privatised utilities. It has said it would replace the separate offices of the regulators with a single body, something also favoured by the Liberal Democrats. In this grand regulatory office would be panels of experts, making the regulators more anonymous, and easier to remove if they failed to come up to scratch.

WINDFALL TAX

Labour has said it would levy a one-off windfall tax on the privatised utilities. It has not said how much the tax would raise but £5 billion is the common assumption in the City of London. Private studies done at S.G. Warbury, the finance house that advised the government on much of its privatisation programme, indicate that the utilities have already accounted for a burden of that scale.

There is no doubt that Labour's windfall tax would be harder to administer than the Conservatives' windfall tax on the banks in 1981. Some Conservatives have floated the suggestion that Labour's plans would become bogged down in the courts.

Independent legal opinion indicates the windfall tax would be within the law, though it would have to be carefully designed not to discriminate unfairly and so fall foul of European Union regulations.

TRAINING

Labour would use the revenue from the windfall tax for training schemes for the young and for the long-term unemployed. Under 'Target 2000', as Labour would call its new scheme, specific levels of literacy, numeracy and skills in using technology would be set. Employers would have to give young people who had not attained the standards six hours a week off for study. Employers who took on younger workers would also get a rebate.

Labour would also oblige unemployed people under 25 to train or do socially useful tasks in return for their unemployment benefit plus some extra pay. A repeated refusal would mean benefits being cut.

The Conservatives would extend pilot schemes where the unemployed would have to perform socially useful tasks.

Labour has, however, backed away from a pledge to impose a 'training levy' on employers despite seeing untrained workers as one of the prime causes of British economic difficulties. One of the reasons often cited is the alleged inability of the market to deliver good training – firms acting in their own self-interest may assume other firms will train workers, knowing they can then hire them as needed – this is known as 'free-riding'. Labour had said it would levy all employers to raise money for training across industry, but has now dropped this pledge. By contrast, the Liberal Democrats propose taxing any firm not spending 2 per cent of its wage bill on improving workers' skills.

The difficulty for all parties is that the better the training, the more costly the scheme. Making the unemployed clean up graffiti or tidy canal banks in return for benefit costs the public purse relatively little. More ambitious schemes cost substantially more.

SMALL BUSINESSES

There is one matter on which all politicians agree: small businesses are a Good Thing. The two main parties have vied with each other to offer measures to cut the late payment of debts, something which small businesses say cripples them. The Conservatives said they would make it easier to get money through the courts; big companies and government departments would have to publish their record on payment of debts. Labour promised that big companies and government agencies would be compelled to pay interest on debts if they were paid late, a move welcomed by bodies representing small businesses but criticised by others, like the Confederation of British Industry, as likely to cause more problems than it would solve.

Just as small businesses are a Good Thing so red tape is universally acknowledged as a Bad Thing. The Conservatives have made much of cutting it – John Major charged Michael Heseltine – 'Tarzan' – with 'cutting through the jungle of red tape'; 'bonfires of red tape' were promised. In the end, a 'Deregulation Taskforce' was set up and some rules were simplified. For example, health and safety regulations prescribing the exact distance between the rungs of ladders were replaced by broader rules to 'ensure a safe working environment'. The Conservatives say this unglamorous but important policy would continue.

Labour retorts that 70 per cent of the thousands of regulations reviewed by the Deregulation Taskforce were actually introduced in the first place by the Conservative government. Many in the party, particularly in the unions, say that 'one employer's burdensome regulation is another employee's protection at work'. Simplification of regulations is to be applauded and will be continued, they say, but the interests of employee and employer have to be balanced.

DEVELOPMENT AGENCIES

Plaid Cymru and the SNP concentrate their industrial strategy on calling for greater powers for the development agencies in their countries. There can be no conclusion on whether Labour's assemblies in Cardiff and Edinburgh would attract firms that wanted to be nearer centres of power – as some in the Northeast and Southwest of England fear – or repel businesses south and east of the English borders in fear of additional interference, including tax-raising interference in Scotland.

It is fair to say that the nationalist parties, as well as the Liberal Democrats, have more in common with Labour than they do with the Conservatives. All three see free markets as potentially harmful. In the event of a hung parliament, none of the parties on whom Mr Blair might depend would find much to offend them in Labour's industrial policy.

WHICH WAY FOR INDUSTRY?

Voting is not just about bald pledges in manifestos. It is also about the leanings of politicians in parties with a range of overlapping policies. It is about reading the way they would actually jump in power rather than the way they say they would when they are trying to get it.

The Conservatives say they have a proven sympathy for private industry so why hand power to people who have a history of hostility to it? Labour, on the other hand, argues that it has changed, and that it offers a fresh, sensible scepticism which lets it look at problems unencumbered by destructive dogma.

A string of speeches by the Shadow Chancellor, Gordon Brown, early this year, underlined the Labour leadership's belief that the old class basis of politics, with the two bigger parties each representing employee or employer, had gone.

It is not clear, though, whether leaders of industry believe him. It is clear, however, that some feel they can live and do business with Labour, if not embrace it wholeheartedly. Their doubts are about some policies and about how far down in the party the conversion goes. At the same time, the old love affair with the Conservatives is probably not what it was. Some business leaders were offended when they were criticised by the Deputy Prime Minister, Michael Heseltine, in January, for lending their names to a report commissioned by a left-leaning group.

Who wins may well turn on the mood of the times: in 1979, Jim Callaghan felt he had been swept away by an irresistible sea-change in public attitudes; in 1964, Harold Wilson caught a mood of modernity with his talk of the 'white heat of technology', Tony Blair is trying to catch a similar mood this time with his video-link press conferences and a deal with BT to put every school on the internet.

There has been pain and insecurity since 1979. There have also been improvements which few would now undo. There has been redundancy in privatised industry but also reduced cost – and reduced prices. If the economic 'feel-good' factor really is one of the key factors in deciding the election, where the crosses of many individuals go in polling booths will each reflect their own very distinctive experiences of employment and unemployment. Despite the broad convergence of party policies, this remains one of the very few areas of the election where the parties are offering genuinely different strategies – and that in turn is likely to fuel much of the rhetoric of the campaign.

THAT SINKING FEELING

INFLATION, DEFLATION AND POLITICS

Peter Jay

Peter Jay is Economics Editor for BBC News.
After six years as a civil servant in the Treasury,
in 1967 he became Economics Editor of The Times.
In 1977, he was appointed British Ambassador to the
United States, a post he held until 1979. Thereafter
he was Chairman and Chief Executive of TV-AM
(1980-83), Editor of Banking World *and presenter*
of 'A Week in Politics' (1983-86), and Chief of Staff
for the Maxwell Group of Companies (1986-89).
He took up his present position with the BBC in
1990. He has won many awards and honours, including in 1993 the Royal
Television Society Home News Award for his coverage of 'Black Wednesday'.

'It's the economy, stupid!' When Bill Clinton encapsulated what he saw as the key election issue in his first presidential campaign in 1992, he put himself in the mainstream of conventional opinion about what it is that mainly determines electoral behaviour and awards success to one party or another in most modern democracies.

But the 1990s have witnessed a change in the UK, if not yet in the United States. John Major won the election in 1992, at what was very close to being the worst possible moment in what was itself an exceptionally adverse economic cycle. The recession in the early 1990s reached its deepest point about a year after the election. But by the spring of 1992 the main impact had already taken its toll and was fresh and vivid in the minds of the electors. The further deterioration over the next year was small.

Labour's failure to win clearly made a deep impression on those who are now the party's leaders, though all the lessons to be drawn from it are still not clear. John Major's victory in these conditions should have made everybody re-examine their assumptions about the central importance of the cyclical status of the economy in determining election outcomes, though the explanation may merely be that Labour, by offering no clearly differentiated expansionist alternative, simply failed to play the card that might have taken the trick.

SHATTERED ILLUSIONS: THE REALITY OF 1997

It certainly seemed that whoever won in 1992 faced a very rosy future. The economy was so depressed, that it could safely expand relatively quickly for more than a whole Parliament. That certainly looked like a winning formula for the 1997 election, especially as things developed in the twelve months after the election. The problem of ERM membership was resolved on 16 September 1992 by the fulfilment of the usual consequences of such attempts to defy the laws of economic gravity. And the problem of the government's deficit began to be addressed by Norman Lamont's last budget in March, 1993.

The government and the economy now looked set for a long comfortable cruise to at least cyclical balance: no recession; no boom. The depth of the hole made by the 1990s recession meant that the economy could expand quite briskly for most of the rest of the decade without any risk of over-heating and general inflation (rather as between 1981 and 1987, before it all went wrong).

Then came Kenneth Clarke. Appointed in May 1993 in the wake of a press campaign against Lamont, he immediately went out of his way to attack his economic inheritance, focusing on the £50 billion deficit in the then current year. In the first 'unified budget' at the end of November, he added further tranches of tax increases, on top of those announced by Mr Lamont, as well as tightening control of public spending.

By the time of his summer forecasts 19 months later, after a 'neutral' budget in November 1995, slow growth and some allegedly mysterious shortfall in revenue, the government's optimism about the reduction of its borrowing had been distinctly toned down, as Evan Davis has described in his earlier chapter.

BRITISH HEAVYWEIGHT CONTEST: CLARKE v GEORGE

Mr Clarke also deemed it wise to announce, as an extension of the system established by Mr Lamont for making monetary policy decisions 'transparent', that the minutes of his monthly meetings with the Governor of the Bank of England would be published about six weeks later. He thereby handed what was widely thought to be a powerful weapon of suasion to the Governor, since evident disagreement between the authorities about the course of monetary policy might be expected to have dire consequences in the foreign exchange and gilt-edged markets.

Between the autumn of 1994 and the spring of 1995 the governor exercised his prerogative to advise interest rate increases in the name of conforming to the government's stated inflation target (1-4 per cent for the annual change in the Retail Price Index, excluding mortgage interest payments, falling to 2.5 per cent by the end of the Parliament).

The governor, Eddie George, was also keen to win back for the Bank of England some of the independence which it lost fifty years earlier. He may have believed that a strong anti-inflation posture would reinforce the Bank's claims to resume its old powers over interest rates.

Interest rates were increased on Mr Clarke's authority in September and December of 1994 and in February of 1995 by a total amount of 1.5 per cent to 6.75 per cent. But in May, 1995, he rejected the governor's advice to raise rates yet again. For the governor the affair did not work out well.

With the recovery stopped and going into reverse, Mr Clarke welcomed evidence of low growth and dormant inflation as finally vindicating his rejection of Mr George's advice on interest rates. He referred continuously to what he called 'sustainable growth', by which he meant that output was not falling in absolute terms and that, precisely because it was rising so slowly, there was no danger of being blown off course by inflation.

This may seem a bit like describing malnutrition as 'sustainable weight-watching'. But it did not stop the Chancellor from eventually recognising the need for interest rate cuts – by a total of 1 per cent between December 1995, and June 1996, at least once against the advice of the Governor – to arrest the slow down and to try to restart the recovery.

The Chancellor was happy to accept applause from the inter-national organisations whose deficit-busting zeal increased with every publication. The IMF in the summer of 1996 actually described the state of the British economy as 'enviable', which so tickled the Chancellor that he departed from precedent and published the IMF's report, saying that he would continue to do so in future.

But the IMF warned that there could be no tax cuts, unmatched by extra spending cuts, in November 1996's pre-election budget. In the event, Mr Clarke cut spending by £2 billion and taxes by £1 billion net, including a 23p basic rate of tax as a further small step along the road to the target 20p rate.

Mr Clarke clearly no longer believed, if, indeed, he and the Prime Minister ever had believed, that with one budgetary bound the Conservative party could be free of its re-election difficulties, perhaps also persuading himself that the voters' minds would be better concentrated if they had to travel hopefully towards the 20p basic rate horizon than if they arrived at it without the trouble of first re-electing a Conservative government. Perhaps this was not a time to be seen hacking merrily at the tax base. The Chancellor may even have had an eye also on the Maastricht convergence criterion which indicates a maximum budget deficit in 1997-98 of just under £25 billion, well above his forecast £19 billion, but not beyond the reach of the kind of forecasting error that has been seen in some recent years.

THE BLIP: IS INFLATION BACK?

Attention now focused on the threat to the medium-term economic outlook from the 'blip' in inflation seen in the figures for October 1996, announced shortly before the budget and continued into the RPI for November, announced in December. The percentage change in the RPI over twelve months (excluding mortgage interest payments) – colloquially referred to as the underlying rate of inflation and the explicit object of the Chancellor's inflation targets – which had been coasting down to 2.8 per cent in the four previous months, edged up to 2.9 per cent in the twelve months to September and then to 3.3 per cent in the twelve months to October and again in the twelve months to November.

Examination of the figures at the end of 1995 suggests that abnormal factors may be at work in the figures for the months of November, December, 1996, and January, 1997. But if it is not a blip, and the governor turns out to have been right, then it will not just be the outlook for interests rates and growth in 1997 and beyond which grow darker.

Far more seriously, this would suggest that growth has not merely shown no gain in consequence of the economic reforms of the 1980s, but has actually slumped. The implication would be that the historic average long-term growth rate since the economy last reached the inflationary ceiling, in 1988-89, has suffered a sharp retardation from about 2.3 per cent a year to only about 1.7 per cent. This would be equal with the much derided period between 1974 and 1979, and otherwise lower than any cycle since the nineteenth century.

THE 1980s EXPERIENCE: ALL FOR NOTHING?

The implication that the reforms of the 1980s may have been counter-productive in terms of economic growth and efficiency would, if sustained by continuing evidence of inflationary acceleration from the autumn of 1996, administer the biggest shock to conventional economic wisdom in Britain for many decades.

Meanwhile, the Labour party is also courting the approval of the deficit-busters, imposing upon itself just about every rule of fiscal rectitude that anyone has dreamed up in modern times, even if they are not obviously compatible with each other. Labour are not playing the expansion card. All progress must be found on the supply side (making workers cheaper and/or more flexible, not making employers more confident).

And then there is Europe. The new government will have to decide – one day – about the Euro. The consequences of that decision could outweigh everything else. Indeed, inside a single currency there could be no 'macro-economic policy', if that is defined as setting interest rates, exchange rates and fiscal balances, since these matters would be largely governed by European institutions.

But that is for the future. For the moment, Britain's politicians wrestle with their fear of inflation, born of the harsh lessons of the 1970s and 1980s, and fret over signs of future inflationary pressures. Neglecting the eminent political wisdom of seeking to grow the economy over time at its realistic potential is becoming the error of the 1990s. It may be that few people care very deeply about the margin of economic prosperity forgone. It may also be that even fewer people realise how deflated the economy actually is.

ISSUES WHICH WILL
HELP DECIDE
THE ELECTION

LIVING AT EASE?
THE PARTIES' POLICIES

WELFARE, FAMILY LIFE AND FOOTBALL

A NATION AT EASE?

Niall Dickson

Niall Dickson is Social Affairs Editor for BBC News. Before joining the BBC, Niall worked as a teacher, then became Publicity Officer for the National Corporation of the Care of Old People, and in 1980 he was Head of Publicity for Age Concern in England. In 1981 he became Editor of Therapy Weekly, *going on to become Editor of the* Nursing Times *until 1988, when he joined the BBC as Health Correspondent. He became Chief Social Affairs Correspondent a year later. In 1995, he became Social Affairs Editor.*

When he moved to 10 Downing Street in November 1990 John Major vowed to create a nation 'at ease with itself'. Emphasising his own humble origins he signalled his wish to create a classless society. The implication was clear – his premiership would be less confrontational, more harmonious than that of his predecessor. More effort would be devoted to reducing divisions and tensions.

However, politicians are more often servants than masters of powerful social forces, a fact which may help to explain a paradox that has been a source of considerable frustration for the government and its supporters. The electorate that will shortly go the polls has never known such prosperity. In spite of this, everywhere there is talk of unease – even among those who have 'never had it so good'. Seldom a day goes by without reference to the elusive 'feelgood factor'.

This malaise, if that it be, extends beyond the narrow economic issue of consumer confidence – some of that certainly has returned. It lies at the heart of how people feel about themselves, about their prospects, and about the society in which they live. In a word many people feel insecure and, ominously for politicians, the public appears to hold them at least partly responsible.

The causes are straightforward enough. Insecurity has grown as a result of a more fluid labour market, which has largely dispensed with the concept of a 'job for life'. The result is a greater emphasis on performance which has left even the competent worried about their futures. Whether these concerns are justified or not is unimportant in this context – what matters is perception; they feel insecure. This is compounded by increasingly fragile family structures and a widespread view that crime, even violent crime, is a real threat. In 1971, 80 per cent of 7 and 8 year olds went to school on their own – by 1990 only 9 per cent did so. Parents are more reluctant to let their offspring out of their sight.

At the same time, many traditional support mechanisms have contracted or disappeared. The cohesive working-class community, (where children played in the streets) the trade unions and the church all provided social glue and a sense of well being – their influence has declined sharply. Instead, small nuclear families are left to cope on their own – they tend to be more mobile, less rooted in their communities, and more likely to be separated even from their immediate relatives.

And to this more uncertain world must be added question marks over the long term future of the over arching support mechanism – the welfare state. The post-war belief that government would be there in times of need, is evaporating. Again, whatever the reality, many believe the state will offer minimal support should they fall on hard times.

A key challenge for all the parties then is to find ways of restoring a modicum of security in the minds of voters – the problem is, they have to do this without producing plans that would lead to large and unpopular tax rises.

CHANGING BRITAIN

Today's social attitudes reflect radical changes in the composition of the electorate over a relatively short period. Within a generation, the number of people aged 80 and over has more than doubled. More women than men are now economically active – from a world in which men worked and women stayed at home to rear children, we have moved to one in which there is a growing divide between households with two incomes and those with none.

The electorate now would be almost unrecognisable to politicians of the 1960s and 70s. More people than ever live alone – partly, but not wholly, as a result of the ageing of the population. Two out of three homes are now owned by their occupiers – that compares with just over half in 1981. Council housing, once the mainstay of the British social system, has gone into sharp decline – in the mid-70's local authorities were responsible for half the new houses in the UK, by 1994 just one new home in 70 was council built.

Divorce, once a relative rarity, has shot up by 700 per cent since the 1960s. Family breakdown has fuelled the growth in one parent families – by 1995, one child in five lived with one parent – three times as many as in the early 70s. And by official definitions Britain has become middle class – most voters will be from social classes ABC1.

The politicians are faced with a more complicated and fluid social picture – old certainties of social status and resulting voting behaviour have been weakened.

DIFFERENCE AND DEFERENCE

The irony is that the social and economic changes that have brought increased wealth have also created increased dependence. The benefits system, designed mainly to provide temporary assistance for those who fell on hard times, has become a mainstay for many. Most of the benefits bill goes on the elderly, who account for 45 per cent of the total, although the biggest rise in recent years has been on payments to the sick and disabled which between 1982 and 1995 increased threefold to more than £20 billion. The remainder goes to families and the unemployed. The growing cost of social security might suggest a degree of income redistribution, but changes to the system and the switch from direct to indirect taxation have conspired to ensure that growing inequality has continued largely unchecked over the last 20 years.

In the last couple of years there are signs that the income gap between rich and poor has stopped widening but it remains greater than at any time since World War II. This is partly because incomes at the top, and to a lesser extent in the middle of the income distribution, have shot ahead, and partly because the bottom 20 per cent of the population have seen little or no real increase in their standards of living.

Claims that the 'poor are getting poorer' need to be treated with caution – the composition of the lowest income groups has changed. Fewer pensioners, more unemployed and more self-employed make up today's poor – so it is less clear that a particular group has become poorer than that the nature of poverty has changed. That said, the

Conservative government's decision to end the link between benefits and earnings in the early 1980s has inevitably meant that many of those on social security have not shared in the growing wealth of the country, and that the gap between those with work and those without has widened.

The political parties differ on whether inequality matters. Labour, the Liberal Democrats, Plaid Cymru and the SNP argue that a more unequal society is a less healthy one, less at ease with itself and less likely to be economically successful. However, it is unclear how far the main opposition parties would go to reduce inequality, either through taxation or through the social security system. Neither is committed to restoring the link between benefits and earnings, although the Liberal Democrats have said they will increase a number of benefits, including Income Support for young people.

The Conservatives are more sanguine about greater inequality. For them, growing income differences are the product of economic success – not a cause for concern, providing there is a safety net for those who cannot support themselves.

What they and the others accept is that a substantial number of young people at the bottom are not currently equipped or motivated for the post industrial world – for the major parties, finding ways to lift this group out of their predicament through education and training has become a social and economic priority. Few politicians are yet talking about ghettos or even an underclass, but there is a recognition that some communities, left behind when heavy industry moved away, have been beached.

In one important respect, though, John Major's vision of a more classless society does appear to be being realised. Britain has become less deferential – respect for those who in the past might have been deemed to have a higher social status has declined with even the traditional professions of law and medicine being challenged as never before. Whatever obligations voters may feel they have towards others, those others are less and less likely to include people who are better off than themselves.

WORK AND WELFARE

Faced with this changing social landscape the government's preoccupation has been pragmatic – to find ways of slowing down the seemingly inexorable growth in the benefits bill. Until 1995, social security ministers resisted Treasury demands to cut levels of benefit arguing that they were already 'modest' enough. Instead they have concentrated on giving help to those deemed to be in greatest need – restricting access (or 'targeting' as the government would describe it) rather than cutting the amounts claimants receive. Hence Invalidity Benefit has been replaced by Incapacity Benefit, which is taxable and subject to a tighter and simpler medical examination of fitness to work. Unemployment Benefit has been replaced by the Jobseeker's Allowance, payable for six months rather than a year, and with tougher rules to encourage claimants to get back into the labour market. On the other hand, extra help has been provided for low-income families in work – Family Credit Benefit is intended to make it worthwhile for parents to take lower paid employment.

BENEFITS AND YOUNG PEOPLE – AT-A-GLANCE

CONSERVATIVE	LABOUR	LIB-DEM
Have stopped paying benefits to 16 and 17 year olds.	Gordon Brown has proposed that child benefit currently paid to those over 16 still at school should be ended. The proposal may now be quietly dropped.	Propose restoring full benefit entitlements to 18-25 year olds and entitlement to Income Support for 16-18 year olds.
	Get 250,000 under 25 year-olds off benefit and into work by using money from a windfall levy on the privatised utilities.	Give all 16-19 year-olds the equivalent of at least two days a week education or training.

The government has also taken steps to curtail the benefits bill in the longer term – by 2020, men and women's pension ages will be brought together at 65 thereby saving billions in women's pensions.

Labour by contrast has opted for a so-called decade of flexible retirement – men and women would be able to retire from the age of 60, but on a reduced state pension. The party says the cost would be the same. Labour's scheme does offer more choice, but it would almost certainly increase the number of pensioners on lower incomes.

The overall impact of the government's measures has been to slow down the growth in benefit spending, not cut it and the projected figure for 1996/97 – £90 billion – makes social security by far the largest departmental budget in Whitehall and more than double the entire cost of the National Health Service.

The government has deliberately avoided a full-scale one-off benefits review which could have helped to coalesce pressure groups in opposition. Instead, it has engaged in a 'benefit by benefit' review, restricting argument to the merits of each reform. The result has been a somewhat muted debate further muffled by the fact that differences between the parties often lie in the detail.

At one time Labour was committed to restoring the link between benefits and earnings but now it too is concentrating on ways of encouraging people out of dependency, rather than spending more. The Conservatives stopped benefits paid to 16- and 17-year-olds arguing that they could stay at school or go on a government training scheme. The opposition was appalled – the Liberal Democrats say they will restore the payments, but Labour has proposed what some regard as an even tougher regime. Single people under 25 would have to make a choice between a job, training or education – staying on full benefit would not be an option. The shadow chancellor, Gordon Brown, has also proposed that Child Benefit now paid to those over 16 still at school should be scrapped and the savings targeted at poorer households with young people in education. Internal opposition, as well as the ammunition this 'teenage tax' gave the Tories, seem to have caused a rethink, and the proposal may now be quietly dropped.

In spite of the rhetoric, the differences between the main parties on social security are not as great as they were. All remain committed to a mix of means-tested and universal benefits. There is also consensus on the desirability of encouraging individuals to make provision themselves wherever possible – as one Labour spokesman put it, high social-security spending should not be seen as evidence of success but a sign of failure.

In both Labour and Conservative ranks there are those who believe that continuing to pay Child Benefit to all mothers does not represent the best use of scarce resources – but neither party has yet dared to propose abolition or means-testing, and Labour seems to have ruled out taxing the benefit as impractical and likely to alienate middle-income voters.

On the face of it the clearest difference between the parties lies with the state pension. In an extraordinary move just weeks before the election was announced the Conservatives produced a succession of social policy initiatives in a determined effort to show that the government had not run out of ideas. Chief among them was a far reaching plan to privatise the state pension for those about to enter the workforce, to phase out the state's second tier pension SERPS (the State Earnings Related Pension) and to offer instead a guarantee that should private provision fail for anyone the state would step in to provide the equivalent of today's basic state pension. Thus the government would no longer be a central funder and provider of incomes in retirement but would instead revert to being a regulator of private pension funds and a safety net for those unable to look after themselves.

Although the Conservatives' changes would be introduced over forty years they represent another significant step towards redefining the role of the state in social policy. They insist that they are not proposing to abolish the state pension and in a sense that is right – it will still be there in a new guise as a guaranteed minimum. But the responsibility for ensuring that elderly people have adequate income in retirement would shift from the state to the individual.

All the politicians know that the relative value of the state pension is likely to be reduced over time anyway and that as such its importance will diminish – nevertheless the government's opponents will be able to make much of their commitment to retain the basic pension in its present form in perpetuity. What they are unlikely to point out is that as earnings rise the pension will in any event fall further and further behind general living standards because it is no longer linked to earnings and no government is going to be able to revert to that – had it been linked only to prices since it was introduced it would be worth around £23 today instead of more than £60. In spite of the rhetoric then, the importance of the basic pension looks certain to continue to decline. Given Labour's new emphasis on public-private partnerships and its backing for individual savings, it seems inevitable that the state pension will increasingly be regarded as no more than a small but useful foundation on to which elderly people will be expected to add their own savings and pension.

There was a time when political parties would go into elections promising an immediate pension increase, or a boost for Child Benefit – today, the emphasis has switched to tax cuts and claims of financial prudence. Hence cracking down on benefit fraud (officially estimated at £1.4 billion a year) is backed by all parties as is the idea that social security should, if possible, be a hand up rather than just a hand-out. There is little talk of making benefits more generous, and seemingly little appetite among those not receiving them to pay more to achieve this. The welfare debate has moved from competing claims of generosity and profligacy to an argument about who can run the system most efficiently and reduce the burden on the taxpayer by lifting claimants out of dependency whenever possible.

In addition, the Conservatives have begun to develop a new minimalist vision of welfare in which the state offers minimum guarantees while at the same time providing incentives for those who helps themselves.

LONG-TERM CARE

This principle has been applied in the government's last minute proposals for long term care aimed at addressing the deep anxiety among many middle aged and older people who have built up expectations that the welfare state would be there to support them in return for the national insurance contributions they made during their working lives. Instead when they have found themselves needing long term care they have bumped into a means-tested system run by local authorities, in which elderly people are admitted to private residential and nursing care – those with more than modest means are required to sacrifice their homes and savings to pay the cost of the fees. In the mean time, the National Health Service has been quietly divesting itself of free long-term care places.

LONG-TERM CARE FOR THE ELDERLY – AT-A-GLANCE

CONSERVATIVE	LABOUR	LIB-DEM
Propose that people should take out insurance to fund their long-term care.	Support the establishment of a Royal Commission to work out a fair system for funding long-term care of the elderly.	Believe a 'national consensus' is needed to establish a viable, long-term system to finance long-term care.

Faced with mounting anger, not least among its own supporters, the government initially increased the amount elderly people could retain before they were required to contribute – in 1996, the threshold went up from £8,000 to £16,000. It has also sought to clarify the distinction between free health care and means-tested social care. In one of its last acts before the election was called the government went further producing a scheme in which those who took out a private insurance policy for long-term care could have their home and savings protected after the insurance had run out. In return for the individual taking out insurance the state would apply a less punitive means test allowing them to keep more of their assets. Like some of the other last minute initiatives in the social sphere the long-term care scheme was an electoral gamble – it may have reassured some Conservative supporters but it also raised the profile of an issue others might have preferred to forget.

Labour has promised a Royal Commission into the whole question of long-term care. It would examine who should provide and fund it. However, it is difficult to imagine a new government whatever its complexion, agreeing to invest large sums of additional public money into this area. In the longer term the solutions look certain to come from individuals making provisions of one sort or another for themselves and their families.

RACE

Ethnic minorities remain a relatively small proportion of the UK population – just over 5 per cent. At one time, race and immigration were more significant election issues, but while they still command public attention they no longer arouse the same passions. The handling of applicants for political asylum is the one issue that has threatened to alter this modest equilibrium. The government has responded to a rapid growth in applicants by attempting to speed up the process. It has also identified countries where it claims the risk of political persecution is minimal or non-existent and from which it would not normally accept political refugees. The opposition parties have accused the government of using the asylum issue to play on racial prejudice – a charge that is vehemently denied. Labour has supported a number of high-profile cases but it too has backed tight immigration laws, and there is no indication that any of the main parties would significantly change the flow of people into the UK.

When the Conservative backbencher Nicholas Budgen – who represents Enoch Powell's old Wolverhampton seat – attempted to divide the party leaders on immigration during question time just before the campaign, both Mr Major and Mr Blair quickly asserted their determination to be seen to be at one on the broader principles of race relations.

But poverty and race still go together: a non-white individual under 65 is nearly twice as likely to be in the poorest fifth of the population as a white person in the same age band, and in this age band the non-white is half as likely to be in the top fifth. Unemployment among young people from ethnic minorities is 31 per cent compared with 20 per cent for whites. None of the main parties in Britain, however, supports positive discrimination on the grounds of race. There are of course significant differences within the ethnic minority population – Indians for example, are likely to be better off than Bangladeshis or West Indians, and educational achievements among some Asian communities exceed the white population.

The question of relations between the police and sections of the black and Asian populations – again, especially among young people – has divided the parties with the Conservatives tending to back the police where officers have allegedly assaulted suspects in unprovoked attacks. The degree of suspicion and alienation among black youth is such that many of them regard all politicians with equal disdain.

FAMILY VALUES

Politicians, like everyone else, have struggled to make sense of the social turbulence around them. The rising tide of divorce and the growing number of one-parent families (partly but not wholly caused by family breakdown) and the increases in youth crime and school exclusions have caused some to hark back to seemingly more stable and happier times.

This view appeared to be enshrined in the government's hapless slogan 'Back to Basics' with its implied objective of returning to values that had been lost in the new order. Since the ignominious dropping of the theme in 1993, amidst accusations of 'sleaze' and sexual impropriety, the Conservatives have been careful to avoid being seen to promote personal morality in this way. Even the decision to freeze and phase out special benefits for lone parents cited arguments about equity (why should one set of claimants get more than another?) rather than any ethical claim about the undesirability of encouraging more single mothers. Likewise, when a White Paper last year proposed to make it easier for women to have their baby adopted, this was proffered as a desirable alternative to abortion – ministers denied any suggestion that they wanted to discourage lone mothers from choosing to bring up their own children.

The leaderships of the two main parties are content to say that two parents are generally better than one, but are quick to reassure that this should not be taken to imply that one parent cannot do an excellent job. Moral rectitude can cost votes as well as win them, and insulting large numbers of parents who have found themselves on their own – for whatever reason – is no longer seen as good politics. If there is one thing politicians have learned during the last few years it is that the family is an area where wise policy-makers fear to tread. The catch is that there seem to be an increasing number of times when there is no alternative but to intervene.

THE CHILD SUPPORT AGENCY

Few government creations have inspired such vitriol as the Child Support Agency. Established in 1991, it is an attempt to ensure that parents fulfil their financial obligations to their children even if they are not the principal carer. The aim was to achieve a fair settlement between the state, the parent with care and the so-called absent parent, with the interests of the children being paramount.

From the outset the CSA was a public relations disaster. It attracted criticism from lone parents, who pointed out that they were not receiving the maintenance to which they were entitled; from fathers and their second wives, who claimed to be driven to penury by excessive CSA demands, and from men wrongly accused of fathering children they had never heard of. There are some signs that the earlier chaos has been replaced with a modicum of order and the past year has seen fewer hostile headlines. However, opposition to the CSA remains strong among the 200,000 people who have had to deal with it in the last four years. The government has acknowledged that serious mistakes were made both in policy and implementation and has made a number of changes – in particular, through a series of concessions made to second families. The CSA has saved the tax-payer £1.5 billion through reduced benefit payments, but it remains deeply unpopular. Its electoral impact will be limited unless further stories arise during the campaign but there certainly will be parents (especially fathers and second wives) whose hatred of the CSA is sufficient to stop them supporting the Conservatives.

For this group, Labour are unlikely to be the beneficiaries – while criticising many aspects of the CSA and arguing that it should do more for children (and, by implication, less for the Treasury), Labour has consistently maintained that the CSA is the right solution to the modern problem of child maintenance. The Liberal Democrats, by contrast, are pledged to scrap the CSA and return to a courts-based system which would allow for discretion in individual cases.

DIVORCE

Government frustration in its attempts to reform the divorce law in England and Wales is another key social policy that is likely to affect the lives of millions, yet will probably have minimal electoral impact. This is partly because the divisions are not neatly down party lines and partly because most of those who will be affected in time are for now ignorant of the fact – the new law will not come into force before the end of 1998.

The main opposition to the current reform has come from the Conservative backbenches, where an alliance of Roman Catholic and traditionally minded MPs and peers objected to the extension of the principle of so-called 'no-fault' divorce and to the original government proposal that such divorces could take place after a 12-month waiting period. That has now been amended so that all divorcing couples will have to wait for a 3-month cooling off period, followed either by a 9-month period for reflection or a 15-month period if one party asks. for it or where they have children under 16. The government has sought to portray its reform as a means of putting the interests of children first and to suggest, if anything, that the 18-month waiting period could encourage couples to get back together again. The hope is that the change will curb rather than fuel the divorce rate, which has begun to plateau after years of relentless growth. Ministers also want to halt the relentless rise in the cost of legal aid which has almost trebled in England since 1988.

Opponents of reform believe the Act will lead to more, not fewer, divorces. The difficulty for those wishing to back them is that none of the main parties is offering a distinct alternative. Critics within the relationship counselling sector and the legal profession have also complained that the new system is likely to be underfunded, and that some seeking a divorce (especially women) will end up without legal representation, and will suffer as a result.

A NATION TOGETHER?

There have been brief moments in the last few years when the United Kingdom has lived up to its name – the national lottery has provided an activity in which the vast majority of the population can take part simultaneously. However frivolous, it has been a talking point, a focus of mutual interest. Typically, though, its success has been marred by disputes over the size of the organisers' profits and by arguments about which good causes should benefit. Whatever political advantage the government might have hoped to gain from launching such a popular venture will have been more than offset by these squabbles in its wake.

And in England at least, the success of the Euro 96 soccer tournament – in particular the nail-biting contribution of Terry Venables' team – achieved a momentary feel-good factor which some politicians, for a while, actually thought might kickstart a more general revival, with potential benefits to the government. Ever since England's World Cup win in 1966, the year of Harold Wilson's second election victory, political folklore has it that sporting triumph favours incumbent governments – the evidence is sketchy at best.

The VE and VJ Day celebrations in 1995 likewise appeared to bring young and old together, inspired by memories of a period when a single national achieved so much – the collective silence was respected throughout the country. And the massacre of small children at Dunblane Primary School united the nation in mourning – for a moment, politicians earned respect for the dignity with which they attempted to express a shared anguish.

It did not last long. The subsequent row over the abolition of handguns split the government from the main opposition parties with their call for a total ban. Yet in spite of some of the nationalistic outpourings over the beef crisis and the fishing dispute with Spain, the sense of UK nationhood appears weak – not because there is any strong affinity with Europe, nor even because of frustrations in Scotland and Wales, but perhaps because at least some of the social cement that once held this country together has begun to crack. Thus far there is little evidence that any of the political parties has captured the imagination of the electorate in the task of repair and renewal.

CLASS WARS

THE GREAT EDUCATION DEBATE

Mike Baker

Mike Baker is Education Correspondent for BBC News. He joined the BBC in 1980 as a graduate news trainee. He was appointed a Regional Political Correspondent in 1981, a Parliamentary Correspondent in 1984, and in 1988 he became a Political Correspondent, before taking up his current postion.

Just as the political debate over education appeared to be settling down after the radical changes of the Thatcher years, the choices of secondary schools by two not-so-ordinary London households for their sons re-ignited the issue. The choices by Tony Blair and Harriet Harman of, respectively, an opted-out school and a selective school, are bound to be referred to time and again by the Tories in the general election campaign.

The Conservatives will press the charge of hypocrisy, saying Shadow Cabinet members choose schools for their own children that they wish to deny to others. Harriet Harman's choice is particularly sensitive as it highlights a division over selection within the Labour party that, in its own way, resembles the Tories' own problems over Europe. Many on the Left want a clearer commitment to abolition of the remaining 160 or so grammar schools. However, the official policy, representing something of a fudge, is to base such decisions on referendums of local parents.

The intensity of the debate over selective education was further fanned by the government's introduction of an Education Bill in autumn 1996 which sought to require all schools to consider annually whether to introduce selection. It also proposed to allow greater freedoms for schools to select some of their pupils by ability or aptitude without having to go through the formal process of changing status. Opted-out schools would be allowed to select up to half of their pupils in this way. The Conservatives will want to focus attention on selection and parental choice. The notion of a grammar school in every town, floated by John Major but greeted rather coolly by Gillian Shephard, is one that might well reappear during this election campaign.

Whatever the issues, all three main parties now see education as a potential vote-winner and schools could well receive the attention afforded to the NHS at the last election. After all, Tony Blair has said his top three priorities are 'education, education and education' and has promised that a big Education Bill would be at the top of a Labour government's first Queen's Speech.

The Liberal Democrats are hardly shy on education either, having long planted their campaign banner on a promise to spend more on schools even if that means raising taxes. The other parties, less keen on specific spending pledges, have kept pace with a rush of initiatives, many verging on the gimmicky. Labour and Tories slugged it out with calls for more homework, an issue normally left to schools. Unusually, the teacher unions agreed with the Tory view that Labour was wrong to propose national minimum amounts of homework. Soon after, though, it became clear that instead of a minimum of 90 minutes homework a night, the Conservatives wanted pupils 'on parade' after school. Their plan to promote school-based military cadet corps amazed most teachers as all but a tiny handful of state schools

CLASS WARFARE – AT-A-GLANCE

CONSERVATIVE	LABOUR	LIB-DEM
Total education spending on schools, colleges and universities has increased in real terms by 31% in the decade to 1995.	Doubt over Gordon Brown's proposal to scrap child benefit for 16 to 18 year-olds, diverting £700m to education and training.	Promise to raise taxation by a penny, to increase education spending by £2 billion.
Argue that there is no direct connection between class size and standards.	Will phase out assisted places scheme to limit class sizes to 30 or under for 5, 6 and 7 year-olds.	Work to reduce primary school classes to more than 30.
Want more schools to opt out of local authority control.	Rename opted-out schools and bring their funding in line with other schools.	Return opted-out schools to local authority control, but allow them more independence.
Encourage schools to specialise and diversify.	Require schools to agree admission policies with local authorities.	Oppose the wholesale expansion of grammar schools, but leave decisions about selection to local communities.

abandoned them years ago. However, as has become the pattern on education, Labour felt obliged to support the initiative out of fear of being seen as soft on discipline. Not for a very long time have Labour and the Tories been crowding into the same narrow area of education policy, tough on discipline, academic rigour and standards. Luckily for both parties, most school pupils are too young to vote.

For, despite the intensity of the rhetoric, the reality is that Labour and Tory education policies have converged over the past few years. Their plans to raise standards by closing failing schools, targeting inadequate teachers and setting improvement targets, are now similar. Yet, as in so many areas, the closer they have become, the harder they try to appear distinctive.

Just a few years ago, the Tories seemed readier to talk about anything else but education. Under John Patten, the government's raft of education reforms appeared to be heading for the rapids. The National Curriculum was unravelling, the national tests for children at 7, 11 and 14 were being boycotted by teachers and class sizes were mushrooming. The government's unlikely saviour was a quiet and modest knight. Sir Ron Dearing slashed the content of the national curriculum and persuaded the teachers to oversee the tests. He did not save Mr Patten's political career but he laid a solid base for the next Education Secretary, Gillian Shephard.

She was an unusual choice: unlike many of her predecessors, she arrived at the Department for Education already knowing a lot about schools. As a former teacher and school inspector (and wife of a retired head teacher and NUT member), she understood the practical realities of the chalkface. This has sometimes prevented her responding with maximum enthusiasm to some of the ideas from the Downing Street policy unit and, in the cruel world of internal party politics, has led to occasional sniping from colleagues that she has 'gone native'. Unlike her immediate predecessor, Mrs Shephard also managed to praise teachers without patronising them. Yet, while the curriculum and testing are no longer such damaging issues for the Conservatives, she has not been able to dispel concerns over other key issues, such as funding, standards and discipline. These, along with the Tories' chosen areas of selection, opting-out and nursery vouchers, are the issues likely to dominate during the election campaign.

FUNDING

The outbreak of parental protest over school-funding cuts in 1995 sent a tremor through the government and shook many Tory back-benchers. Mrs Shephard battled hard in the next two public spending rounds and emerged with some more money. But with growing numbers of pupils in schools, the cuts are not over and class sizes continue to rise. It is not inconceivable that new pockets of protest could burst out right in the middle of the election as figures for local funding emerge.

Education 'cuts' are hard to assess. A few schools have been forced into drastic measures, such as sending children home early. But some of the more alarmist predictions of job losses failed to come true. Nevertheless, although the exact number is hard to establish, figures from the local authorities suggested some 9,000 teachers' jobs went in the summer term of 1995 alone. However, the government points out many new jobs were also created in the same period.

The election may well see a repeat of the rows over whether central or local government is to blame for inadequate school budgets. In the Commons in March 1995, the Prime Minister blamed town hall bureaucracy, saying there were two administrators for every three teachers. As this sort of charge is often repeated, it is worth a closer look.

According to the Local Government Management Board 376,665 teachers and 316,244 other staff are employed in education in England and Wales. 162,000 of the latter were not 'administrators' but cleaners, caretakers and groundsmen, most of them part-timers. A further 110,000 were, according to the Department for Education's evidence to the Pay Review Body, bursars and secretaries employed in schools. Further inspection reveals that the alleged administrators included staff such as educational psychologists, welfare officers, and youth workers. So the final ratio of teachers to Town Hall administrators is more like 9:1 than 3:2.

The row over funding is a dangerous one to arbitrate. However, the Audit Commission reported that between 1994/95 and 1995/96 the average funding per pupil rose in cash terms by 0.9 per cent in primary schools, and by 0.5 per cent for secondary schools. These figures, the Audit Commission noted, were 'statistically significantly less' than the recent teachers' pay award (2.7 per cent) and the retail prices index (3.5 per cent). The same report also confirmed the trend towards larger classes. One way of showing this is through the pupil–teacher ratio, although this does not indicate exact class size as it includes head teachers, deputies and other staff who may not be teaching all the time. The figures show a steady rise since 1992 (see Table 1). An international comparison by the OECD (1992) showed the UK had one of the worst pupil–teacher ratios among advanced countries, with only Turkey and Ireland having a higher ratio. Those with a better ratio included France, Germany, Spain, Australia, Italy and the Scandinavian countries.

TABLE 1: CLASS SIZES: PUPIL–TEACHER RATIO IN PRIMARY SCHOOLS (ENGLAND AND WALES)

1988	1989	1990	1991	1992	1993	1994	1995	1996
22.1	21.9	22.0	22.2	22.2	22.4	22.7	22.8	23.2

Source: Department of Education and Employment and Audit Commission

The Conservatives argue that there is no direct connection between class size and standards. While it is true there is no definitive evidence from Britain, a large-scale research project in Tennessee suggests that much smaller classes do benefit the youngest children. Labour has said it will phase out the government's scheme of subsidised places at independent schools and use the savings to limit class sizes in infant schools. The Conservatives, who favour expanding the assisted places scheme, say any savings Labour might make would have little effect on class sizes. So funding will be a key issue. The Conservatives will argue that total education spending on schools, colleges and universities has increased in real terms by 31 per cent in the decade to 1995. However, the number of young people in education has risen during this time. The Liberal Democrats' promise to put 1p on income tax to pay for education would raise about £2 billion. Labour, of course, has been wary of spending pledges – even Gordon Brown's proposal to end Child Benefit for 16-18 year olds to raise an extra £700 million for education and training now seems doomed.

In the end, though, most voters who are parents will judge the situation according to what they know about their own children's school budget. Ironically, this is where the Conservatives' reforms could rebound on them. In the past, the funding argument was a political football between town halls and central government. Now that school governors have budgetary control they are a strong, local voice that parents tend to trust because they know them as fellow parents. If governors point the finger at central government, they are likely to be believed.

STANDARDS

Concern over standards was stoked by the annual report of the Chief Inspector of Schools in England in February 1996. He said 'overall standards of pupil achievement need to be raised in about half of primary and two-fifths of secondary schools'. He also repeated his belief that around 15,000 incompetent teachers should be sacked and urged primary school teachers to give greater emphasis to traditional aspects of teaching such as mental arithmetic and phonic skills in reading.

However, the big question – whether standards have risen or fallen over the past few decades – remains unanswered. A major inquiry carried out for the government in 1996 reported that a lack of past examination scripts made it impossible to give a definitive answer. Yet the question of whether standards are falling, and who is to blame, is certain to be asked in the campaign, but, as the experts found, it is a complex issue. Certainly there has been a steady rise in the proportion of youngsters getting good examination passes (see Table 2).

TABLE 2: PERCENTAGE OF AGE GROUP WITH FIVE OR MORE GRADES A TO C OR EQUIVALENT AT GCSE (ENGLAND AND WALES)

1989	1991	1993	1995	1996
32.8%	36.8%	41.2%	43.5%	44.5%

Source: Department for Education and Employment

Britain is also producing an increasing number of graduates each year. One in 3 young people now go into higher education, compared to 1 in 8 in 1979 and 1 in 17 in the 1960s. The annual total of new graduates has risen from 133,000 in 1984 to 211,000 a decade later. However, some people would argue that the quality of many degrees has fallen as the quantity has risen.

It is more difficult to assess standards in primary schools. A few years ago a group of educational psychologists caused a stir when they claimed reading standards amongst 7-year-olds were falling. A follow-up inquiry by the school examinations body SEAC concluded that evidence of 'some decline' was found in 19 out of the 26 Local Education Authorities which were able to measure reading standards over a number of years. A further study by the National Foundation for Educational Research found that reading performance had fallen slightly between 1987 and 1991, although not uniformly across all schools. The study of 2,000 children suggested an average fall equal to about two and half months in reading age.

These findings came around the same time that international comparisons found that our young people were performing far worse than their equivalents in other countries in basic arithmetic tests. In tests for 9-year-olds, English pupils came 11th out of 14 countries. English pupils got 59 per cent correct answers, compared to Koreans

who managed 75 per cent. Scottish pupils did rather better scoring
66 per cent. More recently, the Secondary Heads Association
reported that 11-year-olds, tested on arrival at secondary school, were
showing declining scores in basic literacy and numeracy. Two-thirds
of schools surveyed found results had fallen in recent years.

So there is conflicting evidence over whether there has been a
decline in the basics amongst younger children. The explanation
for this could lie with the introduction of the National Curriculum.
The disruptive period of its introduction, and subsequent revisions,
coincides with the fall in reading standards. Many teachers would
argue that the requirement to teach primary pupils nine subjects
plus religious education has squeezed out time for the basics.
The government, though, is more likely to blame poor, so-called
'progressive' teaching methods for any fall in literacy, a view which
has the backing of HM Chief Inspector of Schools in England,
Chris Woodhead.

Perhaps the most curious aspect of the political row over standards
is the way the government and Labour have subtly changed position.
While the Tories were planning major reforms it suited them to
emphasise the evidence of poor standards, but now after so long in
office, they have started to defend the record of schools, since
current standards now reflect on an education system they have
created. At the same time, Labour no longer jumps to the defence of
teachers but now sees political capital in attacking standards achieved
under Conservative governments.

OPTING-OUT

The arrangements for schools to opt-out of local authority control and
become grant-maintained could well change substantially according to
the election result. In simple terms, the Conservatives want more
schools to opt out; Labour wants to rename them and bring their
funding in line with other schools; and the Liberal Democrats want
to return them to the local authority framework. There are over
1,000 grant-maintained schools out of around 25,000 schools in
Britain. They educate around 10 per cent of pupils. There is much
confusion over the nature of grant-maintained schools. They remain
state schools, providing free education but, having opted-out of the
local education authority, they now receive their funding directly from
central government.

Grant-maintained schools come in all forms: selective and
comprehensive, primary and secondary, single-sex or co-educational.

Despite popular misconception, they are not all 'posh' grammar schools. Indeed some schools opted-out in order to maintain their comprehensive status. However, around two-thirds of the surviving 150 grammar schools have opted out. A small number of grant maintained schools have introduced some form of selection since opting-out, with a few becoming grammar schools. It is also worth remembering that the advent of opting-out has increased existing differences between the education systems within the United Kingdom.

Opting-out does not apply in Northern Ireland. There are only two grant-maintained schools in Scotland, (with a third this August) fewer than 20 in Wales, and around 1,100 in England.

SELECTION

The argument over grant-maintained schools overlaps with the even more intense row over selective education. In principle, the Conservatives favour selection by academic ability, Labour and the Liberal Democrats oppose it. In practice, it is a little more complicated.

PARTY PLANS FOR GRANT-MAINTAINED SCHOOLS AT-A-GLANCE

CONSERVATIVE	LABOUR	LIB-DEM
Encourage more schools to opt out	Rename them as Foundation Schools	Return to local authority democratic framework
Encourage schools to specialise and diversify	Require local authority nominated governors	Give greater control over budgets to all schools
Greater freedom over pupil admissions	Require them to agree admission policies with local authority	Return admissions authority to local education authority
Greater freedom to raise private capital	Require them to apply for capital funding through the local authority	

The Conservative right wing has repeatedly pushed for a return of the grammar school system. With great regularity, new initiatives are floated. In March 1996, a Central-Office-inspired briefing led to a number of newspaper stories suggesting the Prime Minister wanted to see a grammar school in every large town. No firm detail emerged, however, and Tory policy emphasises the primacy of local parental wishes.

The Labour party has angered many on the Left by refusing to promise to abolish all the remaining grammar schools. Instead they will hold local referendums, probably among parents of children at 'feeder' schools, to determine whether selective admissions should continue. The Liberal Democrats would leave decisions on grammar schools to local councils.

So, despite the heat of the grammar schools row, the practical differences between the parties are not so great. Each will be led by local opinion. This is probably a wise decision for few local issues are as explosive as school reorganisation. Also, while grammar schools are popular with many parents, secondary moderns are not; and by definition you cannot have one without the other. Most opinion polls show roughly a 50:50 split over selection. However, where they survive, any perceived threat to local schools could be a vote-swinger, although even in these areas many people currently denied access to good schools might welcome them being turned into comprehensives.

NURSERY VOUCHERS

Voters have a very clear choice in nursery education. The government's nursery vouchers scheme is beginning in April when parents can start using their £1,100 vouchers. Labour believes in expanding nursery education, but believes vouchers are unnecessarily expensive and bureaucratic. David Blunkett has promised to abolish the scheme although that will take at least 18 months to achieve. So, much is at stake.

What are nursery vouchers? The name is misleading for a start. They are more correctly vouchers for four-year-olds as they are exchangeable at pre-school playgroups, nursery classes or schools or reception classes at infant or primary schools. The voucher does not confer any entitlement to a place. If there is no nursery-age provision in your area you cannot use the voucher. Nevertheless, the vouchers may prove to be an effective electoral inducement as many parents will feel they are getting something for nothing. Of course, it is rarely that simple. Most of the money for the vouchers has been found by taking money away from Local Education Authorities which were already spending it on nursery education. The more places a council provides now, the more money it loses to the scheme. Only if it wins back those vouchers from parents will it break even.

For a few parents – those who pay for private-sector nursery education or care – there is a direct financial benefit. However the value of the voucher will usually only cover a proportion of the cost at most private nursery schools. Indeed some private schools may not accept the vouchers at all.

The Conservatives believe the virtue of vouchers is that they give spending power to parents not local councils. They think the scheme will encourage new providers to come forward. Labour claimed the money would be diverted from state nurseries into private ones. But just days before the campaign began, a leaked report from the cross party Commons select committee on Education pointed to early evidence of the opposite – that because some primary schools were deliberately starting four-year olds early to take advantage of the vouchers – both state and private nursery schools risked being starved of funding and pupils.

Vouchers are quite likely to be an active issue during the campaign – they come into effect even as the politicians are on the stump, and there is much at stake. The Tories have long wished to extend their market-based vision of education to its logical conclusion – vouchers for mainstream schools. If eventually they are made to work, Conservative enthusiasm – first encouraged by Mrs Thatcher – might mean extending them to older children.

DISCIPLINE

The issue of discipline in schools exploded onto the political scene in late 1996. The teachers' union, the NAS/UWT, raised the stakes when its members refused to teach a number of disruptive pupils. The highest profile case was The Ridings School in Halifax where discipline collapsed so seriously that the school was closed for several days and an emergency inspection team sent in.

At one level, the issue of school discipline offers little scope for party campaigning as there is a broad consensus on the measures required. But we may well see some political mud-slinging over who is to blame when schools fail in this way. Labour and the Liberal Democrats saw The Ridings as an indictment of the government's market-based school system. They point to the presence of grammar and opted-out schools in Halifax and say competition between schools helped turn The Ridings into a 'sink school'. The Conservatives meanwhile prefer to focus attention on the fact that Labour ran the local education authority in Calderdale. It certainly suited the Conservatives that it was a head teacher from an opted-out school who was sent in to revive The Ridings.

THE CAMPAIGN

The education debate is likely to be far more intense and given a much higher profile than in recent general elections. Voters, and parents, will have to watch closely to spot the difference between gimmicks and genuine vision and to decide who is stealing whose policy clothes. A particular difficulty is that after so much rapid change, many voters are still struggling to understand the status quo, never mind further change. Only the Liberal Democrats, though, appear to look back fondly to the pre-Thatcher school system. Both Labour and the Conservatives are campaigning for yet more change. For the Tories the logic is that they are still only half-way to a fully market-driven system. As for Labour, they decided after the last election that they could no longer defend the status quo in education when so much evidence pointed to continuing pupil under-performance in many areas.

Once the campaign is underway in earnest, though, the concern of all parties will be to avoid any banana-skins or incidents like the 'Jennifer's Ear' health row of the last election. The party spin-doctors will want to know every detail of where their own candidates, and those of their opponents, send their children to school. The sons and daughters of politicians would be well advised to pull their school caps down low and avoid talking to strangers with notebooks on their way through the school gates.

TALKING TOUGH

CRIME, LAW AND PUNISHMENT

Jane Peel

*Jane Peel is the Home and Legal Affairs
Correspondent for BBC News. She has worked as
a journalist since 1981, joining the BBC in 1985
as a reporter on Radio Lincolnshire, then moving
to BBC Essex, where she became News Editor.
In 1989 she was appointed as a reporter for
BBC Radio in London and in 1990 to her
present position.*

Thirty years ago, it would have been inconceivable that any political
party other than the Conservatives could claim the mantle 'party of
law and order'. There is now, however, little 'clear, blue water'
between the main parties on the issue – and in particular between
the Conservatives and Labour.

Over the years, the issue of crime and punishment has ebbed and
flowed in importance to the electorate. Particularly brutal crimes and
their coverage in the media have been responsible for upsurges in
public concern, but have never been an election decider.

However, opinion polls suggest two important differences between
the climate in 1997 and that of 30 years ago, or even 18 years ago
when the Conservatives came to power. The first is that law and order
is creeping up the league table of issues considered most important
by voters; the second is that opinion polls suggest Labour is now
considered to be the party with the best policies on law and order
(see Figure 1 overleaf).

The sea-change in Labour party policy dates from Tony Blair's
tenure as Shadow Home Secretary. In February, 1993, he gave an
interview in the *New Statesman*. In it, he established 'new' Labour's
'new' credentials on crime, which answered criticism (from the then
Home Secretary, Kenneth Baker, in February 1992) that Labour was

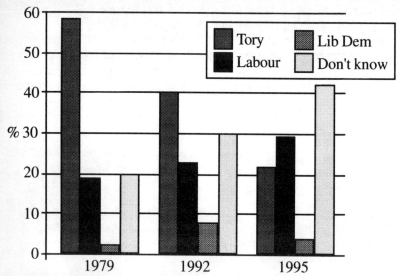

Figure 1 Best party on law and order (*Source:* MORI)

'soft-headed and flabby' on crime. Tony Blair said: 'There are no excuses for crime ... but ... where a community suffers poor education, bad housing, lack of employment or training opportunities, and broken families living in sub-standard conditions, it is more likely to produce criminals than communities where hope and opportunity exists for all.' He went on: 'We should be tough on crime and tough on the causes of crime.'

Just two weeks later, John Major gave an interview to the *Mail on Sunday*, in which he put law and order at the top of the Tory agenda, and at the centre of his 'Back to Basics' campaign. He called it his 'crusade against crime' and said 'Society needs to condemn a little more and understand a little less'.

Since then, the two main parties have been vying with each other to see who can be the toughest on crime, with the Liberal Democrats filling the position of the main opposition to both of them on law and order.

If anything, the arrival of Jack Straw as Labour's Home Affairs Spokesman signalled a further hardening of the party's approach. This one-time left-wing student radical was now calling for the streets to be reclaimed from aggressive 'winos, addicts, and squeegee merchants' (September 1995) – something even the Home Secretary thought was too tough. Jack Straw also suggested that neighbours who made too much noise should be locked up.

Much later, Tony Blair re-entered the fray. In January 1997 he
gave an interview to the *Big Issue*, the magazine sold by the
homeless. In it he supported the New York idea of 'zero tolerance'
where the police clamp down hard on the most minor of infringe-
ments, arresting graffiti artists, beggars and the like, on the basis
that tackling petty misdemeanors will lead to a drop in serious crime.
(The American experience suggests there is some truth in this,
although there are other factors which may have helped reduce crime
in New York).

Mr Blair said we should be 'intolerant of people homeless on
the streets'. The interview prompted a quick response from the
Conservatives. The Prime Minister said Mr Blair had stolen his
clothes – Mr Major had spoken out against aggressive begging
two years earlier and the Labour leader had then accused him
of being petty and vindictive. There was some truth and some
massaging of the quotations going on here. It was a clear
indication that a general election was approaching fast, and
that Labour had moved so far to the right on law and order that
in some areas they were becoming indistinguishable from
the Conservatives.

Labour's decision to make this huge leap (and it must have been
a careful and conscious one) sprang from a recognition that it was
Labour's own supporters who had the most to fear from crime.
The 'working class' in inner cities are more likely to be the victims
of crime and to suffer from the anti-social behaviour of others.
Although in the past Labour had not taken this approach, for the
new-style party it must have seemed obvious that to appeal to their
natural constituency in this way could be advantageous.

The government's response has been to accuse Labour of
hypocrisy, of changing their clothes for electoral gain, and to point
to all the occasions on which Labour has voted against its numerous
attempts to legislate for a tougher criminal justice policy. (There have
been 34 Criminal Justice Bills introduced into Parliament since 1979).
The Deputy Prime Minister, Michael Heseltine, even went as far as to
call Labour 'the villain's friend', in a BBC Radio interview in January
1996. It was a sign that the Conservatives, like their opponents,
continued to view law and order as a key political battleground.
And many more such signs were to follow. In March 1996, a tragedy
on a huge scale struck the people of Dunblane. The murder of 16
pupils in a primary school along with their teacher touched
everyone. The political parties united in grief – at least for a time.

FIREARMS

Thomas Hamilton killed his victims at Dunblane with guns he held legally. Michael Ryan had the done the same at Hungerford nine years earlier. Then, the Thatcher government had acted to ban some firearms from private ownership (although not the type which killed most of the Hungerford victims). This time it was going to be different. Dunblane could not be allowed to happen again.

The government set up an inquiry under Lord Cullen. But even before his recommendations became known the rows began. Shooters' groups, MPs, the police, and a new single-issue pressure group set up to support the Dunblane families and fight for a ban on all handguns, began to use an eager media to publicise their views. Labour stole the Tories' thunder at their party conference when they gave a platform to an eloquent proponent of the anti-gun campaign. Labour then announced they would support a total ban on handguns. Of the various political parties and interested groups, there were some who held the middle ground, but it was largely a case of those who wanted all handguns prohibited versus those who did not.

When Lord Cullen's report was published in October 1996, it was immediately overshadowed. Cullen himself proposed sweeping changes to the firearms licensing system, to make sure individuals like Thomas Hamilton (and indeed Michael Ryan before him) could never legally own a weapon. But he stopped short of recommending a ban on handguns, suggesting instead changes to the ways they were stored.

That was not enough for the government. It announced it would ban all handguns except .22 calibre (the smallest kind used in Olympic competitions). So anxious to get this into law was the government that the Home Secretary, Michael Howard swiftly published a Firearms Bill, announced that all gun owners would have to give up their newly-illegal weapons by April 1997, and said all Conservative MPs were expected to vote in favour of the measure.

There was no question of Labour thwarting the passage of the Bill and the opposition came rather from within Tory ranks, with support from the Liberal Democrats, and the House of Lords. The opponents wanted more compensation offered to those whose weapons, and in some cases livelihoods, would be destroyed. When the House of Lords successfully passed an amendment to compensate gun clubs, Labour's Jack Straw immediately offered the Home Secretary help to reverse the defeat when the Bill returned to the Commons for final approval. With this style of co-operation there was little danger of the Bill falling.

CRIME FIGURES

Although the firearms issue has caught the public imagination as a
political issue, thankfully, it is unlikely to have a major impact on most
people's lives. Crime in general, however, does, though in reality the
fear of crime far outweighs the likelihood of it actually happening.

Home Office figures released twice a year show recorded crime
in England and Wales (separate figures are published in Scotland*).
They cover all the crimes recorded by the police. They do not cover
all the crimes reported by the public, and certainly not all the crimes
that actually occur (different police forces have different ways of
recording crime, and some offences are never reported).

The unreliability of these figures has not stopped their publication
becoming a political battleground, with each party using them to seek
support for its approach. Labour and the Liberal Democrats were
rather thrown off guard when the figures for 1994 and 1995
suggested the inexorable tide had ebbed and was beginning a retreat
(Figure 2). This appeared to be a remarkable achievement for the

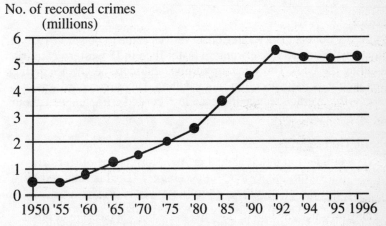

Figure 2   Recorded crime, England and Wales (*Source:* Home Office)

Home Secretary, who had inherited a tricky situation. The figures for
1995 showed he had presided over three consecutive annual falls in
recorded crime – only the third time this had happened this century.
However, in the last few months of 1995, crime began to creep up
again, and the opposition parties immediately grasped the opportunity

* Many of the policies on Law and Order will be specific to England and Wales because
of the different legal system in Scotland and, to some extent, in Northern Ireland.

to attack the Home Secretary for his failure to make an impact on crime, despite tough policies.

In September 1996, new figures showed a small rise of 0.4 per cent in overall recorded crime. Although burglary, theft and car crime continued to fall marginally, violent crime went up by 10 per cent (although violent crime accounts for only 6 per cent of all recorded offences).

WHAT THE PARTIES SAY ABOUT CRIME FIGURES

Conservatives

Crime has been rising throughout most of the industrialised world since the 1950s. In this country, the average annual increase in recorded crime has been around 6 per cent, but in the three consecutive years to 1995, recorded crime fell – the largest sustained fall for 40 years. This is a milestone in the fight against crime, is a credit to the work of the police, but no reason for complacency. More needs to be done.

Labour

Crime has doubled since the Conservatives came to power in 1979. Between 1987 and 1993, it went up faster than in 16 western countries including the USA. There is more crime, and more people are getting away with it as the conviction rate is falling. Labour's record was better – the average annual increase in recorded crime under Labour was only 3.4 per cent.

Liberal Democrats

There is still far too much violent crime. More police officers are needed in the community and a much bigger effort is required by empowered local communities to improve crime prevention. The Conservatives have failed to provide the police officers they promised, and Labour makes no clear commitments to provide adequate resources for crime prevention.

WHAT THE PARTIES SAY THEY WOULD DO OR HAVE DONE TO PREVENT CRIME

Conservatives

• Encourage crime prevention by direct or indirect funding of local initiatives.

- Promote partnerships and identify the best ways of reducing crime.

- Have launched a National Crime Prevention Agency to look at what works.

- Set up a National Crime Squad, with the help of security services and MI5, to fight serious and organised crime.

- Have encouraged and will continue to encourage more use of closed circuit TV, including help to fund schemes.

- Target resources on people who are repeatedly victims of crime.

- Increase the use of special constables, neighbourhood and street watch schemes.

- Have set up a ministerial group on juveniles to look across all government departments at how to identify children at risk of becoming offenders.

- Have funded programmes to tackle truancy.

- Will provide an extra £180 million to recruit 5,000 extra police constables by 1999.

Labour

- Make policing based more on a close relationship between police and the community, including patrols in residential neighbourhoods by known local officers.

- Give local authorities a statutory responsibility to develop community safety and crime prevention programmes (in conjunction with the police).

- Encourage neighbourhood initiatives to prevent drug dealing.

- Better physical security in high crime areas, e.g. locks, bolts and closed circuit TV.

- Introduce various policies to strengthen family relationships in response to research which suggests links between family background and crime.

- Tackle truancy early

- Offer training for those with few job prospects, targeting those most likely to offend.

- New laws to prevent racial harassment and violence with tough punishments.

Liberal Democrats

- Create partnerships between local councils, police and voluntary groups.

- Improve physical security in high crime areas, e.g. lighting, closed circuit TV, but with strict codes of practice to make sure civil liberties are respected.

- Improve pre-school education, parenting skills training, work with young offenders.

- Give local authorities a statutory responsibility for crime prevention, and require planning authorities to consider community safety.

- Consider legislation to force employers and landlords to take account of employee and community security.

- Propose the setting up of a Royal Commission to investigate strategies for combating drug misuse.

- Make schools more effective in tackling bullying and truancy.

- Give everyone, particularly the young, the opportunity for one or two years' community service for environmental projects, crime prevention etc.

- Provide resources for an extra 3,000 beat police officers.

POLICE BILL

The Police Bill started its life rather quietly. The measures to give the police the statutory right to break into properties and plant bugging devices were intended to make legal something the police had been doing for many years without the backing of legislation. The Liberal Democrats were vehemently opposed, claiming there were insufficient safeguards to protect the civil rights of innocent people. Labour were all set to support the Bill, but that was before eminent legal figures and elder statesmen, including the former Labour Prime Minister, Lord Callaghan, spoke out against it.

The main objection was that the Bill would allow these covert police operations to be carried out without the authorisation of the courts and could lead to abuse of the system. There was nothing to prevent confidential lawyer–client or journalist–source conversations from being recorded for means other than to prevent serious crime.

Labour's front bench cottoned on to the growing anxiety about the Bill and decided to withdraw their support. Amendments by Labour and the Liberal Democrats insisting on some form of judicial approval for the bugging operations succeeded in the Lords. The withdrawal of Labour support meant the Home Secretary had to concede that additional safeguards may have to be introduced.

SENTENCING OF OFFENDERS

Of all the law and order measures introduced in the last session by the government, the Crime (Sentences) Bill was their flagship, and, appropriately for such an important measure, it attracted a certain amount of controversy.

The Home Secretary, Michael Howard, said at the Tory party conference in October 1995 that he wanted to put honesty back into sentencing, and he warned potential criminals: 'If you don't want the time, don't do the crime'. It was to herald the biggest change in sentencing practice for years; it marked a radical change in the government's own thinking on sentencing policy; and it led to the biggest outcry ever heard against government policy from England's judiciary, headed by the most senior judge, the then Lord Chief Justice, Lord Taylor. His successor took over where he left off when the proposals reached the Lords more than a year later. One of the reasons for the judicial fury was that the proposals would fetter the discretion of the judges, who until now have had great scope in deciding the sentence that should be passed, according to the individual circumstances of the case.

Unabashed, Michael Howard fleshed out his far-reaching proposals in a White Paper, entitled *Protecting the Public – The Government's Strategy on Crime in England and Wales,* published in April 1996. (This paper, as its title suggests, was far more than a a document detailing the government's thinking on sentencing. It covered a wide range of issues and many observers saw it as the Conservatives' election manifesto on law and order). The Crime (Sentences) Bill followed on 25 October 1996. Its proposals included:

- The end of automatic early release for prisoners. Offenders will be able to earn a limited discount, but otherwise will serve the whole sentence passed by the court.

- Rapists and other violent offenders who commit a second offence will face automatic sentences of life imprisonment. They will be released only when the Parole Board assesses that it is safe to do so.

• Persistent burglars and hard drug dealers (those with three separate convictions for similar offences) will face minimum prison sentences of three years and seven years respectively.

LOCKING THEM UP – AT-A-GLANCE

CONSERVATIVE	LABOUR	LIB-DEM
Propose ending automatic early release for prisoners.	Require the court to explain what the prison sentence imposed actually meant. Believe it is necessary for prison order that the chance of early release should remain.	Set up a Sentencing Advisory Committee to encourage parity and ensure more sensible levels of sentencing.
Propose life imprisonment for rapists and other violent offenders who commit a second offence.	Propose unlimited sentences for anyone convicted of rape whether for a first or subsequent offence.	Abolish the mandatory life sentence for murder.
Recommend minimum prison sentences of three and seven years for persistent burglars and drug dealers respectively.	Introduce fast-track punishment for persistent young offenders by halving the time from arrest to sentencing.	

In response to the unprecedented anger of the judges, a concession was offered. Judges would be free not to pass the automatic life or minimum sentences in 'exceptional circumstances', where it would be unjust to do so. That was not enough to appease the judges, and the Bill faced considerable opposition in the House of Lords (which counts a large proportion of judges and ex-judges among its number). It had first been through the Commons where it was opposed by two former Home Secretaries – Douglas Hurd and Kenneth Baker. The Liberal Democrats also voted against – but with Labour declining to do so, it passed through the Commons with a majority of more than 200. Labour wanted amendments to 'improve' the Bill in a number of areas, but were not willing to help defeat it and face accusations that they had gone soft on crime. In particular, Labour wanted more supervision for offenders once they were released from prison.

In the Lords debate in January, it was a different story. Led by the new Lord Chief Justice, Lord Bingham, the judges, Law Lords and some Conservative peers mauled the Bill. Lord Bingham called it flawed, radically unsound, indefensible, indiscriminate, and likely to lead to injustice. If that was not enough, he said it would not reduce crime, protect society, be cost effective, or work in practice. His speech lasted half an hour and there was not a single word of support for the Bill in it.

The opposition ensured that some changes were likely when the

Lords committee which would scrutinise the Bill line by line began its work, but the government were in no mood to compromise on their flagship Bill and it moved towards becoming law largely intact.

'PRISON WORKS'

Despite its brevity, this was one of the most controversial statements ever uttered by a Home Secretary. 'Prison works' – Michael Howard declared to the Conservative party conference in October 1994. It seemed to contradict every piece of Home Office research carried out in recent years, and even the Conservatives' own views until then, which had been based on that research. Just four years earlier the government had concluded that prison was 'an expensive way of making bad people worse' (Source: White Paper on crime, 1990).

What Mr Howard went on to say, though, was that 'prison works' because while offenders are in jail, they are not out committing crimes. Few could or would even try to disagree with that, but those two words were to be used frequently by his opponents to criticise what had become a much harsher penal policy. The Home Secretary himself, was to use it as a stick with which to beat anyone who looked like advocating a liberal penal policy.

The change in the government's prisons policy included the introduction of more austere regimes for inmates, mandatory drug testing in jails, and the proposal to establish boot camps, like those in the USA, which give young offenders a mix of education, and military-style training. Labour and the Liberal Democrats remain firmly opposed to the idea of boot camps.

The effect of the Conservatives' prison policy can be seen most starkly by looking at the change in the prison population in England and Wales. In 1997, it was higher than it has ever been. Figure 3 shows how the rise in the population was reversed after Conservative policies promoting more use of community penalties and less use of prisons were implemented following the 1991 Criminal Justice Act. It also shows how more recent policies have dramatically reversed that trend. Even before the introduction of harsher sentencing measures, judges and magistrates are responding to the anti-liberal political climate and sending more people to prison for longer.

According to government projections, the prison population is likely to rise by a further 11,000 as a result of the proposed changes in sentencing policy. Some practitioners in the criminal justice field, however, believe this is a wild underestimate, and argue that the increase could be anything up to 30,000.

thousands

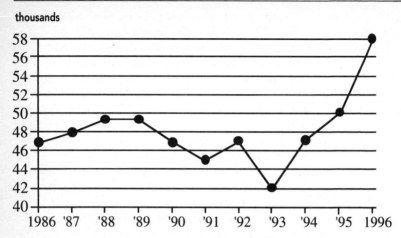

Figure 3 Prison population, England and Wales (*Source*: Home Office)

To cope with the rising jail population, the government is planning to build more prisons (at least 12 more to add to the 135 already in England and Wales). The building programme, with recurring costs, is estimated to reach an annual peak of around £375 million to £435 million by 2011-12. It will be funded through the Private Finance Initiative. This means private sector companies will design, build, finance and manage the jails. The taxpayer, through the Treasury, will then pay the private company an annual fee.

Private prisons, unlike so many other criminal justice issues, divides the parties. The Conservatives believe in them, not least because they say they are cost effective. Labour are opposed in principle, and would take any existing private prisons back into public ownership as soon as they contractually could. In Jack Straw's words – 'I regard privatisation of the prison service as morally repugnant. It is not appropriate for people to profit from incarceration'. The Liberal Democrats do not see privatisation as any part of solving the problems of the prison service, and deny claims that private jails are cheaper than public prisons. They too, are fundamentally against privatisation for moral reasons – arguing that only a democratic state, answerable to Parliament, should have the right to take away the liberty of its subjects.

POLITICS OF LAW AND ORDER

It is clear that attempting to fight the general election on the law and order ticket will not be straightforward. The electorate may have difficulty identifying many distinctive party policies. Even drawing conclusions about the success of the party in power is not easy.

Michael Howard is arguably, the 'toughest' home secretary in 18 years of Conservative government. His policies appeal to those who believe that politicians have always traditionally failed to come down hard on villains. He has even had the benefit of falling crime figures for three consecutive years. In the last Parliament before the election, six major law and order Bills were introduced, championing the victim and coming down hard on the criminal. Although this has not been without political gain, the benefits appear to have accrued more to Michael Howard personally than to the Tories' standing with the electorate as a whole as the party of law and order. As the Parliament dragged to its conclusion, Mr Howard's name was suddenly being mentioned in some Tory circles as a realistic candidate for the party leadership. If this presupposed election defeat, it was also a tribute to Mr Howard's success as a Home Secretary – at least in Tory terms.

Labour, always weak on law and order in past election campaigns, are now happy for it to be raised as an important election issue. The opposition's new approach is responsible for that, as it probably is for the failure of the government as a whole to capitalise on its success. Labour and the Liberal Democrats lay claim to successful efforts to get some of the new law and order measures introduced as Bills (e.g. stalking and restrictions on the sale of combat knives following the murder of headteacher, Philip Lawrence).

Nevertheless, the question 'How important will law and order be in determining the result of the election?' is still a tricky one to answer. There is no doubt that the issue has increased in importance enormously since 1992. Since then, if there has been any real opposition to the Conservatives' measures on law and order it has come from the Liberal Democrats, whose liberal traditions on human rights matters remain largely intact. Because of the similarities between Labour and the Conservatives on some of the major issues it would seem that as in the past, policy on law and order will not be a crucial election decider. But in establishing the electorate's perceptions of what the parties stand for – the shift of 'new Labour' in this area is amongst the most telling. It has Tony Blair's personal stamp from his time with the brief – it is where his ideas of 'modernising' the party have had most opportunity to reach maturity. In short, the dramatic change in attitude on law and order issues is one of the most potent symbols of 'Blairism' and 'new Labour'. The extent to which the electorate has been convinced that the change is genuine will be one of the most important factors in this election.

SAFE IN THEIR HANDS

THE HEALTH SERVICE
Fergus Walsh

*Fergus Walsh is Health and Social Affairs
Correspondent for BBC News. He worked as a
freelance reporter for local stations before joining
the BBC in 1986 as a sub-editor for Radio news.
The following year he became a Radio reporter
and was appointed Home and Legal Affairs
correspondent for BBC Radio in 1988. He moved
to Television News in 1990 and took up his
current post in 1993.*

All the parties will go into this election promising to safeguard the
National Health Service. At first sight, the NHS seems like one of the
untouchables of British politics: it arouses such strong passions
among the electorate that it would be political folly to suggest that it
should be privatised or scrapped. But there is a lot of scope for radical
change to the NHS within the accepted mantra that healthcare should
be free at the point of delivery, based on need, not ability to pay, and
in the past five years the health service has undergone its most
fundamental change since its creation in 1948.

Opinion polls suggest that the electorate would prefer Labour to
run the NHS. It was the post-war Labour government which founded
the health service, and it has long been perhaps the party's strongest
electoral asset. The NHS is in effect a massive nationalised industry –
the largest employer in Europe, so it is easier for Labour to claim that
it cares more about safeguarding its future than a government which
has a long record of privatisation. Nonetheless, Conservative administrations have been responsible for running the NHS for twice as long
as Labour, and Tory prime ministers speak of their unswerving
commitment to it.

A fascinating insight into how health is viewed by some senior
Tories came in Autumn 1994, in a leaked confidential strategy paper

from the party's deputy chairman, John Maples. In it, he said:
'The best result for the next 12 months would be zero media coverage
of the National Health Service'. Of course it did not and could never
happen. Being health secretary is a thankless task and few
incumbents emerge unscathed. Problems often occur when least
expected, often outside political control. Stephen Dorrell has helped
to chart the NHS into calmer waters after his predecessor Virginia
Bottomley had been battered by crisis after crisis. But he has not
adopted a bunker mentality. Instead there have been several White
Papers promising further reforms in GP-led primary care, ruling out
explicit rationing of healthcare, and asserting that the NHS remains
affordable.

When it comes to the NHS, the parties know they have to appeal
to voters' gut instincts. Who do they trust to leave the NHS in the
best shape? Who will safeguard its future? Unlike the economy or
unemployment, health is not usually thought of as a 'switch' issue:
one which on its own makes voters tick a different box. It is nonetheless an important element of any manifesto and election campaign.

So how will the parties fight the election on health? In 1992, things
were much simpler. The opposition parties were committed to
scrapping most of the government's radical changes to the NHS.
This presented a simple choice for voters: stick with the new
competitive NHS run like a business and the promise of better value
for money, or opt for the Opposition's promise of a return to a more
caring public service, free from competition. But Labour and the
Liberal Democrats realise it is now too late to try to unpick the
government's changes and say they would spare the NHS any further
major upheavals. Despite the political rhetoric, then, the health
policies of the main parties have moved much closer together.

FUNDING

Money used to be the main battleground in the NHS. Labour claimed
it would spend more. But the party's determination to avoid spending
commitments means it now focuses more on money it regards as
wasted on bureaucracy, promising to spend it instead on patient care.
Labour has pledged to cut NHS waiting lists and treat an extra
100,000 patients by cutting £100 million of NHS red tape (that sounds
like a lot, but it is less than the NHS spends every day). It remains to
be seen how this would be done, but clearly the party wants to place
as much emphasis as possible on the increased management costs
created by the internal market.

The Conservatives will ask voters to look at their record on health. After social security, health is the biggest area of government spending. Under the Conservatives spending on the NHS has risen by 73 per cent in real terms to over £40 billion a year. Faced with repeated stories about 'NHS cuts' it may surprise some electors that spending has risen by so much. But of course, the twin problems of an ageing population and expensive new medical technology mean that it costs more each year to keep the NHS ship of state above the waterline. In December 1996 Labour's new health spokesman Chris Smith committed Labour to match the government's election pledge to spend an extra £1.6 billion on the health service next year. But with Gordon Brown's tough spending constraints still very much in evidence, he declined to match the Tory pledge to spend more in real terms every year over the lifetime of the next Parliament. The Liberal Democrats say not only will they ensure proper funding for the NHS but they will provide specific extra resources by earmarking the revenues from increased tobacco taxes. These will be used to pay for health promotion schemes: additional resources would also be targeted at coping with the ageing population as well as the costs of improving technology.

The NHS can be viewed as underfunded, in the sense that no government has succeeded in matching the ever-increasing demand for healthcare with adequate resources. The UK spends about 6.5 per cent of its gross domestic product on healthcare – well below the European Union average of about 8 per cent. But there is not always a direct relationship between the level of spending and the health of the nation: the USA spends nearly twice as much on health care as the UK, and yet its system fails large sections of the population.

The Conservatives will point to co-operation with the private sector as a means of saving taxpayers' money and providing a more efficient service. One new area is the Private Finance Initiative. Under PFI, the NHS Trusts and the private sector join together to fund new capital investments, such as hospitals. The hospitals are built privately and leased back to the NHS. The Conservatives argue that this will enable more new building in the health service without the strain on the public purse. PFI has had a difficult birth. Talk of one new hospital a month has proved over-optimistic. Labour see the Conservative model of PFI as a further step towards NHS privatisation and a blurring of the distinction between the public and commercial sector. But Labour's position is made more complex by its acceptance that partnership with the private sector is acceptable when it can be shown to be of benefit to the NHS.

As in previous election campaigns, Labour will allege that the Conservatives are commercialising the NHS with the ultimate aim of privatisation. It is an allegation guaranteed to infuriate senior Tories, and one which they have always strongly denied.

PRESCRIPTION CHARGES

As well as the Private Finance Initiative, Labour also cites huge increases in prescription charges as a sign of creeping privatisation. However, more than four out of five items are prescribed free (a bigger proportion than under Labour), and the money raised from charges makes a valuable contribution to the NHS. Well before the election, the Liberal Democrats made clear their intention to abolish charges for eye tests and dental check-ups, and to freeze prescription charges.

THE STRUCTURE OF THE NHS

The NHS has undergone enormous structural changes since 1991 and, according to the government, these changes are now largely complete. They were aimed at making it more efficient and responsive to patients' needs. The review was prompted by a funding crisis in the late 1980s. Instead of the politically impossible notion of privatisation, the Conservatives created a competitive marketplace within the NHS, aimed at encouraging hospitals to become more efficient.

The government says its reforms have succeeded. More people are being treated than ever before. Productivity *has* increased, but it did under the old system as well. It is difficult to assess how much this is due to the reforms and how much to changes in treatment such as day surgery. Many Trusts do seem better at coping with their finite budgets than in the past although the problems of patients being treated on trolleys and cancelled operations still emerge each winter.

Critics say a huge unnecessary bureaucracy has been created with managers being put before patients. John Maples, in his leaked strategy paper, was pessimistic about the electorate's view of the government's changes: 'People perceive the reforms as clumsy and believe what doctors and nurses say about them, which is almost universally hostile.'

The government would like the political debate to move on to an issue it sees as more fundamental to patients: which party can run the most efficient and highest quality health service?

Fundamental to the NHS reorganisation was the separation of the providers of care from those who fund it. It means that hospitals now compete for funds from the health authorities and GP fundholders who hold the budgets. Whereas at the last election Labour and the Liberal Democrats intended to unpick much of the government's changes, both parties are now anxious to play down suggestions that the NHS might be subjected to yet another cataclysmic change. Labour says it is neither possible nor desirable to turn the clock back and the Liberal Democrats say the NHS needs evolutionary change not dogma-driven upheaval. Both suggest that they would keep the division between the commissioning and delivery of health care, but would end what they see as the commercialisation of the NHS under the Conservatives.

At the last election, Labour planned to abolish the internal market. It says it still aims to do this, while allowing those who buy care on behalf of patients some choice in where to spend their money. In August 1996, Chris Smith became the fifth shadow health secretary in as many years, and by December he was ready to set out how the healthcare market would be restructured. Under Labour, existing health authorities would become largely strategic bodies, concentrating on public health and monitoring standards. Purchasing of healthcare would be done by GP-led commissioning groups (much smaller than health authorities) who would negotiate long-term agreements with NHS Trusts. Labour claims its plans would reduce the number of contracts in the system (and so the level of paperwork) by 90 per cent. The idea is to replace competition with co-operation. The government also seems keen on a move to longer- term contracts, and talk of competition between hospitals is currently being played down. The Liberal Democrats say they would increase the accountability of the NHS to local people by bringing the commissioning of health care under local authority control.

TRUSTS

The Conservatives see the transformation of Britain's hospitals into self-governing Trusts as a major achievement, encouraging innovation and local decision-making. At the last election, Labour planned to return opted-out hospitals to local authority control. But this has been dropped. Now both Labour and the Liberal Democrats say they would make NHS Trusts more representative of local people although they would remain self-managing.

TREATING PATIENTS

The Conservatives will argue that they have created a responsive and efficient NHS which is going from strength to strength. To support this, the party will point to its achievements in cutting waiting lists, and treating more patients:

- More than one million more patients are treated in hospital every year now than before the government changes.

- For every 100 patients treated before the NHS reorganisation, 122 patients are treated now.

- The average wait for non-urgent hospital treatment fell from over 9 months in March 1988 to 4.6 months in March 1994.

- There are about 10,000 patients waiting over 12 months for treatment, compared with 200,000 six years ago.

- Nearly half of those on a waiting list are seen within five weeks and three quarters within three months. (*Source:* Department of Health)

These statistics do not reveal how long it takes before patients can get onto a waiting list in the first place. But in April 1995, under the Patient's Charter the government set targets for all patients to get their first out-patient appointment within 6 months, and 9 out of 10 patients to be seen within 3 months.

The reduction in waiting times is a tangible achievement of the NHS changes. NHS league tables and other pressures from government have helped to focus the minds of hospital managers on reducing long waits. But this success came at a price. Some doctors have complained that targets for waiting times and an emphasis on achieving a five-star performance in hospital league tables has skewed resources away from areas like intensive care and casualty treatment. Improvements in medical technology must take part of the credit for shorter waiting times. Labour claims the figures for those treated can not be trusted because the same patient is often counted more than once as they move from one hospital department to another.

The opposition will remind voters of the extent of hospital closures pointing out that one in three beds have been axed in England alone since the Tories came to power. The closure of much-loved hospitals could make Conservative MPs in some marginal constituencies even more vulnerable. The opposition will also emphasise continuing problems in some areas of emergency treatment, quoting examples of critically ill patients who have had long waits for an intensive care bed.

The Liberal Democrats claim they would guarantee that within three years, no one has to wait more than six months between diagnosis and treatment. Labour has given a pledge that nobody will have to wait more than two weeks for breast cancer surgery, and said it would end other waits for cancer surgery.

BUREAUCRACY

Labour will argue that red tape is strangling the NHS, and claim that the internal market has led to mushrooming administrative costs.
It points out that spending on managerial and administrative staff has increased by £1 billion since the NHS changes were introduced, and argues that some of this could be transferred to patient care.
The government says that much of the apparent increase in the number of managers is the result of reclassifying senior nurses and doctors. The Conservatives will point to the abolition of regional health authorities and the merging of district and family health service authorities in England as evidence of its commitment to eliminating unnecessary bureaucracy.

FAMILY DOCTORS

The vast majority of NHS care is provided by family doctors. They are the gatekeepers of the NHS, and are becoming increasingly important as more and more emphasis is placed on primary care. The creation of GP fundholding – whereby family doctors have their own budgets and can choose where to send patients for some treatments – remains one of the most contentious of the government changes. Although many doctors remain hostile to the system, GP fundholders now cover 58 per cent of the population.

Fundholding has enabled some GPs to get faster treatment for their patients than those of non-fundholders (though the reverse some-times applies). But this enables critics to attack the new system as unfair as it enables some patients apparently to queue-jump because of their GP, rather than the seriousness of their condition. The government denies it has created a two-tier health service while at the same time applauding fundholders for showing how patient care can be improved. Waiting times have always varied around the country but now two people living in the same street, but with different doctors, may no longer have the same access to healthcare.

There has been only a limited amount of research on whether fundholding works, but there is anecdotal evidence that fundholders have changed the relationship between family doctors and hospitals, making the latter more responsive and more aware of patients' needs. A report by the Audit Commission, the government's own spending watchdog, published in May 1996, concluded that fundholding had not produced major improvements across the board.

Fundholding is the one really distinctive area of policy difference between the two main parties. Since Labour plans to abolish the market system within the NHS, it believes there is no place for fundholding or the bureaucracy that goes with it. Labour's problem is that its alternative is complex and may appear to be taking something away from voters who are registered with fundholders.

Under Labour, all GPs would have to join a local commission group which would be responsible for buying healthcare for between 50,000 and 150,000 people. The aim is to ensure that all family doctors have a say in planning services for their local area. Fundholding would be phased out over two to three years, but some fundholders might be allowed to hang on to their own budgets for patient care, if all other local GPs agreed. Stephen Dorrell said GP fundholders would be 'shackled...into a form of chain-gang committee-based commissioning'.

The Liberal Democrats acknowledge that fundholding does appear to have brought benefits to patients, although arguably at the expense of patients of non-fundholders. The party proposes a unified system of funding for all GPs. Doctors would be free to manage their budgets individually, or as part of a consortium of GPs, or to ask their health authority to manage the funds. Fundholders would have to demonstrate that they could manage their own budget effectively.

DENTISTRY

Labour claims that NHS dentistry is in crisis and has been abandoned by the government in a further move towards privatisation. The opposition parties point to the difficulties for adults in finding an NHS dentist in many areas. This problem is particularly acute in Southeast England. But the government says there are more dentists working under the NHS than ever before. While this may be correct, many dentists have largely withdrawn from NHS treatment, although they stay on the health service books. This makes it difficult to rely on any of the bald statistics which are quoted by the parties. The government will point to tangible improvements in oral health, such as the number of 15-year-olds totally free from dental decay, which has increased five-fold in the decade to 1993.

HEALTH PROMOTION

The Conservatives point to significant progress in improving the nation's health. A child born today can expect to live two years longer than one born in 1979, and over the same period, the proportion of babies dying in the first year of life has fallen by almost a half. The government has set targets for improving the health of the nation in areas such as coronary heart disease, obesity and smoking. Voters may find it hard to reconcile ministers' health promotion measures and their refusal to ban tobacco advertising. The government says the voluntary agreement with the industry works well, and with the exception of teenage smoking it should reach its targets for reducing tobacco consumption. Labour and the Liberal Democrats have a much simpler strategy: a complete ban on tobacco advertising.

Labour claims that the government refuses to accept the impact of its economic policies on health. It too will quote statistics: if all infants and children enjoyed the same survival chances as those in social classes I and II, over 30,000 deaths a year might be prevented. Labour says it would offer a co-ordinated approach to health promotion and each government department would be obliged to demonstrate the effect of their policies on the health of the nation. The Liberal Democrats also attack the government for failing to have a comprehensive strategy on health promotion, and they pledge action to reduce poverty and social inequality.

MENTAL HEALTH

In the past few years, a small number of highly publicised killings by severely mentally disordered people forced ministers to question the policy of 'Care in the Community'. That policy, of moving the mentally ill out of asylums, began in the 1960s, but was accelerated in recent years. The vast majority of people with mental health problems pose no danger, and the policy of closing the old Victorian institutions has broad political and medical support, but not enough help has been given to the small group of probably just a few thousand vulnerable patients who, from time to time, need intensive support in the community. The government has come up with several initiatives including greater supervision of patients discharged from hospital. Mental health is seen by many who work in the field as a Cinderella service and it is unlikely to figure prominently in the election. But like other areas of the NHS it always has the potential to grab the headlines. Labour says it wants a moratorium on mental health bed closures pending a review of facilities.

WHOSE VISION?

Privatisation was at the heart of the NHS debate in the 1992 election, and it is likely to be there again this time. Labour argues that the NHS will not survive another term of Conservative government. Its health strategy document talks of two potential futures for the NHS after the next election. The Tory road of more privatisation based on competing health businesses with more charges for services. Or the future with Labour of a modern NHS freed from commercialisation to concentrate on delivering quality services for patients.

The Conservatives reject the privatisation charge. The party will ask voters to look at the government's tangible achievements in health and to accept that it is the best party to manage a modern NHS effectively and efficiently. It will say that Labour's plans will lead to less choice for patients, will be driven by the unions, and will lead to more bureaucracy.

The Liberal Democrats say they would halt NHS bed and hospital closures for a year while an independent audit of facilities is carried out. They also say they would recruit at least 10,000 more nurses *or* 8,000 extra doctors, and claim they will put patients before dogma making health promotion the key plank of policy. The party says that it would make the health service more accountable and get it in better shape to meet the needs of the population.

JENNIFER'S EAR

Politicians who seek to exploit individual patient's problems during the election campaign would be wise to cast their minds back to what became known as the 'War of Jennifer's Ear'. Five-year-old Jennifer Bennett's year-long wait for an ear operation was used as the basis for a 1992 Labour election broadcast on NHS waiting lists. The film did not name her, but two newspapers printed her identity and a furious row erupted over who was responsible since the parents had not wanted any publicity. For hardened political journalists desperate for vibrant copy amidst a lacklustre campaign the controversy was a gift. Neither Labour nor the Conservatives emerged from the affair undamaged. Afterwards, there was some bemusement as to how such a saga could have left its mark as the most memorable event of the entire campaign. Its impact provided a timely reminder of the depth of feeling associated with the health service – and remains as a powerful symbol for party managers, as they go into this campaign, of how easily such a phenomenon can jeopardise an entire election strategy.

ROOF OVERHEAD

HOUSING, MORTGAGES –
AND NEGATIVE EQUITY

Ed Crooks

Ed Crooks is Economics Correspondent for BBC News. He worked for the Institute for Fiscal Studies and the Investors Chronicle *before joining the BBC as a researcher in 1990. After working in television and radio news and for 'Newsnight', he was appointed Economics Correspondent in 1994.*

There is no more potent and universal symbol of the rise and fall of the British economy over the past decade than the rise and fall of the housing market. In the 1980s, people watched the house price bubble grow with amazement and delight – or envy. In the 1990s, hundreds of thousands were trapped in their homes unable to sell; or worse still, have had their homes repossessed because they were unable to keep up the payments on their mortgages.

The declared policies of all the parties are to steer clear of both those extremes. Another housing boom is as firmly rejected as another crash. Michael Heseltine has hailed rising house prices as a sign of economic success, but he was attacked for it. Stability is the watchword in economic management, and stable house prices are an essential part of the package. If the government delivers on its promises, whichever party is in power, the housing market will be governed by the need for somewhere to live, not by hopes of quick and easy profit.

Differences over home ownership, too, are much less than they were. The Conservatives have defined themselves as supporters of 'the property-owning democracy'. Labour has now come round to a very similar position; in a recent speech Tony Blair said 'I am the first to acknowledge the success of the right to buy.' The Conservatives, on the other hand, introduced the 1996 Housing Act which tries to get more private money into the provision of grant-assisted, low-cost housing – a move broadly supported by the opposition.

HOUSE PRICES

Soaring house prices were both a cause and an effect of the 1980s boom. On top of low taxes and mortgage rates, they were another reason for people to spend rather than save. Famously, some people claimed to earn more from the rising value of their homes than they did from their jobs. But bitter experience has taught that the old saying about 'safe as houses' is highly misleading. Housing is, in fact, naturally quite a volatile market, subject to large swings in price in either direction. Like the stock market, it depends on expectations about future prices. If there is a widespread belief that prices are going up, then people will rush to move, and prices will indeed go up.

A gentle increase in house prices is a tricky thing to engineer, as recent experience has shown. At the beginning of 1996, the various forecasts from banks and building societies predicted that prices might rise by 2 or 3 per cent; in the event, they rose more than 8 per cent. The forecasters are now promising about the same again this year – a rise of up to 10 per cent or so – but there is no reason to think they will be any more accurate this time.

We are still, even so, a long way from the conditions of the late 1980s, when house prices rose by 34 per cent in a single year – 1988. And the recovery has been patchy. That's true both in the sense that it has been strongest in London, and generally weaker the further from London you go, and in the sense that not all types of property have benefited equally. Small flats and former council houses, for example, may not have increased in value at all, or even continued to go down. And although prices are higher, the number of people moving house is still low. It began to pick up in the second half of 1996, but last year only about 1.2 million properties were sold in England and Wales, compared with around 2 million a year during the frenzy of the late 1980s.

NEGATIVE EQUITY

Corrections in house prices to bring them back into line with wages and with other prices are a regular occurrence: the difference in the 1990s was that it happened while inflation was low. In times of high inflation, house prices had stagnated while retail prices and wages rose. This time, prices actually fell, leaving unprecedented numbers of people in homes worth less than the mortgages on them.

The number of people suffering from negative equity, as it is known, has fallen as house prices have risen. It was 1.7 million at its peak, and is now down to somewhere around half a million (estimates vary). The Nationwide building society has predicted that by the end of 1998 negative equity will only be a problem for a small hard core of 100,000 households. But the number of people with 'insufficient equity' – in other words who would not have enough left to cover the cost of moving once they had paid off their mortgage – is much greater, perhaps approaching two million.

REPOSSESSIONS

The number of people suffering repossession has also fallen in recent years. It peaked at over 75,000 in 1991, and then declined to a rate of just below 50,000 a year, but has not fallen any further over the past three years. That still means, of course, that almost 1,000 families a week are losing their homes. The number of people in arrears with their mortgage payments has, however, carried on falling – down from over 500,000 at the end of 1993 to less than 350,000 by the summer of 1996.

The Conservatives like to emphasise these positive developments, and point to schemes being introduced by mortgage lenders themselves to help people faced with the threat of repossession or suffering from negative equity. Tony Blair has suggested that Labour would encourage schemes by mortgage lenders to help out people in difficulties. The Liberal Democrats propose a new mortgage benefit, and would 'cajole' lenders to find alternatives to repossession.

MORTGAGE RATES

The mortgage market has been revolutionised by the deregulation of the financial sector since 1979. What was once a long and demanding application process can now be quick and easy. Banks and building societies are eager to lend, to the extent that the Labour party is considering the need for tougher rules to make sure borrowers get the best mortgage for their needs.

Competition between lenders is fiercer than ever. Cash-back offers and discounts have been restricted a little recently, but they are still available for people buying for the first time, moving house, or even just moving their mortgage to a different lender. Mortgage rates are lower than they have been for more than thirty years. But it looks as though this cannot go on for ever, whoever is in power. If interest rates rise further, then mortgage rates will keep on rising too.

The tax breaks attached to mortgages, of which Margaret Thatcher was particularly fond, were greatly reduced in value by the two tax-raising Budgets of 1993. Labour has attacked the changes, but has made no promise to reverse them. The Liberal Democrats say they would go even further, and phase out tax relief for mortgages altogether over the next five to ten years, depending on conditions in the housing market.

SOCIAL HOUSING

The sale of council houses has been the great hidden privatisation. It raised £28 billion – more than the sales of British Telecom, British Gas and the electricity industry put together – and transformed whole communities. And one of its effects has been to polarise the character-istics of typical council tenants and typical home-owners.

Since 1979, 1.5 million people have bought their own council homes. Naturally enough, these have tended to be the better-off tenants, in particular ones with jobs. At the same time, policies intended to target help on those most in need have meant that new tenants have tended to be the poorest and most disadvantaged people. So unemployment among council tenants is now twice the rate for everyone else, half of council tenants are in the poorest fifth of the population, and one council household in five is a single-parent family.

At the same time, rents have doubled in real terms, and the burden has been taken by Housing Benefit. The cost of Housing Benefit rose from £1 billion in 1980 to almost £9 billion in 1993: a four-fold increase even in real terms, allowing for the effect of inflation. It is not just a burden on the taxpayer, inflated by an estimated £2 billion of fraud, but a key to the poverty and unemployment traps. People can find that if they get a job, or work harder and increase their earnings, they are hardly any better off because of the loss of Housing Benefit.

HOUSEBUILDING

While the Conservatives were selling off council houses, they were stopping building them too. Local authority house building is now negligible, and housing associations, private charities supported by public money but independent of Government and (since 1988) able to raise commercial funds too, have grown rapidly. They are now the principal providers of new state-assisted housing.

But in the past few years support for housing associations has been one of the main victims of the new drive for tighter control of public spending. Between 1993 and 1997, central government support for housing associations has been halved. Until now, the number of houses built has kept rising, partly because during the construction downturn, building has been cheaper, and partly because a lot more private money has been coming in. But in the next three years, the number of houses being built will be lower than last year.

The answer for Labour and the Liberal Democrats is to allow councils greater freedom to spend the money earned from council house sales on new building, perhaps through the housing associations. But this apparently appealing proposition gives the misleading impression that the money is just lying idle. In fact, it has been used to pay off the councils' debts, or to earn them interest. There is no real difference between a local authority using council house sale receipts to build more homes, and borrowing more money to do it.

PRIVATE RENTING

Private-sector renting is the 'motherhood and apple pie' of housing: everybody loves it, because it offers more freedom and mobility and promises an escape from the horrors of home ownership revealed in recent years. One of the aims of the 1988 Housing Act was to encourage private landlords, and the Conservatives say it has been a success: the number of people renting in the private sector rose from 1.7 million in 1988 to 2 million in 1994. The house price crash certainly helped – scaring a generation of potential first-time buyers away from the idea of trying to own their own home as soon as possible. In fact demand seems to have run ahead of supply, because private-sector rents have been rising sharply.

Labour and the Liberal Democrats, too, say they want to encourage a healthy private-rented sector to stand alongside owner-occupation and social (in other words housing association and council) housing. But their priorities seem to lie elsewhere: as shown, for example, in Tony Blair's attacks on the Conservatives for claiming to be the party of the home owner, and his assertion that 'the Labour party is trying to support the aspiration of the majority of the people to own their own homes'. The Conservatives, for their part, predict that over the next ten years, 1.5 million more people will buy their own homes, helped by initiatives aimed at today's tenants in social housing.

It has been suggested that we would all be better off if the country were less fixated on home-ownership. In Germany, for example, only 42 per cent of households own their own homes, compared to 68 per cent in Britain: a fact which may help to explain the differences between the two countries in attitudes to inflation and interest rates. But on the present showing, there is no chance of any future government trying to do anything to break up the painful but deep-rooted attachment between the voters and their property.

ISSUES WHICH WILL HELP DECIDE THE ELECTION

PRIDE AND PREJUDICE

A SMALL OFFSHORE ISLAND?

BRITAIN IN THE WORLD

John Simpson

John Simpson is Foreign Affairs Editor for BBC News. He joined the BBC in 1966. He became a radio reporter in 1970 and two years later became the BBC's first correspondent in Dublin. Assignments followed as Common Market Correspondent and Southern Africa Correspondent before becoming Diplomatic Correspondent for Television News in 1978. After spells as Political Editor, presenter of the 'Nine O'clock News' and Diplomatic Editor he was appointed to his present position in 1988. He specializes in East-West relations, the former Soviet Union, Iran and Afghanistan. In March 1991 he was named Royal Television Society Journalist of the Year (an award he shared with John Cole), and was awarded a CBE in the Gulf War Honours list in June 1991.

International standing is a curious commodity, very hard to obtain and surprisingly hard to lose as well. Japan and Germany have grown rich and strong, and yet they count for much less on the world stage than economically weaker countries like Britain or France. In Britain's case, our position in the world has undoubtedly slid in recent years; and yet anyone who travels widely will have seen signs that our international significance in many key ways is as strong as ever. Some of these signs are objective, others merely anecdotal; yet together they add up to something that is impossible to mistake.

There are now more banks with major offices in London than in any other city in the world, and more than at any point in our history. British companies own a greater share of American, German and French industry and commerce than vice versa. More British music and more British books were sold around the world last year than those of any other country. The British Council had one of its best years ever in terms of support for its activities; just prior to a savage cut in its budget. The international audience for British-made television programmes was higher than it has ever been before. In Germany, there are now approaching five million daily viewers of the BBC World Service Television; while in Taiwan, a country with no discernible political or cultural links with Britain, twice as many people watched the BBC as compared with the American CNN.

None of these factors indicates a decline. Nevertheless in political terms Britain's voice has been less sought, and is less audible, than before. We have suffered political set-backs, and we have gone through a gruelling period of internal bickering which has done us nothing but harm internationally. And although foreign opinion traditionally means little in British politics, there is a kind of radiation effect which makes itself felt to the electorate.

VIEWED FROM ABROAD

During the entire 20th century, no British election has been lost or won over an issue of foreign affairs. Prime ministers may have fallen as a result of their faulty handling of some foreign policy issue, the most spectacular case being Sir Anthony Eden's resignation after the Suez debacle in 1956. But that is because they lost the confidence of their supporters in Parliament. No one since Gladstone has gone to the country on anything but domestic policies, and the received wisdom is that only bread-and-butter issues matter to the electorate.

Yet in this case the perceived wisdom is not necessarily right. True, this election will not be decided on what the voters think about British policy towards Russia, say, or an enlarged NATO, or how we should deal with China after the hand-over of Hong Kong. Europe is a different matter; for whether the Europhobes (or even all the Europhiles) like it or not, our relations with the EU are no longer a matter purely of foreign affairs. Every single government ministry in Whitehall now has a department which deals on a daily basis with the European Commission and the European Parliament. Yet not even European issues will be central to the British election, despite the efforts of Sir James Goldsmith's Referendum party.

All the same, foreign affairs do have one very real effect. The voters are not solely interested in whether they have more or less money to spend, whether their children are properly educated, or whether health care and the social services are up to scratch. They also want their country to be well regarded in the wider world. The election of 1983 was fought out on the pros and cons of Mrs Thatcher's monetarist policies and their effect on the country,

yet it was the previous year's victory over Argentina in the
Falklands War which set the tone for the whole campaign; and,
although the Thatcher government had reached considerable depths
of unpopularity before the war, it won the election handsomely.
The 'feelgood factor' is not only the result of improving economic
conditions; it also has to do with whether people feel better or worse
about their country's place in the world.

Since the 1992 election the only wars John Major has fought have
been within his own party or about beef. They happened to be about
Europe; yet even if by some miracle Europe had been taken out of the
equation altogether the post-Thatcherites in his party could well have
fallen out with the centre and left-wing over something else.
A governing party which is not under the full control of its prime
minister is going to look weak abroad: and John Major's government
has looked desperately weak in the eyes of international observers for
a long time now.

In the space of a few days not long ago *Le Monde* called him
'troubled', 'uncertain', and 'in danger from his own supporters'; *Die
Zeit* said he was 'unlucky-seeming'; *Die Welt* talked of dark whispers
of incompetence; *Corriere de la Sera* questioned his wisdom and his
understanding of Europe; and *Le Soir* of Brussels forecast that he was
certain to lose the election. *The New York Times* and *The Washington
Post* latched on to the divisions in his party and the questions about
his ability to control them. None of these newspapers has anything
approaching a wide readership in Britain; yet the general sense that
the outside world does not regard him as a strong, capable leader has
certainly penetrated public awareness, and helps to reinforce the
reputation he has acquired at home.

The outside world's opinion can be very helpful to a British prime
minister. It was an unfortunate leader-writer on *Pravda* who, in 1980,
first coined the expression 'The Iron Lady' for Margaret Thatcher;
unfortunate, because when her officials heard about it and wrote it
into her speeches and made it part of her public relations pitch, the
leader-writer found himself under criticism within the paper. For a
time, consequently, he was restricted to writing about the power and
oil industries. When Jacques Chirac, then Francois Mitterrand's
prime minister, called her approach to European negotiations 'the
attitude of a housewife' at an EU summit, her officials picked it up
with glee and the British press rallied round her.

French journalists, like those of other countries, have no nickname
for John Major. To them he is merely 'M. Major'; and for some
months when cartoonists in France, Germany or elsewhere wanted

an image of his Britain they have drawn a cow with its eyes rolling crazily. Mad cow disease has become the most conspicuous thing about the United Kingdom during the last year or so, together with IRA terrorism and the break-up of marriages in the Royal Family. It would all have happened to Lady Thatcher if she had managed to stay on this long; it would have happened to Neil Kinnock if he had won in 1992; it would have happened to Tony Blair if he had won an election in 1995. As it was, it happened under John Major's stewardship; he gets the blame, direct or indirect, as a result.

HANDS ACROSS THE CHANNEL – OR THE ATLANTIC?

The foreign reporting of a country – any country, let alone Britain where the journalistic ethos is so rich and noisy – tends to reflect the way domestic newspapers, television and radio see it. As so often happens, therefore, images are created and built up by a kind of circulating movement of opinion: British journalists perceived Mr Major as unexciting and ineffectual, then foreign journalists based in London, which remains the news capital of the world, took it up and reported it back to their own countries; governments abroad were inevitably affected by this view, and made their decisions accordingly; and British journalists based abroad reported it back. There is a mutual reinforcement about all this which has more to do with accepting received opinions than with objective assessment.

President Chirac and President Bill Clinton have both spoken privately of how impressive they find John Major in discussion and negotiation; no doubt many other leaders have found the same thing. Yet because Mr Major's control over his divided party seemed so uncertain, neither he nor Britain were treated as though they counted for as much as they really did.

It is the second time in 20 years that Britain has been in this position. The cause, under the Labour governments of Harold Wilson and James Callaghan, was the same: the controversy over British sovereignty in Europe. For those of us who reported on the agonizings and the hasty patching-together of policy from 1974 to 1979 under an administration with a tenuous majority and no real control over its dissidents, the events of 1992 onwards seemed remarkably, even disturbingly, familiar. MPs who opposed the official line towards Europe regarded the question of Britain's sovereignty as bigger than anything else; it overrode their instinctive loyalty to their parties, and affected whatever else they did or said.

Every government in Europe is now staffed at a senior level by officials and diplomats who remember those days. Most of them expect a Labour government under Tony Blair to be just as bitterly divided as the governments of Wilson, Callaghan and Major over Europe. Most of them believe that the only way a British prime minister can keep control of his or her party is by showing some degree of scepticism towards European political and monetary union, an attitude which automatically rules out a genuinely close relationship with either of the two leading European powers, Germany and France. Britain is too big to be ignored in Europe, but it has shown itself time and again to be too divided and too uncertain about the European issue for either the Germans or the French to find it worth getting particularly close to us. And without a closeness with one or the other Britain will always be isolated and weak within Europe. Outside it, too. The former US ambassador in London, Raymond Seitz, said pointedly as he left that Britain's voice was heard loudest in Washington when it was heard in Paris and Bonn as well.

It is easy for politicians to be carried away by wishful thinking at times of stress. For several years now, Tory MPs have tried to convince themselves that things would change to let them off the single currency hook. When Jacques Chirac won the French presidential election of May 1995, for instance, opinion at Westminster was that France would be much less Europhile as a result; the Foreign Office, knowing him better during his earlier incarnations as prime minister under Giscard d'Estaing and Francois Mitterrand, did not make the same mistake. Many Conservative MPs were equally certain that public opinion in Germany was too attached to the mark for Chancellor Kohl to be able to press ahead with monetary union; but of course it has not turned out that way.

While Lady Thatcher, as prime minister, derided the whole concept ('The emu is a bird which never gets off the ground'), her Foreign Office under Sir Geoffrey Howe and Douglas Hurd took a more feline approach, trying to ensure that the European Union would be enlarged by new applicants like Poland, Hungary and the Czech Republic before monetary or political union could take place; which would make any serious union an impossibility for many years to come. This does not seem to have worked either. British wishful thinking about Europe has repeatedly come to nothing, ever since the days when we confidently expected the collapse of the original Common Market in 1957. Europe has historically been the area where British strategic thinking, Labour or Conservative, has shown itself to be faulty.

By way of contrast - and perhaps contrary to everything that seemed likely to happen when Bill Clinton was first elected president in the United States - the Anglo-American relationship is now strong and thriving. It has long outgrown the awkwardness created by the efforts of some people within the Conservative party trying to find details of Mr Clinton's past as a student at Oxford which might have helped George Bush in the 1992 presidential election. It outgrew the British government's irritation when Mr Clinton made it clear he wanted to do something to get a peaceful solution to the Northern Ireland problem. It even outgrew the sniping from inside and outside the Clinton administration about British policy towards Bosnia. Post-Bosnia, the relationship became so smooth and friendly that Whitehall found itself hoping that Mr Clinton would be re-elected; something that would have seemed distinctly unlikely two or three years earlier. Some British diplomats will be sorry he chose Madeleine Albright as his Secretary of State, given her savaging of British policy in Bosnia a couple of years ago; but even she seems to have accepted the relative chumminess of the link with Britain.

BOSNIA

The re-emergence of the United States on the world stage, after a period during which Mr Clinton seemed to have little interest in or aptitude for foreign affairs, meant that Britain took a back seat once again in several key areas. Most important of these was the former Yugoslavia; and here at least there was an almost audible sigh of relief from the British as they gave up their leading role. The Balkans was the area that turned Douglas Hurd's enjoyment of his job as Foreign Secretary into a sense that it was a gloomy and distasteful burden. Responsibility without power is never fun; and the ludicrous failure of the European Union's peace efforts in 1992 forced Britain and France to play a part which neither of them had the international clout nor the desire for.

It was with a certain bitter amusement that the Foreign Office watched the State Department change its mind after the Dayton Accords had been signed. The Americans always believed that Britain and France were too sympathetic to the Serbs and too hostile to the Croats and to the Bosnian government (which received powerful support from liberal opinion in the United States). When the Americans had to deal with the three main sides in earnest they found the Croats and Muslims just as infuriating as the British and French had. Soon the State Department was accusing the Muslim-led government of developing covert links with America's great bugbear, Iran; even though the links had been pretty clear for a long time.

This was all rather comforting to British *amour-propre*. Yet nothing could hide the fact that British influence in the world had been shown to be weaker than before. If Britain and France had been prepared to take tough military action earlier, the climb-down in favour of the Americans would not have been so obvious. Yet there were very real dangers in a purely European power becoming involved in a punitive military action within Europe, and the results of failure might have been even worse. In Yugoslavia, as Douglas Hurd observed, it was always a case of 'damned if you do and damned if you don't'.

TIES OF COMMONWEALTH

Our European obsessions sometimes make it hard for us to remember that there is a wider world. We seem rather to have turned our backs on the Commonwealth now, even though, since the return of South Africa, it has become one of the biggest as well as one of the wealthiest of transnational institutions, second only to the United Nations itself in many ways. France, which assiduously develops its relations with its former colonies in ways that suit both it and them, finds this act of national forgetfulness of ours hard to understand. This year the last major part of Britain's one-time empire, Hong Kong, is being handed back to China, in remarkably good shape. Its economy has once again been rated the freest in the world (compared with China's position at number 126 in the same ranking), violent crime is down by a half compared with 1993, and corruption is at its lowest since the 1960s. The dispute over China's evident dislike for the democratic systems which Britain has belatedly introduced has not damaged the reputation of the last colonial governor, and Chris Patten's approval rating in Hong Kong is still above 60 per cent. It looks as though the hand-over, far from being a mournful period which will mark Britain's decline as a world power, will in fact turn out to be a celebration of the better side of imperial government.

BOXING ABOVE WEIGHT

As Foreign Secretary, Douglas Hurd was given to claiming that Britain 'boxed above our weight' in international terms, thanks to world-class foreign and intelligence services. Both of those helped, for instance, to ensure that British relations with post-Cold War Russia have been good; Britain, alone of Western countries, first spotted Mikhail Gorbachev as the coming man, and first assured

Boris Yeltsin of full support at a time when he thought the tanks of the coup plotters were heading for his White House. These things count for a great deal in international affairs.

What counts for more, however, is political strength. Ever since he won the 1992 election, Mr Major has been noticeably short of that; and in international terms Britain has lacked it as a result. Two or three years ago the big question in British foreign policy was, whether we and the French would be able to hang on to our permanent seats in the Security Council at the United Nations. That was finally settled in Britain's (and France's) favour; yet it has not, after all, helped to make either of us more powerful internationally. Disregarded in Europe, and not of much account elsewhere, we are in danger of boxing below our weight for the first time in decades. And yet the extraordinary thing is that our influence as a world financial and cultural centre – *the* world financial and cultural centre, in many important ways - is unlikely to be affected.

THE CONTINENT CUT OFF
EUROPEAN DIVISIONS
John Sergeant

John Sergeant is the Chief Political Correspondent for BBC News. His journalistic career began in 1967 on the Liverpool Daily Post and Echo *and in 1970 he joined the BBC as a Radio news reporter covering events from around the world and, for seven years, reported on Northern Ireland. In 1979 he was appointed Political Correspondent specializing in the European Community and the European Parliament and in 1988 he took up his present position. He won the British Press Guild award for 'Best Outside Broadcast' of 1990 for the coverage of Mrs Thatcher's 'I fight on' announcement outside the Paris Embassy. He has also presented, on an occasional basis, a wide variety of programmes including 'Today'.*

Of all the issues in the general election Europe is likely to be the most difficult for the main parties. Both the Tories and Labour will be tempted to play it as simply as possible. The Conservatives will wish to paint Tony Blair as the 'soft touch' on Europe, the man who will give in to Brussels. Labour will stress how the Tory civil war on Europe has made it impossible for them to represent the national rather than the party interest. Only the Liberal Democrats will be able to summon up a straightforward, strongly pro-European platform, but even some of their leading figures disagree and according to opinion polls, many of their supporters are downright Eurosceptic.

The public mood is uncertain. One of the party experts said recently: 'I have given up asking people about Europe – their views are so contradictory.' But what the politicians say about Europe could have a vital effect on the outcome of the election. For a long time it looked as if the main parties would succeed in relegating the arguments, by suggesting that crucial decisions, in particular over a single currency, were still a long way off. That is no longer the case. Europe may not fit neatly into the great battle between the Tories and

Labour, but with so much now at stake, the parties will have to give European issues more prominence than ever before.

EMU: THE BIRD WHICH WILL SOON FLY

This year is the qualifying year for those countries wishing to take part in EMU (economic and monetary union). At Maastricht in December 1991, partly at the insistence of John Major and the then chancellor, Norman Lamont, strict conditions were laid down to see that only those countries whose economies were coming together – or 'converging' – would be allowed to take part in the single currency.

The rules, including keeping budget deficits to below 3 per cent of national output, became known as the 'Maastricht criteria'. Next spring, it's likely that at a European summit hosted by the UK it will be decided which countries have qualified. It will be a political decision; no country will have a veto on the outcome. The countries taking part will, according to the treaty, agree to the irrevocable fixing of exchange rates on 1 January 1999 and three years later their own notes and coins will be withdrawn in favour of Euro notes and coins. Apart from losing the Deutschmark, the French franc and so on, this would mean that interest rates would no longer be decided on a national basis, and member governments would not be able to allow their currencies to be devalued. Economists disagree over the importance of devaluation as a policy tool. Politicians worry about the loss of sovereignty involved.

Proponents of a single currency believe that it would enormously boost trade within Europe and it would allow the Euro to compete effectively across the world with the American dollar and the Japanese yen. In Britain, the argument is often put simply: 'Can we afford to be left out?'

HOW EUROPE SHOULD BE RUN:
THE IGC DECIDES

The other big decision is even closer. In June 1997, at a European summit in Amsterdam, the long-drawn out series of negotiations called the IGC (Inter-Governmental Conference) is due to end.

The original idea was that moves towards economic and monetary union would have to go hand in hand with political changes. The Germans, for instance, have always stressed the need for political union. The German Chancellor, Helmut Kohl, has denied that he is in favour of a 'United States of Europe' but the mainstream Continental view is of a more closely integrated Europe, with more decisions taken at a European level. There is general agreement that the enlargement of the EU – nearly doubling its present membership – is bound to lead to some changes in the way the institutions work.

Britain has insisted that the EU should remain a partnership of nations, and that there is no need for any diminution of the national power of veto in key areas, including asylum and immigration policy, but negotiations have been stalled, not least because the other governments are waiting for a possible change of government in Britain, and the prospect of more flexibility in the British approach if Tony Blair takes over from John Major.

THE ERM CRISIS: THE MARKET DECIDES

At the last general election, in the spring of 1992, all the main parties supported Britain's membership of the European exchange rate mechanism. It was famously described in 1992 by Lady Thatcher's one-time economics adviser, Sir Alan Walters, as a half-baked policy. He meant that in more than one sense. Sterling was linked to the other currencies, but it was not fully-baked EMU, for the pound could still be forced out of the system, through massive speculation on the foreign exchange markets. To the enormous embarrassment of the government, that is what happened in the autumn of the same year.

The shock is still being felt, particularly within the Conservative party where the ERM experience proved to be a defining moment for the growing band of Eurosceptics. The widespread official view that interest rates would have to rise as the pound went down was confounded and for many (although not the Chancellor, Kenneth Clarke), sterling's exit from the ERM is seen as the moment when the economy finally began to look up. But the political damage was considerable, with opinion pollsters convinced that it was a blow to the government's fortunes from which the Tories have still not recovered*.

THE CONSERVATIVES' 'WAIT AND SEE' POLICY

Even during the Maastricht negotiations, John Major had to make sure that other members of the cabinet were prepared to endorse his position. Otherwise, there was always the danger of resignations and that the party would split. By insisting on a formal opt-out on the single currency and on the Social Chapter he made it possible for the

* See Boundaries, Polls and Chicken Runs, pp.244–257.

treaty to be signed, and there was at least sufficient acquiescence among senior figures for it not to impede a Conservative victory in the election which followed a few months later.

During the long drawn-out Parliamentary battle to have the Maastricht Treaty ratified what was often described as 'the great fault line' of British politics became visible to all. It was far more obvious on the Tory benches than among opposition MPs. At this stage, most Labour Eurosceptics were not very influential within their own party, and the doggedly determined Tory Eurosceptics proved to be masters of publicity. They were fully prepared to stand up against the government, in the end having to be forced into line when the issue was treated as a vote of confidence. It was the only way the provisions of the Maastricht Treaty, as negotiated by John Major, could become law. He had to threaten a general election in order to win the vote.

THE BATTLE WITH KENNETH CLARKE

The 'wait and see' policy on a single currency carried the Conservatives through the last general election without much difficulty. Merging Europe's currencies into one was a much more distant prospect and many leading figures were as convinced that nothing would come of the idea, as were the British officials in the 1950s who left the Messina talks early, not expecting them to lead to the setting up of the Common Market.

For pro-Europeans in the Cabinet, such as Kenneth Clarke, that historical precedent was one of the main arguments to justify keeping open the door to a single currency. If only, they would claim, Britain could have been involved directly in those negotiations, then mistakes such as the Common Agriculture Policy would have been avoided. In a similar vein, only by sticking with the talks on setting up a single currency could we be sure that it might ever be a system suitable for Britain.

As the general election has drawn closer, many in the cabinet have felt restless about the self-imposed restrictions of the 'wait and see' policy. A year ago the Eurosceptics in the cabinet, who include Michael Portillo, Michael Howard and Peter Lilley, were helped by John Major to win a tactical victory over the pro-Europeans who include Michael Heseltine and Kenneth Clarke. They succeeded in reaching cabinet agreement on a referendum on a single currency if it was ever supported by a Conservative government, but it was quite a struggle and at one stage Mr Clarke threatened to resign. The policy debate has continued in various forms, with more than 100

Conservative candidates announcing at the end of last year that
whatever was in the official manifesto they would pledge to vote
against a single currency if they were elected. However the official
wait and see line has held, as it has on the Labour side.

LABOUR'S 'WAIT AND SEE' POLICY

Labour starts from a different position – they are, in principle, in
favour of a single currency – but in practice they have just as many
get-outs as the Conservatives, if they want to use them. Labour have
always argued that their decision would depend on the way economic
and monetary union would work in practice. They have insisted in the
past that the Maastricht criteria were not in themselves an adequate
test of the real convergence of the economies involved.

As of last autumn, they too will only let Britain take part if it has the
backing of the British people in a referendum. Labour's old formula
was that either a general election or a referendum would be suitable
but, helped by pressure from John Prescott and Robin Cook, the new
formula was accepted by Tony Blair and Gordon Brown, and later by
the whole shadow cabinet. This puts a further barrier in the way of
any early decision by a Labour government to join a single currency.
Not only does a referendum have to be won (unlike, for instance in
Germany and France, where a parliamentary vote could suffice), it
would also be necessary to establish an independent Bank of England.
To achieve all this and meet the deadline of 1 January 1999 might be
asking rather a lot of the first Labour government in nearly 20 years.

SO HOW PRO-EUROPEAN WOULD LABOUR BE?

Tony Blair once told his party conference that he would not allow
Britain to be isolated, but he has since refined that view. He will not,
he says, allow Britain to be isolated for the sake of it, but only if that is
the most effective way to fight for British interests.

Labour are well aware that British opinion has become more
Eurosceptical and that if the Tories succeed in painting Mr Blair as
the 'poodle of Brussels', then the election could be lost. However
Tony Blair is determined that Labour should be seen as constructive
Europeans. They will castigate the Tories for so often trying the
patience of the other member states that when a real crisis occurs,
such as over beef, only minimal help is given.

On certain key policies Labour and the Tories are sharply at odds.
A Labour government would be prepared to consider removing the

national veto, that is allowing for majority voting, in some areas of industrial, regional and environmental policy. Above all, Labour would remove the opt-out on social policy negotiated at Maastricht. They would accept the Social Chapter.

THE SOCIAL CHAPTER: A THREAT OR A PROMISE?

Throughout the parliamentary battle over the Maastricht Treaty, Labour and the Liberal Democrats could oppose the Bill and join forces with the hard-line Eurosceptics because the treaty, as negotiated, included the opt-out on the Social Chapter. Both parties are in favour of a common EU social policy and they see it as a way of giving British workers the same rights as those on the Continent.

The Social Chapter, in its present incarnation, is not very exciting. It specifically excludes controversial issues, such as pay and the right to strike. (Labour's minimum wage policy is not part of the Social Chapter.) The only major decision reached under its provisions is an agreement to establish works councils in larger companies. But for the Tories, the Social Chapter has always represented the worst of the Continental approach to business. It is not what it contains at the moment, they argue, but what it will contain in the future. It would burden companies with extra costs and regulations. As a pet project of the former European Commission president, Jacques Delors, it is, in the words of Lady Thatcher, simply a case of 'socialism by the back Delors'.

The fact that all the other countries, including many led by non-socialists, support the Social Chapter appears to have had little effect on the passions it has aroused in Britain. The arguments are bound to take up a major part of this election campaign.

FISH AND BEEF: A MEAL FOR THE EUROSCEPTICS

The BSE crisis, particularly the world-wide ban on British beef exports, and the continuing arguments over the effects of the Common Fisheries Policy have given rich pickings to the Eurosceptics. They have been able to highlight the fact that in these areas Britain has given up the right to act independently. But the major parties are not suggesting that there should be a dramatic change in either the beef market in Europe or the fisheries policy.

Pro-Europeans on both sides of the Commons point to the need to pool sovereignty in these areas, even if this means that on occasion Britain's room for manoeuvre is highly restricted. However, the opposition parties will use these issues to argue that Britain's power within the European institutions has been severely curtailed as a result of the Conservatives' negative attitude towards Europe.

THE LIBERAL DEMOCRATS: ARE THEY THE TRUE EUROPEANS?

Paddy Ashdown, on the face of it, has the easiest path to tread. His party conference last year fully backed his pro-European policy and his commitment to a single currency and a more closely integrated European Union could hardly be in doubt. But not all leading party figures are so enthusiastic, and the leadership are all too aware of those opinion polls which show that a majority of Liberal Democrat supporters harbour Eurosceptical doubts. However party strategists were convinced of one simple point: the worst thing they could do was to change policy, as a weaker European policy could easily be portrayed as a weaker Liberal Democrat party. One of the essences of third-party politics is the need to establish the party's identity; and on that basis the Liberal Democrats relish their pro-European image. The other party leaders may trim, just a little. Mr Ashdown is unlikely to do so.

THE OTHER PARTIES: A MIXTURE ALMOST AS BEFORE

The big difference this time may be provided by Sir James Goldsmith and his Referendum party. They certainly managed to scare Tory party managers last year; and they were a factor in encouraging the main parties to firm up their referendum plans. They will pay for, and probably receive, plenty of publicity, and they received the boost late in the Parliament of, fleetingly, having their own MP – the defecting Sir George Gardiner. But they will still have to compete around the fringes with the UK Independence party, who argue for withdrawal from the European Union.

The Ulster Unionists will continue to take a Eurosceptic line, but the nationalists in Northern Ireland and those in Scotland and Wales are all firmly pro-European. For them 'independence within Europe' is a concept which has found strong voter appeal. However, it is not the main issue for these parties.

HOW THE CAMPAIGN MAY GO

For many on the Conservative side, the great advantage of Europe as an issue is that it can be used as a weapon to hurt the other side. They would like to force Labour on to the defensive, to suggest that the great choice is who would be most effective at representing British interests: Mr Blair or Mr Major? It would be yet another way of highlighting the Labour leader's lack of experience.

But Europe, of course, is a double-edged sword: the more prominent it becomes as an issue, the easier it is for Labour to depict the Tories as divided. Within the Conservative ranks, there are many who will not flinch from stating their different views, particularly if they believe that the Tories will lose the general election. This is the great fear of the Conservative party managers. They have to ensure that all their leading figures keep their eyes on this election, not the one that would follow if a defeated Tory party was looking for a new leader.

Europe could be the issue on which the election turns. For the main parties, it is full of danger as well as opportunity; and now, at last, most people agree on its importance.

FLYING THE FLAG

CONSTITUTION, DEVOLUTION & CHANGE
Huw Edwards

Huw Edwards is a Political Correspondent for BBC News and frequently presents the One 'Clock News. He joined the BBC as a News Trainee in 1984. He has been at Westminster for the past 11 years, first as Parliamentary Correspondent for BBC Wales, and then as Political Correspondent for Network News. He specialises in reporting and analysing constitutional policy.

> *It is a programme of change so profound and so threatening that it must remain at the heart of serious political debate between now and the general election.* (Brian Mawhinney MP, Conservative Party Chairman, speech to Conservative Political Centre, February 1996)

The trumpet that sounded in the dying days of the 1992 campaign is indeed destined to sound a good deal more. Home Rule, Devolution, Subsidiarity, call it what you will. Some would have us believe that the constitutional burst was loud enough to secure victory for John Major last time round. More to the point, perhaps, Mr Major seems to have convinced himself that this was so.

Labour's package of constitutional change, diluted though it may be, is seen by Conservatives as one of their best hopes of swinging millions of votes in so-called Middle England, not least because Labour's proposals have implications for English taxpayers. When Tory billboards proclaim the 'New Dangers' of 'New Labour', it is this raft of constitutional changes – above all others – that voters are invited to feel queasy about.

The Liberal Democrats, who have made so much of the running in this field, now stand shoulder-to-shoulder with Labour after agreeing a joint approach to constitutional reform in March of this year.

The Scottish National Party and Plaid Cymru, both preaching the virtues of self-government for Scotland and Wales, present problems for Labour, Liberal Democrats and Conservatives alike.

Unless Labour promotes its plans with unprecedented confidence, the terms of the British campaign debate will once again be those set by the Conservatives. Labour, portrayed as the great wreckers of Britain's constitutional fabric, egged on by the even more irresponsible Liberal Democrats, bullied by the menacing nationalists, will do battle with the guardians of the British nation, the Conservatives. This time, the chances are that millions of voters will engage in the constitutional debate to a rare degree. Connoisseurs of the constitutional debate in Scotland and Wales know that this can only mean one thing... a spectacular bust-up.

DEVOLVING POWER

SCOTLAND

Every credible survey of opinion shows that a hefty majority of Scots demand a greater say in their own affairs. These demands vary in intensity. A long, unbroken period of Conservative rule has landed Labour in a dominant position. Despite this, the SNP has secured strong support for its policy of an independent Scottish state within the European Union.

Labour's tricky problem in the election campaign is to convince nationalistic Labour voters that it believes in a strong Scottish Parliament, while reassuring millions of conservative-minded voters (in Scotland, and more electorally significant, in England) that such a Parliament would be perfectly capable of working smoothly within the UK. Labour's risky solution to its electoral vulnerability has been to embrace a referendum on its plans, after years of denying the case for any such test of public opinion so soon after a general election.

The Conservatives have the uphill task in Scotland of insisting that their very modest proposals meet the high level of demand for greater self-determination.

The Liberal Democrats – whose demands for a fully federal constitution have long been a feature of British politics – now embrace Labour's more cautious approach. They hope *this* will bring about the first step on the road to more radical change.

It is a fascinating mix of policies, and should make for further lively exchanges, spiced up by the fact that the debate has moved once again from a purely Scottish stage to a British one.

SCOTLAND AT-A-GLANCE

LABOUR	SNP	CONSERVATIVE	LIB-DEM
Scotland within UK	Independent Scotland (but Head of State remains HM Queen)	Scotland within UK	Scotland within UK
Parliament elected by Additional Member System (part-PR)	Parliament (elected by PR)	Scottish Office, Scottish Grand Committee	Parliament elected by Additional Member System (part-PR)
Limited legislative, tax-raising powers	Full sovereign legislative powers	Beefed-up role for Scottish Grand Committee, with right to interrogate senior ministers; limited transfer of powers from Westminster to Edinburgh	Limited legislative, tax-raising powers
Legislated for within Labour's first year, subject to pre-legislative referendum in first months of government	Independence Settlement to be put to referendum in Scotland	Prospect of limited extra powers of scrutiny for Scottish MPs	Legislated for within first year of government, subject to pre-legislative referendum in first year of government
Parliament strengthens European ties via Committee of Regions	Scotland becomes full member of EU, UN	Scottish Office makes further economic links with EU and Committee of Regions; Scottish Office ministers go to Euro Council of Ministers	Parliament strengthens European ties via Committee of Regions

THE SCOTTISH DIMENSION THIS TIME ROUND

England and Scotland, Wales and Northern Ireland together are far, far greater than the sum of their parts. (John Major, 1992 campaign).

From this assertion stems all current debate. The Tory attack centres on three main areas: tax, the threat to the Union, and fair representation.

The Tartan Tax

The Scottish Parliament will have the power to increase or cut the basic rate of income tax... by a maximum of 3p in the pound. This will give it a greater degree of independence. ('Key Proposals for Scotland's Parliament', The Scottish Constitutional Convention, November 1995).

Thus was born the 'Tartan Tax'. Michael Forsyth, the Scottish Secretary, mounted an effective campaign against it – and this will be the populist dynamic driving much of the election campaign north of the border. Thanks to the tax-raising powers of Labour's Parliament, Scots would find themselves 'double-taxed', say the Tories.

The overall plan is that of the Scottish Constitutional Convention, a multi-denominational grouping (including Labour and the Liberal Democrats) which took six years to produce its vision of the future. That vision did not last long as a cast-iron Labour policy guarantee. In a remarkable tribute to effective Tory campaigning, Tony Blair put a big question mark over the future of the entire enterprise. In June 1996, he reversed the promise not to hold a referendum in Scotland and Wales on Labour's plans. This caused understandable upset among the Labour workers who had been pleased with the previous policy of using a general election victory as a mandate for constitutional change. Even worse for those workers was Mr Blair's decision to make the Scottish voters answer two questions; the first seeking approval for the devolved parliament, the second seeking specific approval for tax-raising powers.

The Liberal Democrats were also very unhappy, not least because they had not been consulted on the change. However, by March of this year, they had reached agreement with Labour on a joint approach to constitutional change. This embraced the two-question referendum – and a parliament with fewer powers than the Liberal Democrats had originally hoped for.

In retrospect, Labour's startling U-turn should not have caused so much surprise. The signs were all there, months in advance. Tony Blair was in the process of making all problematic policy 'watertight', and this was his way of defusing the inevitable Tory attack about 'imposing' a tax-raising body on the Scottish people. The tax-raising powers had already been undermined, in any case. In a classic piece of 'New Labourism', Tony Blair had sought months earlier to distance himself from the policy he had inherited from his predecessor, the fully paid-up devolutionist John Smith.

In reality, no Scottish Parliament would dare use this [tax] power unless parties had pledged to do so in an election... nobody in Scotland should pay a penny more or less in tax unless it has been voted for. (Tony Blair, John Smith Memorial Lecture, February 1996).

This was Labour's tentative answer to the deliberately provocative Tory ploy of equating a limited tax-raising power with an actual pledge to raise taxes. But Mr Blair did not think this made the policy sufficiently 'watertight', hence the new reliance on a referendum. The new policy certainly makes life more difficult for Michael Forsyth and the Tories, who had long been demanding a referendum.

Their horrified expressions on learning of the Blair about-turn spoke volumes.

But Labour has also made itself vulnerable to attacks from the Scottish National Party – accusing Mr Blair of 'appeasement', of caving in to Tory propaganda, and of lacking the self-confidence to take its plans to their logical conclusion ... independence. Any further dilution of Labour's plans will be a gift to the SNP's propaganda machine.

The Threat to the Union

Constitutional change does not, in my view, threaten the Union. Indeed, it will enhance it. (Gordon Brown, Labour News Release, January 1995)

Arguing this particular case can be rather difficult for Labour in view of the SNP's assertive campaign.

My party will do all in our power to convert (Labour's) proposed Mickey Mouse parliament into a normal one as enjoyed by other members of the European Union. (Winnie Ewing, SNP MEP, January 1995)

While the SNP argues that a parliament with limited powers is a timid first step towards independence, Labour insists that satisfying this particular Scottish demand will help quell the calls for separation. This is manna for the Conservatives. While the Tartan Tax can still feature in the Scottish campaign, the threat to the Union will be put before the voters of England – the biggest 'New Danger' presented by Mr Blair. There is little evidence of any widespread English interest in the democratic condition of Scotland or Wales (indeed, interest within Wales and Scotland is patchy). But the prospect of damaging the 'unity' of the United Kingdom is far more likely to shift votes in Middle England.

Back to West Lothian...

And back to the late 1970s, when Labour MP Tam Dalyell (then MP for West Lothian) voiced concern about Scotland's representation at Westminster in the age of a Scottish Parliament. He's still voicing that concern.

Why should Scottish MPs at Westminster be able to vote on purely English matters while English MPs will have no say over matters devolved to a Scottish parliament? (Tam Dalyell, *Glasgow Herald* January 1994)

More eminent Labour figures have also made the point. Robin Cook, a prominent battler against the 1979 proposals, often made the case himself. But Cook's great rival, Gordon Brown, has little patience for this particular obsession. In a speech in January 1995, he explained that because devolution for Scotland and Wales went 'hand in hand with the offer of greater regional democracy throughout Britain, what has been called the West Lothian Question should not, in my view, be a barrier to proceeding with change'. This is a rare example of a front-line Labour politician tackling this issue head-on. Tony Blair seems increasingly unwilling to adopt this line himself, not least because the 'offer' of English regional reform is not a policy with which Blair appears comfortable.

One ultimate solution might be to restrict the voting rights of Scottish Westminster MPs to those issues affecting the UK as a whole, and not specifically England and Wales. Another solution might be to cut down the number of MPs Scotland sends to Westminster. The current 72 is an over-representation, in any case. There are an average 54,000 electors per MP in Scotland; 69,000 in England.

So far, Labour has published no plans to change the current position. It does not intend to tackle the West Lothian Question in the context of its manifesto plans. Indeed, George Robertson has said he sees no case for change. The vulnerability of the plans before an English electorate is plain. Scotland cannot be seen to be getting some kind of special treatment, thus putting English regions at a disadvantage (primarily of the economic kind). But an eventual reduction in the number of Scottish MPs at Westminster is not hugely acceptable for a Labour Party that depends on its Scottish contingent for survival.

WALES

Scotland and Wales have distinctive historical and political traditions. Scotland had its own Parliament (until 1707) and still retains a separate legal and judicial system, quite different from Wales. Our proposals are not, therefore, a carbon copy of the proposals for a Scottish Parliament. ('Shaping the Vision', Labour Wales, May 1995)

The Welsh still bear the scars of 1979 and the St David's Day referendum, which graphically exposed the division within Labour's ranks in Wales. It was a memorably poisonous contest, even by Welsh standards.

The prospect of another referendum fills many Welsh Labour members with horror. It might be fair to speculate that Ron Davies, the Shadow Welsh Secretary, would not have chosen this policy

WALES AT-A-GLANCE

LABOUR	PLAID CYMRU	CONSERVATIVE	LIB-DEM
Head of State, HM Queen	Head of State, decided by referendum	Head of State, HM Queen	Head of State, HM Queen
Wales within UK	Self-governing Wales in United Europe	Wales within UK	Wales within UK
Assembly 60 members; (AMS, part-PR)	Parliament (PR)	Welsh Office. Welsh Grand Committee, with better scrutiny of Welsh issues. Welsh Select Committee, with improved role	Senedd/Assembly, 60 members (AMS – part PR)
Pre-legislative referendum in 'first months' of Labour government			Pre-legislative referendum
Very limited law-making powers No tax-raising powers	Full law-making powers	Clampdown on quangos Greater role for WGC, with prospect of grilling senior ministers	Very limited law-making powers No tax-raising powers

voluntarily. But if Tony Blair has doubts about the case for Scottish devolution (as many insist he does), his commitment to the Welsh scheme might be even more shaky. Labour's plans for a Welsh Assembly will be the focus of the coming campaign in Wales. It will be impossible to avoid the shadow of 1979. The Conservatives are still happy to quote its overwhelming 'No' result as if Welsh opinion cannot possibly have changed in the 17 years that followed.

Labour is understandably cautious when it reads opinion polls indicating a solid majority in favour of some sort of devolved power. In many cases, this is nothing more than a loud raspberry blown at successive Conservative governments, not one of which has earned anything like majority support among the Welsh.

As so often, Wales is faced with more modest versions of things on offer elsewhere. Labour is proposing a far more modest version of its Scottish proposals, though no doubt the hope is that as the Welsh Assembly settles down, it will demand the powers claimed by its Scottish cousin. Ron Davies scored a notable victory when he secured a PR-based election for the Assembly, very much against the wishes of a majority of the Welsh Labour Executive. This was again a central factor in securing Liberal Democrat support for the plans. But the Liberal Democrats' compromise has been seized on by Plaid Cymru as evidence that the Welsh Liberal Democrats have caved in to Labour's wishes.

Plaid Cymru sets out the same ambitious goal of independence as shared by the SNP (though Plaid prefers the term self-government), but it proposes a more modest rate of progress towards that goal.

Wales = Quangoland

The Conservatives are in a weak position in Wales, and are saddled with a record of massive quango-creation that has characterised the years since 1979. From April 1996, there were more quango appointees in Wales (over 1,400) than elected councillors (1,273). The budget allocated to those quangos was as large, if not larger, than that allocated to Welsh local government. To add to the Tories' problems, there is a widespread perception that of the 400 or so annual quango appointments made by successive Tory Secretaries of State, many have been blatant party appointments. Labour, Plaid Cymru and the Liberal Democrats all agree that one of the primary functions of a devolved Welsh body would be to call to account the quangos and the Welsh Office itself. There seems little doubt that this is a popular campaigning line.

The real interest in so much of the Welsh debate lies in the Labour–Plaid Cymru tussle, where Labour is forced to defend the decision not to offer Wales the same as Scotland. The decision to go for a part-PR system is seen as one way of creating a more 'inclusive' democratic system of the kind often preached by Mr Blair. The signs are that Labour is preparing to grant the Assembly limited legislative powers in certain areas. This might well satisfy the more cautious Welsh electorate. If not, Plaid Cymru might well gain ground with its plans for a self-governing Wales within a United Europe, though the current appetite for such reform is less than voracious.

THE ENGLISH REGIONS

The Northern Group (of Labour MPs) supports devolution for Scotland, but our price is devolution for England. (John McWilliam MP, December 1995)

This is where Labour's constitutional intentions have changed most since Mr Blair was elected, and where Conservative charges of a swelling local bureaucracy seem to have caused unease for 'New Labour'.

The change in Labour's stance has been dramatic. It went into the last election promising a massive increase in local institutions.

Each region would acquire the equivalent of a Scottish or a Welsh Office. (Devolution and Democracy, Labour Party, 1991)

THE ENGLISH REGIONS AT-A-GLANCE

LABOUR	CONSERVATIVE	LIB-DEM
Regional Chambers (indirectly elected)	Emphasis on local government, including creating Unitary Authorities	Regional chambers (indirectly elected)
Optional 2nd step: elected regional assemblies, where local demand is proven	Consider ending capping of local authorities	Optional 2nd-step elected regional assemblies where demand is proven (likely use of referendums)
(likely use of referendum)		
Principal function: economic development and ties with EU	Strategic role for local government as enabler, not provider	Principal function: economic development and ties with EU

By the time *'A Choice for England'* was published in July 1995, the plans were of a more modest kind, reflecting Tony Blair's widely-rumoured scepticism in this area. Labour now proposes 'regional chambers' for those ten regions covered by a Government Integrated Regional Office (IRO).

The regional chambers would consist of nominated representatives of elected local councils. Looking farther into the future, an optional step of directly-elected regional assemblies would be available for these regions in which demand for them is strong. (*A Choice for England*, Labour Party, July 1995)

Assessing local demand will involve referendums, probably in those areas where Labour MPs are demanding them. Mr Blair seems to have moved towards the Liberal Democrat stance, where the fully federal UK structure they propose is underpinned by the principle of 'change-if-there's-demand'.

In England, the process should proceed only as fast as the demand for it justifies. (*Here We Stand*, Liberal Democrat White Paper, 1993)

Crucially, Mr Blair has to contend with a determined group of Labour MPs (notably in the Northeast, led by the former Chief Whip Derek Foster) who are utterly determined that their area will not suffer the disadvantage of living in the shadows of a powerful Scottish Parliament. They have promised trouble if they don't get their way, which is presumably why Jack Straw, the Shadow Home Secretary, has seen fit to extend a few olive branches.

Those regions like the North, the Northwest, the Southwest, where there is popular consent, will be able to move ahead quickly within our first term of office to establish elected regional assemblies. (Jack Straw, Labour Conference, October 1995)

All of this delights the Tories, who are convinced that most English voters do not want what Conservatives insist is another tier of government. The Conservative case is that local government throughout the UK has been transformed, more recently with the introduction in some areas of all-purpose unitary authorities. They claim this involves less bureaucracy and reduced cost. In addition, the Conservatives insist that 'true' devolution of power has been a feature of reforms in education, health and housing, where decision-making has been 'devolved' closer to the service-users.

OUR VOTING SYSTEM

Accountability, strong government and a 'fair' distribution of seats cannot easily be reconciled. (Conservative Campaign Guide, 1996)

The Liberal Democrats have put electoral reform at the heart of their far-reaching reforms for a federal Britain. In doing so, they battle against the Conservative party and much of the Labour Party. The joint agreement in March of this year saw Labour and the Liberal Democrats agreeing on the setting up of a Commission on voting systems. This would recommend an appropriate system of proportional representation for electing MPs; and this would be put to the people in a referendum. The hope is that this might be done in the first term (5 years) of a Labour government. Mr Blair himself is instinctively against PR for Westminster elections and he has said so in recent months.

PROPORTIONAL RERESENTATION: THE PARTY OPTIONS

LABOUR	LIB-DEM	CONS	SNP	PLAID CYMRU
Commission on voting systems; Referendum: PR for Euro-elections	Commission on voting systems; Referendum: PR for Euro-elections	First-past-the-post stays	PR for Scottish Parliament	PR for Welsh Parliament

For the Liberal Democrats, the past 17 years have shown the first-past-the-post system to be 'grotesquely distorting'. In 1983, the Conservatives secured a majority of 144 with 42.4 per cent of the vote. In 1992, the Conservatives secured a majority of just 21 with 41.9 per

cent of the vote. This mismatch between party support and
representation, say the Liberal Democrats, is still more marked in
local and European elections.

Labour's Plant Commission reported in 1993 and advocated a
supplementary vote system for Westminster elections. With one eye
on the possibility of having to work with the Liberal Democrats,
Mr Blair has been careful not to slam the door shut, and may yet find
room for compromise, despite his evident misgivings:

> *'I believe a referendum is right so that people can decide what is the
> best electoral system for this country'.* (Tony Blair, *The Observer*,
> July 1994)

What is not clear is the timing of any such referendum, and Mr
Blair has been careful to avoid making any specific promises here.

The Conservative case is clear. They believe that first-past-the-post
provides stable government, and supports the link between MPs and
their constituents. And yet...

> *'Within the Conservative party, discussions continue about the relative
> merits of both systems'* (Conservative Campaign Guide, 1996).

That might well be the case for European Elections, but there is no
hint of change for electing MPs to Westminster.

BILL OF RIGHTS

> *There is a growing public demand in Britain for constitutional reform,
> and recognition that the British system of human rights guarantees is
> inadequate.* (Archy Kirkwood MP, Liberal Democrat, speaking in the
> Commons, May 1991).

Britain already has a Bill of Rights. It was passed into law in
December 1689 after the Glorious Revolution. In legal terms, this is
simply another Act of Parliament which could be repealed by
Parliament if it wished. It is this failure to preserve our freedoms in a
grand declaration of constitutional principles which drives the
campaign for a 'new' Bill of Rights. But opinion is sharply divided as
to the desirability of such a Bill.

> *It [the 1689 Bill] has helped preserve our freedoms for over three
> hundred years. It refutes the argument that our freedoms can only be
> properly protected if somehow the principle of parliamentary sovereignty
> is constrained.* (David Willetts, *Modern Conservatism*, 1992)

BILL OF RIGHTS AT-A-GLANCE

LABOUR	CONSERVATIVE	LIB-DEM
European Convention on Human Rights to be incorporated into UK Law	Status quo	European Commission on Human Rights to be incorporated into UK Law
Human Rights Commission to implement law		Human Rights Commission to implement law

The Conservatives reject the case that Britain's sovereign hereditary monarchy, in partnership with an unelected second chamber, constitutes an undemocratic, anachronistic set-up.

The Liberal Democrats have been the prime movers behind the campaign for written legislation protecting freedom of speech, freedom of association, and freedom of information (more of which later). Britain does not have a written constitution, and therefore, they argue, basic human rights are not guaranteed.

The main Conservative case is that it is precisely this flexibility – the lack of a written constitution – that should recommend it to this and future generations. They argue that the definition of freedom of speech, should, for example, rest in the hands of the people (as in Parliament) and not left to the interpretations of lawyers.

In his leadership campaign, Tony Blair supported 'entrenching clear rights for every citizen in a Bill of Rights for Britain'. In this first instance this would go no further than the incorporation into UK law of the existing European Convention on Human Rights. The Liberal Democrats have agreed with this as a first step, together with the appointment of a Human Rights Commissioner.

THE OTHER PLACE

It is no bad thing for our Constitution that the elected House of Commons has a counterpoint and conscience which does not derive from the same elective process. (Dr Brian Mawhinney, Conservative Party Chairman, February 1996)

The extent to which the Conservative leadership is prepared to defend the constitutional status quo has surprised some of the party's most experienced MPs. Dr Mawhinney's defence of the hereditary peers was seen as a gaffe by Labour, whose own research indicates that this is one of the few areas of genuine public appetite for reform. And yet, Labour's immediate proposals have been heavily diluted. The prospect of an elected second chamber has become more distant. In the first instance, Labour would remove the voting rights of

REFORMING THE LORDS AT-A-GLANCE

LABOUR	CONSERVATIVE	LIB-DEM
Hereditary peers not allowed to sit and vote	No change	Hereditary peers not allowed to sit and vote
Life peers to be created to tackle 'imbalance'		Life peers to be created to tackle 'imbalance'
Committee to recommend steps to democratic 2nd chamber		Committee to recommend steps to democratic 2nd chamber

hereditary peers, and recently, Robin Cook and Robert Maclennan, announcing their joint agreement, proposed that many new peers should be appointed to ease the passage of legislation.

This area of reform of the Lords saw a good deal of hard bargaining between Labour and the Liberal Democrats. The prospect of an elected 2nd Chamber is still there, but with no meaningful timetable attached to it.

FREEDOM OF INFORMATION

We will enact a Freedom of Information Act to attack secrecy wherever it exists, public or private sector. (Tony Blair)

Those who view the UK as an excessively secretive state see great merits in a Freedom of Information Act. In its various forms, this would include statutory access to information held by government and other public bodies. This would, it is argued, give greater confidence in matters of public health and safety. While the Tories reject proposals for a full-scale Freedom of Information Act, John Major prides himself on the anti-secrecy measures he has implemented since the early 1990s. These measures were designed to complement the Citizen's Charter initiative, which is aimed at giving people a guaranteed standard of service from public bodies. The Tories do not think that full statutory provision is the best way of achieving greater openness. Labour and the Liberal Democrats both support a Freedom of Information Act.

Before anyone gets too excited by the prospect of an election campaign driven by lively debate on the relative merits of a Freedom of Information Act, beware. It is true that the public consistently states in opinion polls that a written constitution and freedom of information are eminently desirable. That much is beyond doubt. But a supplementary question on the public's real priorities reveals something different.

FREEDOM OF INFORMATION AT-A-GLANCE

LABOUR	CONSERVATIVE	LIB-DEM
Freedom of Information Act, general right of access to official information held by public bodies	Right of access to health and safety information	Freedom of Information Act, general right of access to official information held by public bodies
Tightly defined reasons for keeping information secret	New code for civil servants	Tightly defined reasons for keeping information secret
	New powers for Parliamentary Ombudsman	

These policies are not big vote winners – or losers. They are not issues which swing votes in any great numbers.

This makes Tony Blair's tactics rather more understandable. He has been busy scaling down Labour's promises in this area, keen for a future Labour government – the first in over 20 years – not to get bogged down in the constitutional mire. His deal with the Liberal Democrats is meant to keep his legislative plans under control, and less vulnerable to any rebellions in his own ranks.

However, if some unpleasant material hits the ventilating system he'll scale things down further still.

ONE NATION?

A SCOTTISH PERSPECTIVE

Brian Taylor

*Brian Taylor is Political Editor of BBC Scotland.
He began his journalistic career with the* Press and
Journal *in Aberdeen. Then followed five years as a
lobby correspondent for Thomson Regional
Newspapers before his return to Scotland.
He joined the BBC in 1985 as a reporter on the
nightly news programme, 'Reporting Scotland'.
He was appointed Political Correspondent in 1988
and Political Editor in 1996.*

'THE SCOTTISH QUESTION'

This is not just an argument about a Scottish Parliament. That is just
a symptom. Think of it rather as the 'Scottish Question', much as
Gladstone thought of the Irish one. The real problem is much more
difficult to define: prompted by a feeling that Scottish concerns are
not adequately or separately addressed; boosted by collective folk
memories from the Union of the Parliaments in 1707; manifested by
the search for an outlet other than Hampden or Murrayfield for
Scottish nationhood. In short, an issue of Scottish patriotism.

The classic error in observing Scottish politics is to assume that
this frequently ill-defined feeling of patriotism has relevance only for
the Scottish National Party with its objective of an independent
Scotland within the European Union. In truth, this mood has an
impact upon *all* the parties seeking popular support in Scotland.

For the SNP, obviously, it is the starting point, the original dynamic;
although its leader Alex Salmond believes the party must offer much
more than an enthusiastic rendering of 'Flower o'Scotland'.
He positions his party on the Social Democratic Left, seeking to
relate independence to the everyday concerns of Labour-voting
Central Scotland.

For the Liberal Democrats, Scottish home rule is a century-old creed. In effect, they suspended their ambition of a federal Britain for the gain of an interim deal with Labour – a deal which features the cherished Liberal Democrat goal of a proportional voting system. Their hope is that reform might be catching, and PR might spread to Westminster.

The Scottish patriotic mood has a big impact on Labour too – although the party's reply to the Scottish Question has varied. Keir Hardie founded the party on a solid home rule platform – but that remained largely in abeyance while leaders like Clement Attlee pursued centralised objectives in areas like welfare. Neil Kinnock's conversion to the cause proved less than skin-deep, while John Smith's commitment was beyond question. And Tony Blair's abrupt decision to hold a referendum (despite firm pledges not to) has raised hackles, and aroused deep suspicion.

The return of the Stone of Destiny to Scotland was no fanciful whim. Michael Forsyth did not wear his kilt to the *Braveheart* film premiere in Stirling because he thinks he has fetching knees. The apparent support for the Gaelic language and Highland culture is part of a pattern. The Conservatives' 40-year variable voting slide in Scotland, if nothing else, tells them that they cannot afford to set themselves utterly against the underlying mood which they believe devolution represents. In essence, they are attempting to realign the Tories with Scottish popular sentiment: employing Scots words in posters, for example, and even recalling the Scottish Tories' Jacobite origins. The Conservatives are fond of stressing that they have been responsible for many of the administrative acts of devolution to Scotland – including the establishment of the Scottish Office and the creation of the post of Secretary of State. Their most recent experiment in this vein has been to enhance the role of the Scottish Grand Committee – which comprises all 72 MPs from Scotland – with more meetings across Scotland, rather than purely at Westminster, and sporadic opportunities to question senior ministers.

THE SCOTTISH QUANGOCRACY

The so-called 'democratic deficit' lying at the heart of the home rule campaign is most frequently cited in the context of the quango state. Figures supplied by the House of Commons Library suggest that in 1995-6 there were a total of 212 non-departmental public bodies in Scotland wielding either executive or advisory power. This total includes 68 NHS bodies. Their one characteristic is that they are unelected. Labour, the SNP and the Liberal Democrats also contest that they are unaccountable. The gross expenditure attributed to these organisations was £9.3 billion – with £5.9 billion contributed by government. This latter figure is calculated as some 42 per cent of central government spending. This is estimated to be roughly twice the relevant percentage for the UK as whole – although it is stressed that this bald figure is potentially misleading, as there are significant tranches of UK spending such as social security and defence which impact upon Scotland, but are not distributed through quangos.

No one suggests that the entire quango network – which includes a range of advisory bodies – should be dismantled. But opposition politicians have offered a range of suggestions for altering their nature. In particular, Labour has warned the three water boards appointed by the Scottish Office that they will be dismantled on day one of an incoming Labour administration. The party envisages replacing them with new authorities comprising locally elected members. In addition, Labour has suggested that NHS bodies might be 'democratised' by the accession of further elected members. It is claimed that reforms of the internal market might release funds for patient care. That is disputed by the Conservatives who claim that Labour has failed to specify any sources of additional funding for the NHS. The Tories further claim that Labour would be hamstrung by competing demands from Labour-dominated local authorities.

THE SCOTTISH ECONOMY

Forecasters point to the Scottish economy sharing in the UK upturn – but perhaps lagging a little relative to the most recent changes in the rest of the country. On this question of potentially changing perceptions, the December 1996 commentary by economic analysts at Strathclyde University's Fraser of Allander Institute notes that from the late 1980s until 1994, 'the Scottish economy performed better than the UK'. They add that 'Scotland did not experience a recession in the 1990-92 period but has recovered more modestly'.

The government's own *Scottish Economic Bulletin* noted in September 1996 that 'independent forecasts of the Scottish economy are for GDP growth to be broadly comparable to the UK rate in both 1996 and 1997'. This contrasts with figures – charted by the *Bulletin* – showing Scottish growth commonly ahead of the UK figure from 1988 to 1993. The Fraser of Allander Institute notes that 'Scotland continues to grow less strongly than the UK as a whole'. But Fraser of Allander anticipates that 1997 and 1998 'will be a period of strong

growth in output and employment which will engender a fall in
Scottish unemployment to less than 7 per cent of the workforce'.
This is based on a forecast of continuing export-led recovery – allied
to relative strength in Scotland's main markets, including England.
The institute estimates that Scottish exports will grow by 7.75 per
cent in 1997 and a further 11 per cent in 1998. This issue of exports is
critical. The Scottish economy – now transformed from its earlier
reliance on coal, steel and shipbuilding – is now more heavily
dependent on exports than the remainder of the UK from long-
established industries such as whisky through to new growth sectors
such as micro-electronics.

The Conservatives plan to make considerable play of the inward
investment partly generated by government agencies such as Locate
in Scotland. The *Scottish Economic Bulletin* notes that in 1992/93
there were 65 such projects bringing £352 million of investment and
generating or protecting 8060 jobs. The comparable figures for later
years are: 1993/94, 95 projects, £588 million, 11,070 jobs; 1994/95, 97
projects, £1,127 million, 12,330 jobs; and 1995/96, £981 million, 12,560
jobs. *The Bulletin* discloses that in latter years the trend has been for
Asia Pacific investment to predominate by contrast with earlier
American prominence, citing for example the £260 million investment
in Lanarkshire by Chunghwa for a picture tubes factory promising
more than 3,000 jobs. But opposition parties can be expected to raise
a series of question marks over the Conservatives' vision of the
Scottish economy. There are 'local rivalry' questions over the siting of
investment – with brownfield sites in relatively deprived areas like
Glasgow apparently losing out.

More generally, there are demands for action to help relative
blackspots like parts of urban Dundee and Glasgow plus rural areas
such as sections of the Highlands and the southwest. There are
questions too over Scotland's new employment profile – with claims
that declining unemployment is partly a factor of jobless males
dropping out of the labour market, while new recruitment is often
female, part-time and white-collar. There are concerns voiced that
Scotland is becoming a 'branch plant' economy with relatively low
wages for assembly workers rather than high-grade research and
development jobs. The Conservatives insist that claim is being
addressed – but opposition parties warn that the Scottish economy is
relatively vulnerable to altered international investment priorities. In
addition, there are claims that constraints in public spending – most
notably in the local government sector – will work through to
substantial job losses.

More generally, the SNP has published details of its planned economic programme for an independent Scotland. It envisages lower business and corporation tax to encourage growth, reduced income tax for the low-paid – with a 'modest' increase in the burden for upper earners. The Nationalists say their plan involves total additional spending of £5.5 billion over four years – with total additional income of nearly £7 billion, including £3 billion from altered tax and social security, £260 million from additional corporation tax through 'economic growth' and more than £1 billion from the proclaimed beneficial impact of the process of independence itself. SNP leaders claim their programme would create 100,000 jobs over four years based upon a competitive advantage to Scottish industry. But rival parties have denounced their plans as 'fantasy figures' – with the Tories in particular pointing to an estimate, published by the Scottish Office, that an independent Scotland would face an £8.1 billion deficit. That estimate is contested by the SNP.

SCOTTISH EDUCATION

In the field of education, the issues in Scotland differ from the rest of the UK. The key debates are funding, pay, pre-school education and the distinctive nature of Scottish Universities – by contrast, perhaps, with the issue of secondary school provision. There are just two self-governing schools in the whole of Scotland – one a secondary in the Highlands, and the other a small Church primary school in Dunblane. A third will follow in August but for whatever reason – satisfaction, complacency, parental caution, the lack of a self-governing tradition – the Tory drive for opted-out schools has failed to make much impact thus far north of the Border. In addition, there is little sign of the controversy over 'grammar schools' which is so virulent elsewhere. For the most part, the comprehensive system appears fairly firmly embedded although there is a debate about selection within schools. There are substantial issues, however. The main teaching union, the Educational Institute of Scotland, is seeking to raise the profile of education funding as an electoral issue. It has claimed that local authorities were obliged to find £80 million savings in the 1996/97 financial year – and that the situation is likely to worsen in the following year. Councils, they warn, are contemplating compulsory teaching redundancies for the first time.

The Tories insist they have made education a priority – and that resources are available, provided councils cut their cloth elsewhere. The Liberal Democrats have promised to devote the product of 1p in income tax to education – either in the UK or in Scotland alone should they share power in a Scottish Parliament. The SNP spending programme forecasts an extra £80 million over four years providing, they claim, an extra 700 teachers. Scottish Labour – in keeping with Tony Blair's overall approach – has promised to prioritise education. A further controversy has been stirred by the Scottish Secretary's suggestion that the present collective bargaining machinery for teachers' salaries should be replaced by an independent pay review body – with discretion to recommend special payments for classroom excellence or teachers who face particular challenges. Opposition parties have condemned this as a pre-election 'gimmick' to divert attention from the wider issue of funding.

But there are other questions: are the Government's nursery vouchers the right way to proceed or should there be more direct funding, as opposition parties suggest? What is the future for Scotland's broadly-based Higher examination system? What might happen to the traditional four-year degree in Scottish Universities under strategic and funding reviews? Would a Scottish Parliament attempt to exert further control over education – diminishing local authorities' power base? Answers to all these might be forthcoming when the campaign is underway.

THE ELECTORAL PICTURE

THE CONSERVATIVES

What, then, is at stake? Well, in straightforward electoral terms three cabinet ministers are facing various degrees of threat to their seats. Michael Forsyth is defending a notional majority of 236 or 0.6 per cent according to the BBC/ITN/PA/Sky Guide to the New Constituencies. Capturing his seat is Labour's prime target in Scotland. The President of the Board of Trade, Ian Lang, is being pursued by the SNP in his Galloway and Upper Nithsdale seat, defending a notional majority of 2,400 or 5.5 per cent. The Foreign Secretary Malcolm Rifkind has more of a cushion over Labour in his Edinburgh Pentlands seat with a notional majority of 4,148 or 9 per cent. Conservative defeat in any of these seats would obviously impact upon the general election – but might also affect any subsequent Conservative leadership contest as all three have featured at various times in lists of potential contenders. Within party circles, Ian Lang is seen as a close and able ally of the Prime Minister, Malcolm Rifkind has developed a certain Euro-quizzical note in his more recent pronouncements, and Michael Forsyth has added a reputation for ministerial competence to his previous image as an aggressive campaigner for free-market thinking.

With regard to Michael Forsyth in particular, the party has thoroughly enjoyed his vigorous harrying of Labour over the so-called 'Tartan Tax': the potential for a future Scottish Parliament to vary personal income tax by up to 3 per cent. He is generally credited with prompting Labour to promise a specific question on tax in any future devolution referendum. Labour argues there are no indications in opinion polls that the Scottish Secretary's efforts – which brought him the accolade of Parliamentarian of the Year – will bring electoral success.

LABOUR

For George Robertson, Labour's Shadow Scottish Secretary, 1996 was a difficult year. This *former* Parliamentarian of the Year found himself on the defensive, particularly during the protracted machinations over Labour's proposed referendum. He freely admits that was tough, but insists that he and the party have now clarified their stance on home rule – and weakened the impact of the 'Tartan Tax' campaign in the process by giving Scots a direct say on whether such powers should be granted. He stresses Labour would campaign for a referendum 'Yes' vote on both questions: devolutionary principle and tax powers. But the episode has left an atmosphere of vague disquiet among the more ardent Home Rulers in Labour ranks. That will abate for the election period and, of course, would vanish should Labour win and proceed to deliver devolution. The party in Scotland would then develop its own policy portfolio in consultation with London. UK Labour defeat, however, would generate particular tension within the party in Scotland.

LIBERAL DEMOCRATS

For Jim Wallace, the leader of the Scottish Liberal Democrats, the referendum episode was also instructive. He was exasperated that Labour failed to consult him over a tactical change which overturned the approach adopted by the cross-party convention. He continues to regard the planned referendum as unwarranted, but this hasn't stopped the Liberal Democrats signing a constitutional deal with Labour, which includes the plans for a two-question referendum. He is also under a certain pressure internally to distance his party from Labour – not least from those Liberal Democrats fighting Tories in marginal seats. But Mr Wallace is adamant that the key gains of the Convention process – and the constitutional Liberal Democrat/Labour deal – should not be abandoned. Expect, though, to see the Liberal Democrat stressing their own perspective – for example, that the number of Scots MPs at Westminster should be reduced post-devolution and that the office of Secretary of State should be abolished.

SCOTTISH NATIONAL PARTY

At the General Election, the party leader Alex Salmond says he will argue for Scotland's interests – and will urge Scotland to follow the 'high road' to independence. But, at the same time, he will not want to close the 'low road': the prospect that a Labour-style devolved Parliament might want to accrue further powers to the point of full autonomy. Salmond is an economist. He can count. Say Labour gains power alongside seven or eight SNP MPs – a modest advance but enough to remind Labour of the SNP's potential. Say Labour sets up its Scottish Parliament – and holds elections to that body under proportional representation perhaps two years down the road from Westminster victory. Say by then Labour is suffering from mid-term electoral blues and the SNP is able to gain a third or more of the 129 seats on offer in that Edinburgh Parliament. A vanguard of forty plus paid activists, arguing daily that the devolved Parliament could achieve so much more if only it had greater power. Now Labour leaders can do their sums too. They claim the party which finally delivered on Home Rule could expect an electoral bonus. Privately, a few Tories north of the Border wonder whether devolution might be the salvation of their party, liberating Scots to vote again purely from economic and class motivation.

Opinion polls frequently suggest that Scottish popular support for independence runs ahead of support for the SNP. Alex Salmond explains this by arguing that there are many Scots who are relaxed about the prospect of independence but perhaps do not yet accord it sufficient importance to choose the most direct route to register this opinion. Salmond is fond of representing independence as a process, talking of Scotland 'becoming independent'. Consequently, while the atmosphere of a general election will undoubtedly affect him, he is reluctant to sound too apocalyptic about the forthcoming contest. There is little overt revolutionary fervour from the man who lists Cromwell as his favourite Englishman. Salmond disliked the sloganising forecast that Scotland could be 'Free by 1993' which was produced by another senior party figure on the hustings at the last general election.

There will be no 'In Heaven in 1997' this time around. Critics say the disappointing outcome at the last election – more than 21 per cent of the vote but only three MPs – demonstrates the need for more fervent evangelism. Salmond takes a more studied approach. In a November 1990 newspaper profile, he was quoted as saying: 'If the party has not achieved its objects in ten years it will want a new leader'. These days – with the millennium approaching – he is understandably less keen on precise forecasts. His job, he indicates, would only be on the line in the absence of a 'substantial advance' for the cause of nationalism. The question of defining that phrase, presumably, can be left until after the election.

For all the leaders, then, this is an election replete with personal as well as political challenges. For Scots, it is an opportunity to deliver a verdict on the government of the UK and the governance of Scotland.

THE DRAGON WITH TWO TONGUES

A WELSH PERSPECTIVE
Glyn Mathias

Glyn Mathias is Political Editor of BBC Wales. After working at BBC Southampton and the South Wales Echo, he joined ITN in 1973, where he served as Political Correspondent, Political Editor, Assistant Editor and Head of Corporate Affairs before leaving in 1994 to take up his current position with the BBC.

THE WELSH PICTURE

We are now confidently predicting a Tory-free zone. (Rhodri Morgan MP, Labour, Cardiff West, June 1996)

For more than 60 years, the people of Wales have unfailingly returned a majority of Labour MPs to the House of Commons. It is a record of political dominance which outstrips that of the Labour party in Scotland, whose ascendancy over the Conservatives was achieved only after the Second World War.

This time around, the Welsh Labour party believes it is on course to match its performance in 1966, when it won 32 of the then 36 seats in Wales. Senior Labour politicians have even predicted that the Conservatives could be wiped off the parliamentary map of Wales at this general election. Such claims are, to say the least, premature. What they are based on, however, is the fact that the Conservatives are defending too many marginal seats for their comfort. And they have to live down their showing in the last Welsh local elections in 1995, when they won just 42 seats out of 1,270.

Broadly-speaking, Wales can be divided into three different geographical areas for electoral purposes. First, and perhaps best

1992 GENERAL ELECTION

	WELSH SEATS	% WELSH VOTE	% UK VOTE
Labour	27	49.5	34.2
Conservative	6	28.6	41.9
Plaid Cymru	4	9.0	0.5
Lib-Dem	1	12.4	17.9
Seats	38		

known, are the old industrial areas where Labour regularly piles up huge majorities. In the Rhondda, Allan Rogers had a majority of nearly 29,000 in 1992, a margin of more than 62 per cent over his nearest rival, Plaid Cymru. There have been occasional threats in the past against Labour's stranglehold on these kinds of seats, but this threat seems to have gone away for the time being.

Secondly, there are those parts of Wales which perform politically much like England – much of Northeast Wales, the Cardiff area and some of the border country. In many cases this kind of territory is more Anglicised, and the swing between the two main parties tends to be more in line with the national trend. Most of the Conservative seats are in these areas – the most marginal seat in the whole of the UK is the Vale of Glamorgan, just to the west of Cardiff, where the Eurosceptic, Walter Sweeney, enjoys a majority of just 19 votes.

Thirdly, there are the rural areas of North and West Wales, where the Welsh language can be in common usage, and where a long-standing radical tradition persists. The parliamentary seats are often complex three-way (or sometimes four-way) political battles, with seats changing hands over the decades. The four constituencies held by Plaid Cymru are to be found here, plus the single Liberal Democrat seat. But the Conservatives can win here as well, notably Jonathan Evans in Brecon and Radnor – if only by 130 votes last time.

PARTY PROSPECTS IN WALES
THE CONSERVATIVES

He is our Prime Minister and we're going to stand shoulder to shoulder with him on the soap boxes at the next election'. (William Hague MP, Secretary of State for Wales, June 1996)

Much will depend, of course, on the position of the political parties nationally, but the vulnerability of the Conservatives in Wales can be seen from the small majorities they are defending. Boundary changes have enlarged the number of seats in Wales from 38 to 40. Two extra seats might end up in Conservative hands (Vale of Clwyd and Preseli Pembrokeshire) on the basis of past voting trends, but they, too, are assessed as marginals.The Conservatives can be reasonably confident of holding only two seats. In Monmouth, Roger Evans reversed a by-election defeat to win with a majority of 3,200 in 1992, and Labour would be doing very well to win in what is pretty solid Conservative territory. Statistically at least – the Conservatives are likely to be safest in the revised seat of Clwyd West, with an estimated majority of just over 7,000. The candidate is Rod Richards, who resigned from his ministerial post at the Welsh Office, after newspaper reports about his private life.

CONSERVATIVE SEATS IN WALES NOTIONAL SHARE BASED ON NEW BOUNDARIES

SEAT	MAJORITY	2ND PARTY	MP
Vale of Glamorgan	19	0% over Labour	Walter Sweeney
Brecon & Radnorshire	130	0.3% over Labour	Jonathan Evans
Preseli Pembroke	603	1.4% over Labour	new seat
Conwy	995	2.4% over Lib-Dems	Sir Wyn Roberts*
Vale of Clwyd	2177	5.0% over Labour	new seat
Cardiff North	2969	6.2% over Labour	Gwilym Jones
Monmouth	3204	6.3% over Labour	Roger Evans
Clwyd West	7313	17.6% over Labour	Rod Richards (new seat)

*Standing down.

PLAID CYMRU

PLAID CYMRU SEATS NOTIONAL SHARE BASED ON NEW BOUNDARIES

SEAT	MAJORITY		2ND PARTY	MP
Caernarfon	14476	(39.9%)	Conservative	Dafydd Wigley
Meirionnydd Nant Conwy	4613	(17.5%)	Conservative	Elfyn Llwyd
Ceredigion	1893	(4.5%)	Lib-Dem	Cynog Dafis (new seat)
Ynys Môn	1106	(2.6%)	Conservative	Ieuan Wyn Jones

We are convinced we will have five parliamentary seats. (Dafydd Wigley MP, President, Plaid Cymru, September 1995)

Plaid Cymru did well in 1992 to win four parliamentary seats. With just 9 per cent of the vote, they won 9 per cent of the seats in Wales – an example of the first-past-the post system producing a proportional result. The reason is that their vote is concentrated in their Welsh-speaking heartland in North and West Wales. Their attempts to expand politically outside these rural areas have met with only occasional success.They have set their sights this time on Labour-held Carmarthen East & Dinefwr, the successor to the seat where Gwynfor Evans achieved his famous by-election breakthrough just over 30 years ago. They believe they are serious challengers here, but Plaid Cymru are really waiting to profit from an anti-Labour swing under a Blair government.

Plaid Cymru are by no means secure in all the seats they hold. While the party president, Dafydd Wigley, has sat for Caernarfon since 1974, building up his majority to more than 14,000, and Elfyn Llwyd looks safe enough in the smallest seat in Wales, Meirionydd Nant Conwy, Ynys Mon (Anglesey) may well prove a difficult three-way fight with Conservative and Labour. In Ceredigion, Plaid may be a little weakened by boundary changes and the end of their alliance with the Greens. In 1992, Cynog Dafis won on a joint Plaid Cymru-Green ticket.

LABOUR

Labour have few vulnerable seats in Wales, and are unlikely to lose any. The closest contest with the Conservatives is in the new seat of Carmarthen West and South Pembrokeshire. Boundary changes have given Labour's Nick Ainger a notional majority of little over 1,000 votes to defend, but the Conservative challenge has been undermined by the *Sea Empress* disaster off Milford Haven.

LIBERAL DEMOCRATS

The Liberal Democrats' only MP in Wales, Alex Carlisle, is standing down, but the party is confident it can hold onto Montgomery, a seat with a long Liberal tradition and a current majority of just over 5,000. They had some near misses in 1992, coming a close second in Brecon and Radnor and in Conwy, and they hope to put that right this time. But both seats will probably prove to be three-way fights with Labour as well as the Conservatives, with the outcome uncertain.

DEMOCRATIC DEFICIT?

Not since Caligula made his horse a senator has such a ridiculous appointment been made. (John Morris MP, former Secretary of State for Wales, on the appointment of William Hague, July 1995).

Much of the political debate in Wales has centred on the incontrovertible fact that the governing party for the last eighteen years has been a minority party in Wales. What significance that has depends on your political point of view. For the opposition parties,

LABOUR SEATS IN WALES NOTIONAL SHARE BASED ON NEW BOUNDARIES

SEAT	MAJORITY		2ND PARTY	MP
Aberafon	21310	(53.2%)	Conservative	Jon Morris
Alun & Deeside	6387	(14%)	Conservative	Barry Jones
Blaenau Gwent	30067	(69.2%)	Conservative	Llew Smith
Bridgend	7326	(15.6%)	Conservative	Win Griffiths
Caerffili	22672	(45.4%)	Conservative	Ron Davies
Cardiff Central	3465	(8.1%)	Conservative	Jon Owen Jones
Cardiff South & Penarth	10425	(21.9%)	Conservative	Alun Michael
Cardiff West	9291	(20.3%)	Conservative	Rhodri Morgan
Carmarthen E & Dinefwr	5490	(12.5%)	Plaid Cymru	Dr Alan Williams
Carmarthen W & Pembroke S	1310	(3.1%)	Conservative	Nick Ainger (new seat)
Clwyd S	8332	(19.5%)	Conservative	Martyn Jones
Cynon Valley	21364	(56.2%)	Conservative	Ann Clwyd
Delyn	3178	(7.2%)	Conservative	David Hanson
Gower	7048	(15.1%)	Conservative	Gareth Wardell*
Islwyn	24728	(59.5%)	Conservative	Don Touhig
	92 general election result not 95 by-election			
Llanelli	17271	(37.5%)	Conservative	Denzil Davies
Merthyr Tydfil	26713	(60.3%)	Lib-Dem	Ted Rowlands
Neath	23975	(52.8%)	Conservative	Peter Hain
Newport E	9899	(23.6%)	Conservative	Roy Hughes*
Newport W	7779	(17.1%)	Conservative	Paul Flynn
Ogmore	23827	(56.6%)	Conservative	Sir Ray Powell
Pontypridd	19797	(40.5%)	Conservative	Kim Howells
Rhondda	28816	(62.7%)	Plaid Cymru	Allan Rogers
Swansea E	23482	(52.5%)	Conservative	Don Anderson
Swansea W	9478	(21.6%)	Conservative	Alan Williams
Torfaen	20754	(43.8%)	Conservative	Paul Murphy
Wrexham	7090	(17.5%)	Conservative	Dr John Marek

*Standing down.

LIBERAL DEMOCRAT SEATS IN WALES

SEAT	MAJORITY		2ND PARTY	MP
Montgomeryshire	5209	(15.8%)	Conservative	Alex Carlisle*

*Standing down.

it has led to what they call a 'democratic deficit': whereas the administration of government has been decentralised, with the establishment and growth of the Welsh Office in Cardiff, it is not properly accountable to the people of Wales.

Nonsense, say the Conservatives. Wales is an integral part of the United Kingdom, and Welsh Office ministers are accountable to the people of Wales through Parliament at Westminster. It has not helped the Conservative case that four of the five Secretaries of State for Wales in those eighteen years have not represented Welsh constituencies. Indeed, when William Hague was appointed in July 1995, the opposition parties staged a boycott of his first appearance at the despatch box, protesting at what they saw as the appointment of 'another untried Tory' with no interest in or enthusiasm for Wales.

SECRETARIES OF STATE FOR WALES SINCE 1979

PERIOD OF OFFICE	OCCUPANT	CONSTITUENCY
1979-1987	Nicholas Edwards (Lord Crickhowell)	Pembroke
1987-1990	Peter Walker (Lord Walker)	Worcester
1990-1993	David Hunt	Wirral West
1993-1995	John Redwood	Wokingham
1995+	William Hague	Richmond

On taking office, William Hague took immediate steps to distance himself from the style of his predecessor, John Redwood, whose right-wing views seemed more alien in Wales than perhaps they did in the southeast of England. He spent far more time in Wales – he even learned the words of the national anthem unlike Mr Redwood. His easy-going manner – and his return to the more consensual approach of Peter Walker and David Hunt – helped take some of the confrontational element out of Welsh politics.

DEVOLUTION: DEJA-VU?

It will bring government closer to the people... (Tony Blair MP, Labour party leader, May 1996)

Labour's answer to the democratic deficit, as they perceive it, is to set up an elected Welsh Assembly to which the Welsh Office and the quangos would become accountable. Tony Blair has reiterated a pledge that legislation to set it up would be put through in the first year of a Labour government, either in tandem with or soon after legislation to establish the more powerful Scottish parliament.
The Labour party's devolution plans for Wales are an uneasy compromise between pro-devolutionists in the party and those who, to say the least, are unenthusiastic on the issue. As in the 1970s, Labour has shied away from giving the Assembly primary legislative powers or tax-raising powers. The independently based Constitution Unit concluded: 'An Assembly with executive powers risks incurring the worst of all worlds.'
    The Shadow Secretary of State, Ron Davies, himself a convinced pro-devolutionist, has had to steer a difficult course. He fought to make the Assembly, as he put it, more 'inclusive', and after some

bitter internal arguments succeeded in committing the party to electing the Assembly by proportional representation. This was a central factor in securing a deal with the Liberal Democrats on a joint approach to constitutional reform. It was a prize he extracted from the political mayhem that surrounded Tony Blair's sudden decision to order a referendum on Labour's devolution plans. There was widespread resentment in the Welsh Labour party at the manner in which that decision was made. In reality, it will probably help Labour in the general election, allowing pro-Labour anti-devolutionists to vote Labour in the election and, 'No' in the referendum. But it has put a giant question-mark over whether electing a Labour government would now lead to devolution for Wales. For the Welsh public seem to be more circumspect on the issue than the Scots. Since the four-to-one rejection of devolution in 1979, Labour, the Liberal Democrats and Plaid Cymru claim the public mood has changed.

BBC WALES OPINION POLL

Q. If a referendum was held tomorrow (on Labour's plans for an Assembly), would you vote for or against this proposal?

FOR	AGAINST	DON'T KNOW	WON'T VOTE
55%	28%	10%	7%

Source: Beaufort Research (September 1996).

Given the less than overwhelming apparent support for devolution, it is little wonder that the Conservatives see the issue as good campaigning material. John Major has called Labour's proposals 'a humiliating, patronising slap in the face for the people of Wales'. Plaid Cymru, too, are angry at what they say will be a powerless talking shop. They want more options on the referendum ballot paper, including a law-making Parliament and self-government for Wales. Otherwise, they warn that their support for any Labour government will be in doubt.

THE WELSH ECONOMY

We have created a climate in which the creativity and energy of the people of Wales can flourish. (Prime Minister, John Major MP, June 1996)

It would be wrong to assume that the devolution issue is high on the agenda of the average Welsh voter. Just as on the other side of Offa's Dyke, bread-and-butter issues predominate.

The Welsh economy is Janus-faced. On the one hand, it is attracting record amounts of inward investment, not least the 6,000 jobs being brought to Newport by the Korean electronics giant, LG. On the other, Wales is the poorest region in Britain, in terms of gross domestic product. The fact is that Wales has still to recover from the dramatic decline of traditional industries such as coal and steel. The miners' buyout of the last deep mine in South Wales – Tower colliery at Hirwaun – was a romantic tailpiece to an industrial tragedy. In the South Wales valleys, cohesive communities have been turned by unemployment into some of the most deprived in the European Union, suffering from crime, drugs and social disintegration.

There has been industrial expansion in the Valleys, most notably in Merthyr Tydfil, but the bulk of the inward investment has been along the M4 corridor in South Wales. The Welsh Development Agency is putting past scandals behind it, and is pulling in jobs at a far higher rate than any other comparable British agency. However, politicians from West and North Wales protest that the benefits are not being evenly spread. The Treasury began to get restless over the competition between regions bidding up the levels of grant designed to attract foreign investors. William Hague gave it short shrift, but as the competition gets tougher, it is a problem that is not going to go away.

BIG JOBS: INWARD INVESTMENT SUCCESSES 1994-6

COMPANY	LOCATION	JOBS
Nippon (JULY 1994)	Cardiff Bay (SE Wales)	750
Ford (October 1995)	Bridgend (S Wales)	480
Waferfab (March 1996)	Newport (SE Wales)	768
Legal & General (March 1996)	Cardiff (SE Wales)	463
LG Electronics (July 1996)	Newport (SE Wales)	6106
Sony (December 1996)	Bridgend (S Wales)	1000

The Conservatives say these successes are a tribute to the more competitive economy they have been building in Wales. Labour, while applauding the inward investment, point to the continued unemployment, still above the UK average. Many of the newly created jobs are low-paid or part-time, and research shows that average household incomes in Wales are only about 75 per cent of average incomes per year in England.

Agriculture, still one of the biggest industries in Wales, has been in a continuing state of crisis. Employing around 60,000 people, it has been badly hit by the European Union's ban on beef exports. The BSE crisis, the cattle cull and loss of jobs in ancillary businesses such as transport and meat products are estimated to be causing losses of up to £100 million to the rural economy. The farmers may vent their anger on Brussels, but the Welsh farmers' unions have also described the government's handling of the crisis as inept. The Farmers' Union of Wales even threatened to put up its own candidates at the election.

CUTTING THE CAKE

The people of Wales are being asked to pay more and get less... (Ron Davies MP, Shadow Secretary of State for Wales, December 1995)

At the heart of the political argument in Wales is control of the Welsh Office and its budget of nearly £7 billion a year. As a territorial department, the Welsh Office runs most aspects of government that affect people's daily lives. Public spending in Wales is still governed by what is called the Barnett formula, named after a former Labour treasury minister. This means that Wales gets 6 per cent of any change in comparable spending in England.

The government makes great play of the fact that public spending in Wales considerably outstrips tax revenues from Wales – in other words, that Wales runs a deficit and is effectively subsidised by the rest of the United Kingdom. A calculation by the Welsh Office put this deficit at £5 billion for 1993-4. Labour said this was a reflection of the weakness of the Welsh economy, and that particular year was at the depths of the recession. The Treasury privately calculate the average deficit is nearer £2 billion a year. Like every other government department, the Welsh Office has suffered from the squeeze on public spending over the last few years. William Hague is reported to have fought in Cabinet to preserve the Barnett formula, and argues that Wales has come out of the past two Budgets comparatively better than England. Nevertheless, the Welsh Office budget is being cut in real terms over the next three years.

Broadly speaking, it has been the policy of both John Redwood and William Hague to preserve spending on education and the health service at the cost of other areas of the Welsh Office. Local government appears to have suffered most – the 22 unitary authorities which took over from the former counties and districts in April 1996 had to cope with transition costs amounting to about £140 million.

Over successive years, Welsh local authorities have protested at being forced to cut back on the funding of education and social services in particular, leading to public demonstrations at the loss of teaching posts in the worst-affected schools. Rhondda Cynon Taff, the authority which serves some of the poorest communities in the country, had to cope with a deficit of more than £20 million for 1996-7, and further cutbacks of £12 million for 1997-8. In addition, Welsh council tax payers are now facing bills which are rising more steeply than in England – but historically, local taxes have been lower in Wales.

SHADES OF WELSH OPINION

On so many issues there is no difference between ourselves and the Tories. (Paul Flynn MP, Labour, Newport West, June 1996)

All the political parties, to a greater or lesser extent, advocate different policies for Wales – even, on the margin, some Conservatives. John Redwood as Secretary of State, for instance, initiated his 'Popular Schools' policy, whereby schools which could demonstrate the greatest demand for places could bid for extra funds. William Hague decided to publish a separate *Rural White Paper for Wales*, which among other things initiated a distinctive strategy for the promotion of Welsh food.

The Welsh Labour party's devolution plans clearly provide a platform for a whole range of policies different from the leadership in London. The Shadow Welsh Secretary, Ron Davies, wants to reorganise the big economic quangos such as the Welsh Development Agency; more of the Welsh Office budget would be geared to economic regeneration. But it goes further than that. Attitudes in the Welsh Labour party remain more egalitarian and redistributive, distrustful of 'New Labour' and where it is heading. Paul Flynn, in a moment of anger at the leadership, described some of the party's policies as timid and anaemic. The most obvious resentment is over the party's compromise on grant-maintained schools: with only 16 Welsh schools opted-out, it is seen as a compromise to appease the

ECONOMIC POLICIES FOR WALES AT-A-GLANCE

LABOUR	CONSERVATIVE	PLAID CYMRU	LIB-DEM
Welsh Assembly to boost economy	Enterprise economy	100,000 job creation programme	Employment priority zones
Reform of Quangos, new economic agency	Continued fall in unemployment	2p income tax rise to fund job creation	New training levy
Minimum wage	Continued low interest rates	Reduce National Insurance contributions	Welsh Low Pay Commission

English middle-class – and middle-class Labour politicians. A Labour-controlled Assembly would be likely to try and pressure grant-maintained schools out of existence.

The four parties vary enormously in the extent to which they would intervene to assist the Welsh economy, with Plaid Cymru the most interventionist of all.

THE DRAGON HAS TWO TONGUES!

One issue on which there is now a cross-party consensus is the Welsh language. Legislation was passed in 1993 giving Welsh fully equal status with English and setting up a Welsh Language Board to implement bilingual policies across all public bodies in Wales. The decline in the language has been arrested, not least through the expansion of Welsh medium schools. The language was for long a source of confrontation in Welsh life: now an Act passed by a Conservative government is being implemented by a Board whose chairman is a Plaid Cymru peer. Who would have believed that 20 years ago?

THE WELSH TEST

Labour's stranglehold on so many Welsh seats does not imply that the party faces no great electoral test in Wales. Its ability to enthuse its traditional supporters will be under scrutiny, as will its success in overcoming any backlash from Mr Blair's referendum U-turn.

Plaid Cymru have been less eager than in previous elections to set themselves ambitious targets. Indeed, they have focused on just one extra seat. The most important goal for them will be to boost their share of the Welsh vote into double figures.

The Liberal Democrats face a real uphill struggle. They should hold on to their one Welsh seat, despite adopting an 'outside' candidate, but they will struggle to withstand any increase in Labour's vote, not least in tight marginals like Conwy.

The Conservatives have one main priority – to avoid a wipeout. They should manage it, just, and hang on to a couple of seats. Such a level of support would be serious in any circumstances. But in the event of the election of a new Tory government, it would have grave implications, raising further questions about the legitimacy of Conservative rule.

THE ROAD TO PEACE AND BACK

THE NORTHERN IRELAND PERSPECTIVE

Denis Murray

Denis Murray is the Ireland Correspondent for BBC News. He joined the Belfast Telegraph in 1975, moving to RTE in 1977. He joined the BBC in 1987 as Dublin Correspondent, becoming Northern Ireland Political Correspondent in 1984 and taking up his current position in 1988.

It's almost too obvious to mention: but Northern Ireland is very different.

The electorate here will not vote on the issues that everyone else in the United Kingdom will: the economy, health, education. We will cast our ballots, in the only first-past-the-post election now used in the province, on the same old issues: shades of orange, shades of green, and somewhere in the middle.

Unless there's a hung parliament, none of our MPs will have any say in the formation of the national government, and even then, no say whatsoever in direct terms in the governance of Northern Ireland itself. In 21 province-wide elections since 1969, only twice has Northern Ireland elected representatives to a body that had anything more than administrative or consultative powers. Not since 1973 has there been anything approaching an institution that could be said to govern the province by the direct will of the people who live here.

Northern Ireland was governed from its foundation by a devolved parliament, which was unionist-dominated, and was eventually prorogued by the government in 1972. Ever since then the province has been run by central government, with legislation often in the form of orders in council which allow for minimum debate in the House.

THE FORUM ELECTION

The most recent poll, under a unique and highly complex system, was for a forum which has no powers at all, meets only once a week, and whose only real function was to select the parties with a sufficient mandate to get to all-party talks. In the memorable phrase of a colleague, it was an election, Jim, but not as we know it. To complicate the issue even further, it was the first election held after boundary changes, with one extra Westminster constituency, bringing the province's total to 18.

The most remarkable result was that of Sinn Fein, hitting their highest percentage share of the overall poll ever. Higher even than in 1983, when the party was a fledgling political organisation still benefiting from the backwash of the hunger strikes at the Maze prison in 1981, and which had since looked like its peak.

Some voters from the nationalist SDLP almost certainly changed their traditional vote, in protest at what they saw as government policies designed to obstruct Sinn Fein. The parties that represent the loyalist paramilitary groups won seats in the same way. It's possible that the conditions which produced these results will not apply at the general election, but there are useful indicators as to how that might go.

THE PEACE PROCESS

Lying at the heart of the electoral process for several years has been the peace process. One is tempted to ask, what peace process?

Many Catholics blame the government for the breakdown of the IRA ceasefire, with what they saw as endless prevarication from Downing Street, if not downright obstructionism, over getting Sinn Fein into all-party talks.

The end of the IRA ceasefire in February last year ruled out any possibility of Sinn Fein getting into talks, which made one senior Irish government official remark that negotiations without them weren't worth a penny candle. At the moment, a new cessation appears to be not even a remote possibility – the IRA itself indicated there wouldn't be one before the general election.

What is now in place might be more properly described as a political process: the Stormont negotiations with all parties involved, including those which represent the loyalist paramilitaries, but with Sinn Fein excluded.

That, and the search for peace, will really only impact on the election in one way. The poll here, as ever, is as much about rivalries within the communities as between them: that impact will be in the race for votes among Catholics. The SDLP has started to put clear green water between it and Sinn Fein, after the shock of seeing the republicans produce their best-ever poll performance last year. The SDLP leader John Hume asked the question in a newspaper article: was Sinn Fein in fact targeting his party. And in the same piece he ruled out the possibility of an electoral pact with Sinn Fein, setting out conditions not only about a new ceasefire, but also dependent on Sinn Fein candidates ending their historical abstentionist position from the House of Commons. There was never any possibility of republicans doing that. More recently, Mr Hume demonstrated even greater hostility towards his erstwhile ally in the peace process, saying that a vote for Sinn Fein without a ceasefire would be a vote for terrorism.

Gerry Adams is the hot favourite to regain the West Belfast seat, with Martin McGuiness in with a chance of winning in Mid-Ulster, where the Catholic majority would love to unseat present MP William McCrea of Ian Paisley's DUP. The SDLP candidate will split that vote, but the card likely to be played is the 'vote for the Catholic who can win' one.

On the unionist side, there are negotations between David Trimble, leader of the Ulster Unionists, and Ian Paisley, on seats unionists could lose if their vote is split. Much as the Ulster Unionists would like to take North Antrim from Ian Paisley, they know they can't, but will oppose him for two reasons – (a), it's a safe pro-union seat and they're not risking it falling into SDLP or Sinn Fein hands; and (b), eventually he will not be a candidate through sheer age, and they want some sort of vote base as a springboard to take it then.

In the seats where the sitting MP might lose to a nationalist or a republican, neither unionist party will seek to split the pro-union vote, with the exception of West Tyrone.

The UUP have beaten some concessions on various issues out of the government given their key place in the Westminster numbers game, and while instinctively they would prefer a Tory government, they look back longingly to what they regard as the golden era of Roy Mason, the last Labour secretary of state – a man who believed in a tough security policy.

A NEW SECRETARY OF STATE

Which brings up an interesting question. Who will be the next holder of the post? It won't be Sir Patrick Mayhew, who is retiring from politics at this election – his most obvious Tory successor would be his political development minister Michael Ancram, but that would be a substantial promotion to the cabinet. John Major might favour a more senior figure.

Marjorie Mowlam, the Labour shadow, is insisting that she wants the job, and will get it if Labour win. Now, that will be fun. The first woman secretary of state dealing with arguably the most misogynist group of politicians in Europe? She did the one and only fringe session I've ever seen at the Ulster Unionist conference in 1995, for which they gave her a terrific welcome, but that honeymoon period is over (she told the conference that she is not a Roy Mason), and they now regard her with suspicion. She probably wouldn't even be the SDLP's ideal nomination.

In one year, then, we have the UK general election, Northern Ireland local council election, and an Irish Republic general election. This is possibly a new political landscape for the new millenium, but still dealing with the same old issues, the same old inter-party battles.

A TIME FOR CHANGE?

The Northern Ireland electorate has proved remarkably stable over the years – most MPs have held their seats since at least 1979.

But there are signs of change – there will be at least one new MP, in the new West Tyrone seat, and while the SDLP performed really well in the 1980s to take two seats from unionists, and last time out, West Belfast from Sinn Fein, they will be looking over their shoulders at the republicans this time.

How SDLP performs depends on two things – how the IRA ceasefire stands, and the general state of the peace process. In the Irish Republic for instance, the party that was happy to settle for partition, and stood in the 1920s for an end to IRA hostilities against Britain, was the party of government, until Eamonn de Valera from the opposite camp, founded Fianna Fail, the 'slightly' constitutional party as he called it. Almost ever since, Fianna Fail has been the main party of government there.

So perhaps history may repeat itself, with SDLP voters turning to Sinn Fein, but this could only happen, in my view, if there was an IRA ceasefire. The SDLP's strongest card for years was its deep opposition to violent methods. A full-scale renewal of the IRA's campaign here should mean Sinn Fein's vote dropping back, though the view of its leaders is that its share won't drop much more, but always has the potential to grow.

There was undoubtedly a protest vote in the forum election – one SDLP voter told BBC Radio Ulster that it was only as he picked up the pencil in the polling booth that he decided to opt for Sinn Fein, in protest at what he, and many others like him, see as government obstructionism.

Few Catholics blame the IRA for the end of its ceasefire, much as they might regret it – they blame John Major and a series of what looked to them like new pre-conditions set against Sinn Fein every time it fulfilled the previous one.

On the unionist side, there's a greater choice for voters than for many years, with the small parties which are linked to the loyalist paramilitaries standing. They performed creditably at the Forum election, but still look set to be squeezed by the big UUP and DUP parties at the general election.

Commentators have been looking for the clear messages from the Forum election, since some of the signals are confusing. One theme stands out. I believe that the size of the turnout, much larger than predicted, showed that the electorate of Northern Ireland wanted to give their politicians one clear message – get the negotiations started, and for all our sakes, get them to work.

ISSUES WHICH WILL HELP DECIDE THE ELECTION

CONDUCT UNBECOMING?

A NEW WORD IN PUBLIC STANDARDS

SLEAZE

John Pienaar

John Pienaar is a Political Correspondent for BBC News. He began his career in journalism in 1977 on a south London newspaper. In 1980 he joined the Press Association as a parliamentary correspondent before moving to the Independent *in 1986, becoming political correspondent in 1988. He joined the BBC in his current position at the end of 1991.*

Fairly or not – and whoever said politics was fair – this was the parliament which added the word 'sleaze' to the lexicon of political scribes, and the 'sleaze factor' to the textbooks of political pundits. *The Collins English Dictionary* defines sleaze as something that's sordid or disreputable, and to many people it has become a by-word for almost all that is cheap, fraudulent or just plain nasty in political life and the lives of politicians.

Vague enough to encompass almost any suggestion of misconduct: personal or political, financial or sexual, the 'sleaze factor' has plagued the government almost continually. The phenomenon is hardly a new one. Politics is, after all, the second oldest profession in the world. But it is at least arguable that the vague concept of sleaze has given form to the even vaguer sense of disillusionment with politics and politicians which seems to have taken root in the minds of the British electorate. It may or may not be justifiable, but it is easy enough to explain.

BACK TO BASICS

In the Autumn of 1993 the Prime Minister launched his 'Back to Basics' campaign. It was an attempt to bridge the gulf between

John Major's ideology-free Conservatism (the only -ism he has ever been prepared to acknowledge as his own) and the public and the media's demand for a Big Idea: 'Back to Basics' seemed a good idea at the time. Looking back, the boffins of the Downing Street policy unit were asking for trouble. The concept may have seemed marketable, but it lacked the policies and the strategy to give it direction. The Tory Right-wing adopted 'Back to Basics' as the slogan for a moral crusade, and the trouble began in earnest.

News editors love a running story, and hate to let a struggling administration off the hook too easily. In retrospect, Conservative right-wingers were probably courting disaster by adopting a high moral tone in their interpretation of John Major's early theme of 'back to basic values', but few people could have foreseen the extent of the damage. Over time, the media sought out and magnified stories which called into question the right and qualifications of politicians to set themselves up as arbiters of morality. They also happened to be the kind of stories which sell newspapers. Tales as diverse as David Mellor's affair with a publicity-conscious actress, and his politically fatal decision to accept holiday hospitality from the daughter of a senior figure in the PLO; MPs receiving cash in exchange for parliamentary questions, and even the high politics and low partisan dog-fighting of the so-called arms-to-Iraq affair came to be seen (arguably quite wrongly) as a single phenomenon.

It is worth noting that the public appears to be far more tolerant of its politicians' sexual peccadiloes and misdemeanours than any suggestion of financial impropriety. Misconduct or rule-bending by the government as a whole is another matter. There is no evidence the government suffered much in the public's increasingly cynical estimation from the so-called Pergau Dam affair. The Public Accounts Committee found that £234 million in overseas aid to Malaysia had become linked to an order for 28 jet fighters and other weaponry.

Fleet Street, however, shows no such discrimination. The circulation war at both ends of the newspaper market ensured that any politician straying from the straight and narrow became another example of sleaze.

The exact extent of the cumulative damage is impossible to gauge, though the attempt will occupy many a dinner table and a good deal of air time up to and well beyond the general election. Inevitably, the Conservatives, as the government of the day, suffered the worst of the political pain and much of the damage. The catalogue of sleaze, or at least of media stories loosely filed under that heading, speaks for itself.

CASUALTIES

David Mellor's resignation in July 1992 preceded the government's
ill-fated 'Back to Basics' campaign by a year. That campaign appeared
to open the floodgates. There followed: Michael Mates's resignation
as a Northern Ireland minister over his friendship with the fugitive
businessman Asil Nadir; the fact that Mr Mates sent Mr Nadir a
watch inscribed 'Don't let the buggers grind you down' probably
sealed his fate; Tim Yeo resigned as an environment minister in
January 1994, as did Lord Caithness, the aviation minister. Several
parliamentary private secretaries jumped or were pushed off this
lowest rung of the ministerial ladder including Hartley Booth,
Michael Brown and Alan Duncan. In each case the media linked these
resignations to the 'sleaze-factor'. (Mr Duncan soon returned, though,
as PPS to the Conservative Party Chairman, Brian Mawhinney).

These and other cases reinforced the impression of a government
assailed by ill-luck, an unhappy conjunction of events and, from time
to time, its own questionable judgement. David Mellor's departure
was prolonged by John Major's initial reluctance to bow to media
pressure. Later, the Prime Minister was similarly reluctant to part
with Neil Hamilton over allegations that the Corporate Affairs
minister had taken gifts from the businessman Mohammed Al Fayed.
Mr Al Fayed was to become a thorn in the government's side, with a
stream of allegations against prominent Conservatives. These
included the Treasury minister Jonathan Aitken, who, in turn,
was to leave the Government to fight a libel action against ITV's
World in Action over allegations about his business affairs. He was
subsequently cleared by the Commons Trade and Industry Select
Committee of knowing that the defence firm BMARC was supplying
Iran with naval cannon, via Singapore, when he was a member of its
board. Only after the Hamilton affair had dragged on painfully, did
the Tory hierarchy appear to decide that he had become a political
liability and finally force him out of the government on what
Mr Hamilton's friends insisted were 'trumped up' charges.

Others were dealt with quickly. David Tredinnick and Graham
Riddick were removed as PPSs the moment it emerged that they had
agreed to table parliamentary questions in exchange for money.
From the government's point of view, this was probably just as well.
This was the so-called 'cash for questions' affair of July 1994, and few
stories did more to reinforce the notion that MPs were somehow
cashing in on their privileged status as elected representatives, and
that influence could be bought, sold and brokered by the
mushrooming lobbying industry.

The opposition parties, too, occasionally fell or found themselves enmeshed in the media's net. Paddy Ashdown admitted an extra-marital affair in 1992, before the term sleaze had taken on its present significance. Ironically, his admission appeared to add rather than subtract from his personal standing. Later, when the issue was well and truly established to the Tories' disadvantage, Labour was succesfully targeted over the conduct of several Labour-controlled local authorities. Allegations of nepotism in Monklands were not proven, while claims of political favours in Birmingham did more damage. For a while, the Labour party was forced onto the defensive, but somehow, the issue clung most closely to the Conservatives. The well-chronicled and much investigated allegations that homes were allocated with a view to protecting the majorities of Tory councillors in Westminster have developed into a drawn out political and legal saga.

As the party of government, the Tories always represented bigger game to the editors of Fleet Street and naturally loomed largest in the consciousness of the public. If the sleaze phenomenon was a product of ill luck and ill judgement, the tenacity of the media's pursuit was coloured by malice. Some of this malice was undoubtedly ideological. Much was simply the casual malice of an industry that knows a good story when it sees one. There was also a deeper undercurrent. Many an editor was only too happy to direct a pre-emptive strike against the mere suggestion of tougher privacy laws.

NOLAN

John Major's decision to set up the Committee on Standards in Public Life, under the chairmanship of Lord Nolan was his attempt to lance the boil of sleaze (to mix two messy and unpleasant metaphors). A number of Tory MPs will never forgive him. The cure was every bit as painful as the disease. It only seemed to inflame Tory MPs' sense of injustice and persecution when the Nolan report told them what they knew already, and had for so long been preaching to so little effect. The problem of sleaze was much more a problem of perception than reality. Corruption was, as far as it was possible to tell, still being contained at levels many a liberal advanced democracy would envy. As the Nolan report put it:

> *It was ... clear from a considerable body of ... evidence that much of the public anxiety about standards of conduct in public life is based upon perceptions and beliefs which are not supported by the facts.*

Taking the evidence as a whole, we believe that the great majority of men and women in British public life are honest and hard working, and observe high ethical standards.'

However, as the Nolan report also pointed out, the perception of falling standards had become so deeply rooted as to present a serious problem in itself. In some cases, the closed world of appointments to powerful unelected quangoes for example, the perception of political patronage was reinforced by anecdotal evidence. Something had to be done to prevent the suspicion of sleaze degenerating into an un-quantifiable reality. Now, quango jobs are advertised and the appointments system is far more open. A commissioner oversees the system, and encourages good practice.

Another meeting point between political and commercial life attracted far greater attention. The age-old phenomenon of former ministers quitting politics and being snapped up by city firms and corporations keen to add another big name to their corporate letterhead was targeted as an example of sleaze. The suspicion grew that former ministers were moving into nests they had feathered in office. So whether or not former ministers were taking a 'gravy train' to jobs in the boardrooms of companies they had overseen, or even privatised, in office, those ministers had to be vetted on their way from Whitehall to the City in the same way as civil servants. In fact the new rules would scarcely have delayed any of the ministers most often named as passengers on the 'gravy train'. Lord Young, for example, waited several months before joining Cable and Wireless from the Trade Department. Peter Walker joined British Gas after serving at the Energy Department, but only with a longstay in between at the Welsh Office.

The reforms that caused most resentment to MPs were those intended to expose the earnings of backbenchers where they related to their work at Westminster, usually as 'consultants'. Most were content to codify the ban on MPs peddling their influence, taking cash for questions and the like. But most were also downright hostile to the idea of declaring their consultancy fees. A Tory-dominated committee, set up to translate the Nolan report into new rules for MPs, took the same view. The government left the House to sort it out on a free vote, but ministers, including John Major, sided with the committee and in doing so, sided with the losers. On 6 November 1995, the Commons voted to disclose earnings where they related to the work of MPs. Twenty-three Tories broke ranks with their colleagues, and the next day's headlines proclaimed a

'humiliation' for the Prime Minister. He had voted for secrecy and
been defeated. The bulk of Tory MPs had suffered the same fate;
opprobrium without even the consolation of confidentiality. Some
complained that the entrepreneurial classes would be driven out of
politics, more than a few cursed the Prime Minister for setting up the
Nolan Committee.

Now the conduct of MPs is overseen by the new Standards and
Privileges committee. Its officer, and Westminster's day-to-day
'watchdog', is Sir Gordon Downey. In some ways, the new system is
still on probation. Sceptics wait to be reassured that MPs are capable
of rising above party tribalism in judging and punishing wayward
colleagues. The David Willetts affair went some way to bolstering
the committee's reputation. The committee rebuked the former
minister for apparently prying into the Neil Hamilton investigation.
He resigned immediately, containing the embarrassment to the
government.

FUNDING

One issue was simply too sensitive for the Nolan Committee to tackle,
at least before the general election. Party funding has long been
the source of mutual suspicion between the parties, providing
plentiful ammunition for the partisan dog-fight and latterly, plenty
of ammunition to fuel the public perception of political sleaze.
Asil Nadir's private donations to the Tory party, before the collapse
of his business empire and flight to Cyprus, were the source of only
one crop of headlines which equated the confidentiality of funding in
Smith Square with a shady desire for secrecy. There were many other
examples. Today, the Conservative party proclaims a policy of
refusing anonymous donations, and taking none from foreign
governments or unlawful sources. Labour, the Liberal Democrats and
a core of dissidents within the Tory party itself maintain that there
must be more openness. The situation is complicated by the attempts
of the Tories' opponents to equate business donations, listed in
company accounts but not published by the party, with the honours
awarded to captains of industry. As for Labour, the party's funding
may be more open but it is arguably more vulnerable to the
accusation that influence is available in exchange for financial
support. The trades unions, after all, still retain half the votes at the
Labour conference. Labour has moved to head off criticism by
recasting the system of trade union sponsorship of Labour MPs.
Funds are now to be awarded to constituencies, whether or not they

return an MP to Westminster. By breaking the direct link, the party hopes to counter the impression that MPs are beholden to their sponsoring union, and in some way under the sway of their union paymasters. John Major has refused to expand the Nolan Committee's terms of reference to allow an inquiry into party funding. The opposition parties have demanded such an inquiry. What happens after the election remains to be seen.

SCOTT INQUIRY

The decision to set up the Nolan Committee was not the first time that John Major had established an inquiry to lance a political boil, only to find his backbench troops cursing the cure more than the ailment. The inquiry into what came to be known as the arms-to-Iraq affair, under the chairmanship of the Vice Chancellor, Sir Richard Scott, cast a shadow over the government in general and the career of two ministers in particular during much of the last Parliament.

The facts are well known, not least since they are now documented in a five-volume, 1,800 page report. In essence, the affair revolved around the decision of three ministers – Alan Clark, Lord Trefgarne and William Waldegrave – to redraft the export guidelines for defence-related sales to Iran and Iraq after the ceasefire in the Gulf in 1988. A lucrative market beckoned. The guidelines were redrafted and the way was clear for exports with a civilian application – and in many cases a militarily useful purpose – to reach that market. Then, Iran declared its *fatwah* against Salman Rushdie. Up went the export controls against Iran, and Iraq had the advantage. Meanwhile, MPs were told little or nothing of these twists and turns, despite numerous attempts in parliamentary questions and in correspondence with ministers. Saddam Hussein was bombing Kurdish villages, British hostages were being held in Lebanon and the Foreign Office, in particular, was wary of inflaming public opinion and jeopardizing the prospects for British exporters.

The second act of the drama focused on three businessmen from the Coventry machine-tool firm, Matrix Churchill. They were prosecuted for breaching the export controls against Iraq, and walked free when Alan Clark, who admitted being 'economical with the actualite', allowed the export of weapons-making equipment under the heading of machine tools for general use. The political implications were incendiary. Three businessmen were put at risk of imprison-ment for doing what Whitehall, the security services and the government knew they were doing all along. The managing director, Paul Henderson, turned out to be an MI6 informant.

Much of the evidence was contained in government files, mostly confidential. By convention, the government attempted to protect the confidentiality of its files by producing what are called Public Interest Immunity Certificates. These PIIs theoretically highlight the sensitive nature of papers, and leave it to the court to decide whether to disclose them to the defence and the jury or not. The Scott inquiry found that PIIs tended to be taken by courts at face value, and documents were being excluded as evidence more or less automatically. On this occasion, though, the judge rejected the PIIs, which demonstrated the extent of Whitehall's knowledge. The Scott Report's judgement on these events was as tortuous as it was exhaustive. Ministers cited this or that paragraph to argue the government had been cleared of any 'conspiracy or cover up'. Their opponents argued that MPs had been misled all the same. Either way, William Waldegrave kept his job. So did the Attorney General Sir Nicholas Lyell, who had overseen the Matrix Churchill case.

There was no ambiguity, though, about the culture of government secrecy which Sir Richard identified in his report, and demanded should be changed. He seized upon the argument that ministers were accountable but not necessarily responsible for everything that happened in their department. That, he said, only enhanced their obligation to be frank in their dealings with Parliament. The report provided the opposition with enough ammunition, at any rate, to sustain their demand for resignations. On 26 February 1996, the government carried a technical motion on the Scott report by a single vote. Three Tories had broken ranks and brought the government to the brink of a disastrous defeat. Before long, the legacy of the arms-to-Iraq affair had become clear. There had to be administrative changes in Whitehall, to improve the handling of export applications and the handling of intelligence material. But if the affair had highlighted a culture of secrecy in Whitehall and at Westminster, there had been only marginal changes at most to deal with it. The Public Service minister, Roger Freeman, talks of 'evolutionary and not revolutionary changes'; of the need to keep officials from turning the aspiration of 'open government' into an exercise in damage limitation, in which decision taking and policy discussion is driven yet further underground, and never committed to paper for fear of it somehow reaching the public domain.

The opposition parties cite this affair as a strong argument for their commitment to a freedom of information act. Ministers insist such an Act would be counter-productive. These arguments, like the details and rival remedies for political sleaze, have probably faded in the public's consciousness. Conservative strategists, who for so long were forced into defensive positions on a bewildering number of fronts, may thank heaven for that. But the Opposition parties hope to harness lingering distrust of the political trade to their campaigns on a wide range of issues. This, they hope, will feed into a public sentiment that is considered by Conservative and opposition party strategists alike to be as vague and as potent as the 'sleaze factor' itself ... the notion that it may just be 'time for a change' whether or not the rather disreputable politicians of one or other political colour are to be trusted any more than their rather disreputable rivals.

MESSENGERS TO BLAME

SPIN DOCTORS AND THE MEDIA

Nicholas Jones

Nicholas Jones is a Political Correspondent for BBC News. He worked on magazines and newspapers including The Times, *before joining the BBC in 1972 as a news producer for Radio Leicester. He became Labour Correspondent for Radio News in 1980. After a year as political correspondent for the World Service he took up his current position in 1989. He published a diary of the 1992 election campaign.*

SPIN DOCTOR: *Obsessive political creature; one who attempts to 'turn' news to the advantage of a political party; a press officer to whom almost supernatural powers of persuasion are attributed (or rather non-attributed). Natural habitat – behind scenes at press conferences; within huddle of journalists; on end of phone, bawling. Totally committed to putting a positive gloss on even the most disastrous story.*

An imaginary dictionary definition, of course ... more mundanely, what 'spin doctors' do, day to day, is take the public words of their political bosses – which may on the surface be fairly anodyne or barely newsworthy in themselves – and re-interpret them for journalists in a way that makes the behind-the-scenes subtleties more clear. For instance, a generalised rhetorical attack by a politician may assume rather more importance if the spin doctor provides specific (off-the-record) examples of who's in the firing-line. Or a new form of words for a party policy might be an early indication that that policy may be about to change – the politician isn't yet ready to make that commitment, but the spin doctor can unattributably drop the hint.

This process will be significantly intensified during the election campaign. The atmosphere at the various party headquarters

and among the entourages surrounding the leaders will be a
super-concentrated mix of journalists, some friendly, some hostile,
along with party officials and politicians. Gaining the initiative,
pushing a story in a favoured direction, attempting to increase or
reduce the prominence of a story according to its helpfulness –
all this adds up to a lot of manoeuvring, argument, pressure and not
a little over-excitement.

In one crucial respect, the build-up to the general election has been
unprecedented. Labour and the Conservatives began a significant
expansion of their publicity departments months before they had any
real idea when voting would take place. Both parties realised that
ultimately the effectiveness of their propaganda, as much as the
content of their policies, would be decisive in the final push to capture
the middle ground of British politics.

REBUTTAL

Even as they started to plan for the campaign, Labour's aggressive
approach towards publicity had already paid handsome dividends.
Their skill in using the news media to exploit the government's
unpopularity, and to project Tony Blair, had kept the Conservatives
firmly on the defensive. In order to maintain their supremacy in
attack, Labour were the first to step up their recruitment. They also
invested heavily in new premises and equipment. But another factor
had dominated Labour's pre-election planning. Nagging away at Mr
Blair and the rest of the party leadership was the fear that John Major
could again come from behind, as he did in the 1992 general election,
when the Conservatives' deadly assault on Labour's tax plans was said
to have sealed Neil Kinnock's fate.

During the long wait for Mr Major to go to the country, any
mention of the Conservatives' superiority in negative campaigning
was guaranteed to put Labour's spin doctors on edge. It was the
single issue which raised the biggest question mark over the tactics
which Labour intended to adopt in the final weeks of the campaign.
So great was this concern about the Conservatives' ability to swing
the result of an election by just concentrating their fire on Labour's
potential weaknesses, that it prompted an important first in British
electioneering, the development of Labour's Rapid Rebuttal Unit.
Labour were determined that they would never again be left
defenceless in the face of a Conservative election campaign which
put so much emphasis on the denigration of Labour's policies
and personalities.

A computerised database has effectively become the engine room of Labour's hi-tech media centre at Millbank Tower, a short walk from the House of Commons. Its great value to the party's publicity staff is that it can provide the ammunition with which to mount an immediate counter-attack when the Conservatives or hostile newspapers attempt to misrepresent or distort Labour's policies. Both the Democrats and Republicans pioneered rapid rebuttal units during the 1992 US presidential election. Labour's system is based on the fact-checking procedures used by the Clinton campaign. Whole filing cabinets full of documents have been scanned electronically to provide the database. By searching for key words, the computer can pull out critical information from political speeches, policy statements, press cuttings and government statistics. In the closing days of the parliament, its efficiency was demonstrated – to the horror of traditionalists – when a spokesman at the Commons despatch box used a message received by pager to confront a Tory MP just minutes after he'd asked a question on a subject in which Labour claimed he had a financial interest.

But, however bleak the electoral landscape might appear, Conservative Central Office has demonstrated time and again an ability to turn itself into a highly effective campaigning machine. In previous general elections, its research department has tended to be pre-eminent in helping to wrong-foot Labour politicians. Within months of a computerised database being installed in Millbank Tower, the Conservatives announced that they too had purchased the same Excalibur software, promising their system would be targeted far more towards attack than rebuttal.

Another inner strength of a Conservative election campaign has always been the potency of its advertising. Under the guidance of Maurice Saatchi, Central Office tried repeatedly in the long run-up to polling day to hit on a pre-election slogan to match the Conservatives' 1992 campaign message, 'You can't trust Labour'. In an ill-fated attempt to persuade voters to accept that the economic pain of the recession had been worth it, posters and newspaper advertisements were used to make a high-risk apology: 'Yes it hurt. Yes it worked.' Then, just before the much-publicised launch of Labour's draft manifesto, Central Office unveiled what it hoped would become an enduring theme of their campaign: 'New Labour, New Danger'. Danny Finklestein, the party's research director, was one of the architects of a strategic shift by the Conservatives which recognised that Labour had changed under Blair's leadership but could still be portrayed as being unfit to govern. Finklestein believed it would be possible to sustain and develop their warning that 'new Labour' could be as dangerous as the old version.

Lacking the publicity resources of their two main opponents, the Liberal Democrats had to concentrate their pre-election thinking on sharpening up their policy proposals. They found that of all their many policy commitments, the one which most voters remembered was the 1992 campaign pledge to put an extra penny on income tax to pay for improvements in education. It was reconfirmed weeks before the beginning of this campaign. Just as Labour were saddled with the image of being a party of high taxation, the Liberal Democrats suffered from being branded woolly and over-burdened with policies. As the election approached, party strategists prepared a shortlist of what they hoped would be clear, costed proposals for inclusion in their manifesto. Two contenders for the kind of highly targeted pledges which it was hoped the Liberal Democrats could concentrate on during the election were promises of free eye and dental check-ups, and an increase in police recruitment to put an extra 3,000 officers on the beat.

The Liberal Democrats' problem is often one of managing expectations: being realistic about the number of seats they're likely to win, without risking the morale of supporters. The nationalist parties have similar difficulties: the SNP leadership now regards its 1992 slogan – 'Free by 93' – as unhelpful in raising expectations which were then dashed. This time, they'll talk more cautiously of 'gains for the Scottish people', 'progress and advance' – rather than of any sudden leap to independence. As for their dealings with the media, the SNP is highly sensitive to what they regard as too little coverage from UK-wide outlets, which, they argue, provide people in Scotland with much of their news.

CAMPAIGN STRATEGIES

Great secrecy always surrounds the election tactics of the various parties. Campaign teams for the Conservatives, Labour and the Liberal Democrats have each had to prepare a version of what is known as the 'war book', setting out with military precision the strategy to be adopted until polling day. While the daily themes for speeches and party promotions are flexible, so they can be adjusted as the election gathers pace, the battle lines for negative campaigning tend to be well entrenched. Perhaps not surprisingly, claims and counter-claims about taxation are again likely to become a dominant message in advertising and other forms of publicity.

Of the three party leaders, Paddy Ashdown has consistently expressed the greatest personal distaste for negative campaigning. However, once an election is under way, the Liberal Democrats have demonstrated time and again their aptitude for attacking politics. The great virtue of their position is that they always have the ready-made option of attempting to drive a wedge between the two main parties. Invariably, they tend to portray the Conservatives as a party which cannot be trusted. Warm words by the Liberal Democrats about possible post-election co-operation with Labour will count for little once Mr Blair returns to being an opponent and his party is being ridiculed for a lack of precision in their key policy pronouncements.

Labour's overriding objective will be to keep reminding voters about why they cannot trust the Conservatives again after the way the government misled the country on taxation at the last general election. Mr Blair will argue that a few pre-election Budget reductions should not be allowed to obscure the pain which the Major government has inflicted since 1992 through 22 tax increases. Another constant refrain in Labour's campaign will be that after four successive Conservative election victories, the country needs and deserves a change.

The line of attack being developed by the Conservatives will hammer what are alleged to be the 'back-door taxes' which would flow from a Labour election victory. Instead of achieving the government's aim of strengthening Britain's position as the enterprise centre of Europe, with less regulation than neighbouring countries, a Labour administration would end up destroying jobs, by placing extra burdens on employers through a national minimum wage and by forcing Britain to accept the higher costs imposed by the European Social Chapter. Through concentrating on what they regard as the negative aspects of Mr Blair's vision of a stakeholder economy, the Conservatives believe they can convince the electorate that there is clear blue water between their programme and the policies being put forward by Labour. As in the 1992 election, much will be made of the possible danger that the United Kingdom could break up if separate parliaments were established in Scotland and Wales.

TACTICS

Because there appeared to be every likelihood that the policy differences between Labour and the Conservatives would end up being far less important than in previous elections, the party strategists considered that the image projected by Mr Blair and

Mr Major, and the public's perception of their respective parties, would probably have the greatest influence on undecided voters. This led to all kinds of conjecture about the tactics which might then be deployed.

In a modern, closely fought election where personalities matter as much if not more than policies, the parties become almost totally dependent on the news media for presenting their case to the electorate. The task of the spin doctors is to put the best political gloss, or spin, on the day's political developments. They advise party leaders on the most favourable line to take when explaining or promoting their policies, and then they seek to influence the way this is reported by newspapers, television and radio.

THE SPIN DOCTORS

Labour

- Peter Mandelson MP, Election Campaign Manager; Tony Blair's *éminence grise*; role model for aspiring spin doctors; believes Labour's foward planning will prove superior; confident of holding his nerve however rough the campaign might get.

- Alastair Campbell, Blair's Press Secretary; ex-*Daily Mirror* political editor; aggressive aide-de-camp to Labour leader; no journalist sees Mr Blair without his permission.

- David Hill, Labour's Chief Media Spokesperson; diligent briefer of journalists, with 25 years' experience of Westminster in-fighting.

- Brian Wilson MP, head of Labour's rebuttal unit; former journalist who switched from being transport front-bencher to front-line duty as party's election campaign spokesman at Millbank Tower.

Labour's spin doctors have attracted the greatest opprobrium because of their reputation for trying to bully broadcasters into giving their stories top billing in the all-important news coverage on television and radio. There has been some justification for Labour's practice of shouting louder than the Conservatives. Prime ministers are usually in a commanding position when it comes to the application of the difficult science of news management. Because it is governments which tend to dictate the timing of many newsworthy events, opposition parties are usually left with the task of reacting and often find themselves at a serious disadvantage. In addition, ministers are buttressed by the not inconsiderable support of the publicity staff working within each government department. Therefore, as in 1992, it was only when the general election was finally called that control over Major's media appearances passed from Downing Street to Conservative Central Office.

Tony Blair's success in promoting 'new Labour' and the projection of his own carefully crafted image as a resolute, forward-looking party leader owes much to the assiduous attention of his personal press officer, Alastair Campbell. Should Labour win the election, one of Blair's first likely appointments as prime minister will be to make Campbell the new chief press secretary in Downing Street, where he would be following in the footsteps of another *Daily Mirror* journalist, Joe Haines, who became Harold Wilson's press secretary in 1969.

Campbell enjoys the kind of larger-than-life reputation which came so easily to another celebrated Downing Street press secretary, Sir Bernard Ingham, who established a formidable partnership with Margaret Thatcher during the 1980s. A party leader's personal press officer has to have a finely developed news sense and must be able to thrive amid the daily badinage of press conferences and lobby briefings. Campbell is a fearless operator when it comes to the private arm-twisting which is all part of the cut and thrust of political journalism. Woe betide any reporter, photographer, or cameraman who gets in Blair's way during one of those doorstep scrums which so bedevil prominent politicians in a hurry!

Labour's media headquarters at Millbank Tower controls the party's day-to-day contact with the news media. A staff of over 200, including many volunteers, has been recruited for the campaign. Their task, under chief media spokesperson David Hill, is to organise news conferences, issue press releases, and arrange TV and radio interviews. Labour believe the great virtue of their new media centre is that it brings together on one floor publicity and research staff, backed up by the rebuttal unit, headed by the MP Brian Wilson, himself a former journalist. New campaign themes and storylines can be checked out not only instantly but also collectively, in the hope that this will ensure a co-ordinated response. Preparations for the campaign have been supervised by the party's election planning group, which has been chaired by Peter Mandelson, long regarded as Labour's leading practitioner in the flighty calling of selling politics.

Much to his regret Mr Mandelson found he was left on the sidelines during the 1992 election campaign but, ever since Blair became leader in 1994, he has been back within the inner circle of Labour modernisers and has played a pivotal role behind the scenes. A great deal is riding on his shoulders. There are high hopes within the party leadership that he can repeat his presentational successes of earlier years. Mr Mandelson rose to prominence under Neil Kinnock. He was appointed director of communications in 1985 and, after seeing through the introduction of the red rose as a new party symbol, became the catalyst for the promotional highs of Labour's glitzy campaign in 1987. However, after being selected as the Labour prospective Parliamentary candidate in Hartlepool, he resigned in 1990 as director of communications. He was elected an MP in 1992, and, as he has remarked subsequently, observed with mounting concern what he considered were the mistakes of the 1992 campaign.

One of Mr Mandelson's less publicised attributes, which he regards as being of critical importance in the volatile world of political propaganda, is an ability to hold his nerve during those turbulent occasions when a political party can seemingly lose control of events and appear totally at the mercy of the news media. He believes the confusion and criticism which surrounded the fiasco over Labour's 'Jennifer's Ear' party political broadcast in the 1992 election might well have been avoided had the campaign team remained cool and collected. Mr Mandelson considers it was his determination to hold fast in the face of sustained media pressure in January 1996 which helped Tony Blair withstand demands for the sacking of the Shadow Health Secretary, Harriet Harman, over her controversial decision to send her son to a selective grammar school.

In recent months Mr Mandelson has tried repeatedly to play down his role as a spin doctor. He dislikes the backbiting within the party which his activities have attracted and, in an attempt to establish his authority as a political thinker, set out his critique of the tasks facing a future Labour government in his book, *The Blair Revolution*, written jointly with Roger Liddle. But his prominent position among those drawing up Labour's election tactics has ensured that he remains a target for vilification by the Conservatives, who claim he deploys devious techniques in manipulating the broadcasting organisations on Labour's behalf.

Conservative

- Charles Lewington, Director of Communications; former *Sunday Express* political editor; suave and discreet; highly rated by party insiders.

- Sheila Gunn, responsible for day-to-day liaison with lobby journalists; formerly political correspondent on *The Times*; easy-going, enjoys mixing it with reporters; always ready with advice or a quote.

- Danny Finklestein, Research Director; astute negative campaigner charged with sustaining the campaign slogan 'New Labour, New Danger'.

- Alan Duncan MP, Parliamentary aide to the party chairman; opinionated but assiduous briefer.

After a succession of changes in the chairmanship of his party, it fell to one of John Major's closest ministerial colleagues, Dr Brian Mawhinney, to carry through a much-heralded pre-election shake-up in the Conservatives' publicity machine. He recruited Charles Lewington, political editor of the *Sunday Express*, to succeed Hugh Colver as director of communications. Mr Lewington has generally eschewed the high-profile personal publicity which his Labour counterparts have cultivated, but this does not seem to have been a handicap, and he was soon winning praise from party insiders. He proved adept at advising on how best to exploit gaffes in policy statements and speeches by Mr Blair and the rest of the shadow cabinet. Lewington's apprenticeship on a pro-Tory newspaper had helped him develop a sensitive nose for the kind of news stories which put Labour on the defensive.

Long-established links between Central Office and Conservative-supporting press proprietors always seem to get stronger once an election is called. Because they have been able to rely on an increasingly trenchant anti-Labour stance in most of the mass-circulation tabloids the closer it gets to polling day, Central Office has, over the years, had a tendency to be less adept than Labour at finding ways to gain maximum advantage from political coverage on television and radio. Dr Mawhinney was determined to rectify what he considered was an imbalance in the way the Conservatives were treated by the electronic media. He voiced his concerns about possible Labour bias in several pre-election speeches which were interpreted as something of a warning shot across the bows of the broadcasters. This was followed up by Charles Lewington who launched a forthright attack on the BBC's political journalism in a *Sunday Telegraph* article shortly before the campaign. Dr Mawhinney's other objective was to match Labour's pre-eminence in winning favourable publicity in the regional and specialist press.
He appointed press officers in key centres across the country to re-establish the party's links with local journalists.

Liberal Democrats

- Jane Bonham-Carter, Director of Media Communication; former editor of Channel 4's *A Week in Politics*; previous experience: debunking the quack pronouncements of political spin doctors.

- Judith Fryer, Head of Press and Broadcasting; feisty; holds her own in the push-and-shove of day-to-day contact with the news media.

- Alan Leaman, Director of Strategy and Planning; long-time press officer and adviser to Paddy Ashdown; self-effacing but forceful defender of Liberal Democrats' demand for a fair share of election news coverage.

Few women have made it to the very top in the cut-throat world of political manipulation and managed to stay there. Labour's Joy Johnson lasted barely a year as the party's Director of Communications. In contrast to their opponents, the Liberal Democrats have appointed a succession of female publicity directors who have proved to be doughty performers in the male-dominated world of political journalism. Olly Grender, who was awarded the MBE after her stint running the party's communications department, was succeeded by Jane Bonham-Carter, formerly editor of Channel 4's *A Week in Politics*. Ms Bonham-Carter can rightly claim the longest political pedigree of any spin doctor on the Westminster patch because she is the great-granddaughter of the former Liberal prime minister, Herbert Asquith.

Day-to-day contact between journalists and the Liberal Democrats is in the hands of Judith Fryer, who heads the party's press and broadcasting team. She has become accustomed to the uncertainty which results from continually being upstaged by the two main parties. While some forward planning was possible in preparing for the promotion of the Liberal Democrats' well-established policy commitments on education and Europe, the party's campaign programme had to be kept flexible so that they could respond to a news agenda dictated by Labour and the Conservatives. Unless the Liberal Democrats remained ready to react quickly and make their own contribution to any debate surrounding the dominant topic of the day, they feared they could end up being marginalised in the news coverage, or equally come across as appearing insignificant because of their concentration on fringe issues.

DO THEY REALLY MATTER?

How much impact all this has on voters is impossible to quantify. Opinion poll ratings of the three main parties have rarely shown any significant variation in the long run-up to the election being declared. Nevertheless, up to a third of the electorate is thought to be undecided, providing a key target for the political propagandists.

The party hierarchies believe the way to bid for these voters is to influence the news agenda – no election, according to them, can now be won without the influence of the great spin doctors. This explains the high-profile and prolonged campaigning which has risked making its targets weary before the official campaign had even begun.

The challenge for candidates and voters between now and polling day is to get a clear view of each other, as they peer through the smoke conjured up by the masters of spin.

SURFERS AGAINST SEWAGE

THE POLITICS OF DIRECT ACTION AND THE DISGRUNTLED

Jeremy Vine

Jeremy Vine has been a Political Correspondent for BBC News since 1994. Before joining the BBC in 1987 he worked on the Coventry Evening Telegraph and Metro Radio. For the BBC he initially worked on news and current affairs both for radio and television and on 'Heart of the Matter'. In 1989 he joined Radio 4's 'Today' programme as a reporter. He has also presented 'Today' and 'PM' on Radio 4, 'Newstalk' on Radio Five Live, and 'Newsnight' on BBC Television.

WARREN'S WORLD

His hair is traffic cone orange, his jumper a maze of loose thread. His Holy of Holies is 50 feet of mashed-up slope strewn with wood and broken bricks. Sniffing and wiping his nose with the heel of his hand, Warren talks articulately of fresh fruit, fresh vegetables and rotten politicians. 'They are a waste of time, that lot. I'd rather be on my allotment here', he tells me. 'Politics is nonsense now. I stood as a council candidate for the Greens, but I realised I couldn't change anything that way. This is the future – sustainable living'. A fellow worker, Kate, agrees. 'Whoever wins the election, Labour or Tory, if we're growing our own food we can't be touched'.

They need to be careful here: their allotment is a precarious strip of land above a Brighton railway bridge, almost steep enough for one of them to take a tumble. That said, Warren and his friends never made much of an effort to stop themselves falling off the edge of the political world; Warren speaks for a group called Justice?, which campaigns on specific issues ranging from the Criminal Justice Act, through open-cast mining, to asylum legislation and the Jobseeker's Allowance. He has given up on MPs, Parliament, voting, governments, oppositions and general elections. He uses direct action to get his way. And he is not alone.

SUFFRAGETTE CITY

Do-It-Yourself politics, some are calling it. However, although the phrases 'direct action' and 'single-issue campaigning' have an exclusively 1990s ring, they are not exclusively 1990s phenomena. The families of John and Robert Kennedy are well acquainted with direct action in its most lacerating form (the assassinated President had already acceded to politer forms of pressure: he was a member of the National Rifle Association). In 1887 a newspaper splashed 'SERIOUS RIOTS IN LONDON: POLICE OVERWHELMED' after protests against repression in Ireland on the day that became the first Bloody Sunday. As a student, President Clinton had only one thing on his mind during the Vietnam War; its opponents were the quintessential single-issue campaigners of the modern area. Comb history, and their ilk are the knots that get caught – proud Jarrow Marchers, heroic suffragettes, anti-slavery agitators, peasants with pudding-bowl hairdos who starred in their own Revolt (the first poll tax protests, in 1381; the second came in 1990). The farmer who parked his muckspreader outside Castle Morpeth housing department and sent four tons of slurry belching out onto the windows after a dispute over planning permission was not following a modern fad. There have always been single issues, and there has always been direct action.

Yet something new is happening now – something that deeply concerns thoughtful politicians in the run-up to the election. Direct action has become an industry. Many of its proponents are cut off from Parliament and agitate in the unabashed belief that Parliament is cut off from the people. They are getting ultra-sophisticated in the way they apply pressure. They operate under a vast number of headings, forming a rainbow of different organisations and campaigns. And they cut across social groupings. Single-issue campaigns are no longer run exclusively from allotments.

I KNOW WHAT I WANT, AND I KNOW HOW TO GET IT

Britain has been as creative as any country in the dispersal of weapons of war. Now it is exporting a weapon of peace – our activists currently lead the world in protesting. Meanwhile, in the United States, equally inventive groups use 'monkey-wrenching', the umbrella term for non-violent sabotage – programming computers to tie up a target company's telephone and fax lines, driving nails into the trunks of trees to smash chainsaws used to cut them down, plugging discharge pipes so foul waste oozes back into a factory, pulling up stakes and flags to confuse developers.

As the techniques get more and more effective, and their exponents increasingly tenacious, the political significance of direct action grows. Greenpeace landed on the Brent Spar platform to plead its case in the glare of world attention, handing out TV footage to all takers and forcing Shell into a retreat on the oil rig's disposal that caught John Major with his shoelaces undone. 'The Prime Minister does not deserve to be treated like this,' said Michael Heseltine in pre-leadership contest mode. For others the point was simpler: who needs a political party for a platform when you can have an oil rig?

Fast results breed more groups. The antibodies of politics are multiplying. The way the magazine Squall sets out its driving ideology speaks volumes. 'We present accurate information to those despairing of an increasingly unrepresentative, unaccountable and unimaginative political system' it announces. 'Squall aims to counter a current tide of political helplessness by showing that individuals and relatively small campaigning groups can play an active part in their country's politics'.

A publication with the title *Campaign Guide to the New Opposition* listed such a multitude of single-issue organisations that readers would have been forgiven for wondering if some were invented – New Luddites are in there, challenging 'the legitimacy of science and technology', and offering 'the proud battle-cry for a new generation of non-violent action'. Those who join Psychology Politics Resistance will be put in touch with 'radical psychologists and those active in empowerment work'. The protection of 'the green lung of Leyton and Walthamstow Marshes' is the sole concern of the Lammas Lands Defence Committee, while the direct action proposed by Critical Mass is in the form of 'mass cycle rides through city centres'.

And there, listed in the environment section under 'S', stands the epitome of the single-issue, direct-action group: 'by educating pension-fund managers owning water shares, and the legal system, we work towards clean oceans', explained – yes, Surfers Against Sewage.

NO POINT IN PARLIAMENT?

'These campaigners', the social trends commentator Anthony Sampson wrote in the *Evening Standard* in 1995, *raise awkward questions about democracy: for the battles they have won have been conducted almost entirely outside Parliament, or any organised public debates ... as they extend their own power they have to recognise that they have become part of Britain's informal constitution, more important than much of the flummery which surrounds the Palace of Westminster'.*

So as the election looms, there are key questions about the interface between conventional politics and the world beyond Westminster. Quite how protesters at Newbury – to name one example – would take to being described as an 'informal part of Britain's constitution' is probably best left to the imagination.

Yet they do not underestimate their influence. At one point activists were saying a triumph at Newbury, in the biggest anti-road campaign ever seen in Britain, could cause the government's entire £23 billion 'Roads to Prosperity' programme to collapse. Twyford Down, the M11 link, Thanet Way, Solsbury Hill, Stanworth Valley and the A30 - these are now battle names just as much as headings on some anonymous planner's drawing board.

In the face of the hordes of anti-bypass activists who laid siege to his constituency, the Liberal Democrat MP for Newbury, David Rendel, looked as if he was a dictionary short of the words to address their concerns; the prospective Conservative parliamentary candidate who supplied his farm to security guards found protesters had literally run rings around him – passing themselves off as security staff and handing out leaflets telling the guards they were on poverty pay while their firm raked in vast profits. The Highways Agency spent an excruciating £1.5 million dealing with the unrest. Weeks before the election, smaller-scale protests at the site of A30 improvements near Honiton in Devon made momentary stars of activists like Animal, Muppet Dave and most famously, Swampy, who tunnelled 10ft below ground to stop construction, before moving on to similar work at Manchester Airport's new runway. Labour, meanwhile, faced catcalls for not decrying new roads with sufficient venom. It is almost as if the politicians are out of their depth in the face of hard-core protesters; when the Scottish Office minister Allan Stewart came across a group of anti-road campaigners on the site of the M77 extension near Glasgow, he lifted a pickaxe and was forced to resign.

Michael Dobbs, former Conservative deputy chairman, worried out loud about activists 'displaying little respect for parliamentary democracy'. In a letter to The Times, he reflected: 'It is a pity such pressure groups run so shy of offering themselves for election. Is it simply because they would be so unlikely to succeed?'. A telling point, perhaps – but the problem is that it sounds so much like father talking; no use if thousands of voters are being lured out of the system by the seductive prospect of quick results that bypass the ballot box.

Others are beginning to wonder. Lord Tebbit was making a Euro-dig when he told a radio interviewer that protesters 'have begun to realise there is no democratic way in which the British people can change laws which they find abhorrent and unacceptable', but his indulgence reflects the fact that pressure politics is no longer the preserve of the amputated left: first the poll tax, then the Child Support Agency, then live animal exports triggered demonstrations that dragged the middle classes and the elderly off their floral sofas and onto the streets. In Brightlingsea, lifelong Tory ladies in tweeds were spotted waving placards decrying veal calf exports, and – yet more amazing – alleged police yobbery. The Comte de Chamburn and his wife Victoria, and Celestria Noel, the social editor of *Harpers and Queen*, all let it be known they were off to Newbury. The old Etonian racehorse trainer Charlie Brooks told a reporter: 'People are getting pretty vociferous at dinner parties around here'. The pensioner standing on a pavement with the words 'SOD OFF' scrawled on masking tape across her mouth said nothing, and everything.

HEROES AND VILLAS

Not everyone operates from the outside - or the roadside.

The Michael Dobbs criticism of those who 'run so shy' of standing for Parliament might almost have been taken as a challenge by Sir James Goldsmith, the squillionare who famously owns a Mexican villa and whose extraordinary single-issue campaign on Europe has taken monkey-wrenching and made it fit the rules of the existing system. Anything but shy, and with no allotment in sight, Sir James is thought to be spending around £7 million on his campaign. He aims to trigger a wide-ranging referendum on Britain's place in Europe by fielding candidates in the seats of Tory MPs with views he doesn't like.

The Conservatives, Labour and the Liberal Democrats have all now proposed their versions of referendums – a success for us, the Goldsmith camp roar.

Yet power tactics do not come cheap. They may not even be more effective. Sir James can now boast of being a household name beyond Knightsbridge – in Reigate, for instance, where he has his first and possibly only MP in the defecting Tory, Sir George Gardiner. But by wading into the political arena the tycoon has had to endure conventional mud-slinging ('He is availing himself of his enormous wealth to allow himself an expensive giggle at the expense of the British public' – griped an Evening Standard editorial) and as a result has found it difficult to deliver his message cleanly.

His national poll rating has been microscopic, and while a spread-sheet drawn up by the Tory peer Lord Archer suggests that votes won by the Referendum Party and the similarly sceptical UK Independence Party could succeed in bringing down individual MPs, Sir James and the UKIP leader Dr Alan Sked may well find the end result of all their effort is to marginally increase the majority of a Labour government with a policy on Europe that leaves them spitting.

But they are not alone. As the election approached a number of other groups woke up to the idea of angling for support in the conventional way – and were assisted when the European Court of Human Rights provisionally overturned the British electoral law which stops campaigners leafleting voters to tell them where their candidates stand on a particular issue. Phyllis Bowman, an anti-abortion campaigner with the Society for the Protection of the Unborn Child, secured the ruling after twice being convicted under the existing laws; her solicitor called the verdict 'a trailblazer for all single-issue groups' and 'a blow to all those politicians who seek to avoid the moral debate'. The Campaign for Nuclear Disarmament called it 'brilliant news' too; elections would bring 'greater choice and greater democracy'.

That said, Ms Bowman does not believe that fielding candidates makes a difference, and would rather draw attention to the views of existing contenders with a chance of winning – or losing. That puts SPUC in the uncomfortable position of opposing the tactics of another band of anti-abortionists, the Pro-Life Alliance, who will field around fifty candidates. It has a blacklist of MPs said by its organisers to have 'appalling voting records' on abortion – though the subject has only rarely come up in the Commons since the last election. The Tory MP Edward Leigh supports the sentiments behind the campaign but warns: 'Single-issue candidates get a derisory number of votes, 400 or 500, but hand a weapon to their opponents who say that only 500 people in the constituency are concerned'.

Westminster is not used to being made to pay attention to single-issue campaigners who beat a conventional path to the door. In May 1990, the bye-electors of Bootle gave what was left of David Owen's SDP 155 votes, compared to the 418 won by the Monster Raving

Loony Party. The wheels on the doctor's political vehicle were off within the week.

IN SEARCH OF THE LOST SHEEP

The sudden appearance of single-issue campaigners in the heart of the electoral process suggests that elsewhere in the maelstrom, perhaps even in the tunnels under the A30, there could be seeds of conventional politics. The Liberal Democrat leader Paddy Ashdown would claim to have an insight into the widespread disaffection. His book, *Beyond Westminster* probed the forces that have driven voters away from the mainstream. The perception that ministers lied about tax at the last election – the broken 'read my lips' promise blamed for losing President Bush the White House – must have taken its toll. The catch-all cry of 'sleaze' disfigured umpteen reputations. Poll evidence indicates a collapse of faith in politicians that has driven their credibility terrifyingly close to that of journalists, and after scandals exposing MPs who took money to ask questions or had affairs during moral crusades it is hard to imagine the dusty visages of the new parliamentary standards-bearers, Lord Nolan and Sir Gordon Downey, drawing the disaffected back. The image of the Commons as a leather-lined cell for politicians gone bonkers will take some dismantling.

How ironic it was then, that at the climax of the campaign against the Criminal Justice Bill, which had been largely ignored by London-bound political reporters, enraged protesters scaled the roof of Parliament. Suddenly the TV cameras were panning up to catch them as they showed the nation how they could pull a stunt at the expense of the Westminster machine. Yet by the same token, in physically making Parliament their platform the activists were somehow acknowledging it had a place in their world. 'I must lie down where all the ladders start', as Yeats wrote. Gay demonstrators picketed the Commons while the age of consent was debated. Every week there are new placards outside the building. The egg aimed squarely at John Major's face on the campaign trail indicated, at a stretch, that there is still a relationship to speak of between the elected and the disgusted – even if the two political systems are strained and barely talking.

'THIS IS THE GOVERNMENT WITH THE NON-MIDAS TOUCH'

So will the new politics affect the old? Who will gain and lose most?

The sense of chaos fostered by the work of direct action groups may impact most negatively on the government. Just as the beef crisis was – arguably – born from bad luck rather than incompetence, yet it hit the government for six by creating the impression that the country had gone to pot, so the Conservatives may find they suffer badly from the perception that a shambling coalition of disaffected voters has snatched issues from their control and caused havoc. 'This is the government with the non-Midas touch', said the late Labour leader John Smith, 'in a country where the Grand National doesn't start and the hotels fall into the sea'.

But John Major is never going to be the focus of dissident hatred that Mrs Thatcher was. She sent student politics reeling and had her face on a million protest sweatshirts. Similarly, Labour command no natural loyalty among fringe radicals now. Some are more annoyed by Tony Blair than Mr Major. They find little to choose between them. Same smiles, same suits, same soundbites. It is as much that phenomenon of modern British politics – the sense that the party leaders are gradually grinding down their differences, converging on the centre ground – which feeds fears that when the nation eventually comes to vote, the system itself will pay a heavy price.

YOUNG, FREE AND DISGRUNTLED

At the last general election, 45 per cent of under-25s did not take part. M-Power and Rock the Vote, non-political operations aiming to bring voting back into vogue, have started handing out how-to-register leaflets at pop concerts and comedy venues. Not everyone approves: 'Rock the Vote is addressing the wrong issue', a *Telegraph* reader claimed, saying his student son 'has asked for better politicians'. The organisers would argue that was the point: among first-time voters, today's politicians inspire neither love nor hate.

The centre ground does not crackle with the electricity of new ideas. Where Mrs Thatcher's tenure generated 'Stand Down Margaret', 'She Was Only a Grocer's Daughter,' and 'Tramp The Dirt Down' the last a song by Elvis Costello in which he looks forward to dancing on the Prime Minister's grave, the second perhaps the most bizarre leftist protest title conceivable), John Major would struggle to find any musician mentioning his party through gritted teeth, let alone him. It cuts both ways: the songs that praised Labour in the 80s now sound like all the reasons they were never elected.

Young people in the mid-90s, the conventional wisdom goes, resist categorisation. They don't like left/right labelling. They are hugely disgruntled with politics as it now operates. They are concerned with issues like sexism, racism and animal rights, yet politicians fail to speak about such things. They are not in the least surprised to hear the average age of our MPs is 51, or that there are scarcely more women in Parliament than there are MPs called John.

It does not follow that the young are apathetic. They join marches, and their passion for particular causes swells the ranks of direct action groups. Experience with the transparent gloss of billboard advertising and MTV has given them the nose for a rat, and they sniff out shallow political glitz but, at the other end of the scale, they don't want to be burdened with long-term worries like Europe and the future of farming. The parties could intrigue them by dis-agreeing on more. Yet nothing looks more purposeless than the House of Commons baying at full power.

All is not lost. In the 1992 American election, Rock the Vote claimed to have increased youth turnout by as much as a fifth with the help of stars like Madonna. The effect was said to be a pro-Clinton swing that might well have made the difference between the Democrats winning and losing. Sir James Goldsmith is hardly an anti-establishment pin-up – hardly Johnny Rotten or James Dean – but perhaps his rebel-with-a-cause routine, and those of other recent arrivals, will catch the attention of the young just as the independent Ross Perot seemed to energise the American campaign in which he first surfaced.

Here, Labour now has a commanding lead in surveys that trawl for the intentions of the young – Kinnock and Major were level-pegging in 1992 – but moves between college and home, combined with an age-old bolshiness about registering and a plethora of better things to do when polling day comes, make everything guesswork. A senior Tory at Central Office was not getting in a flap about the registration campaigns: 'We aren't concerned. The main thing is that they take an interest. We think Rock the Vote is genuinely non-political, so let's just leave it at that'. Paddy Ashdown was aglow: 'It is important that young people realise now that decisions made at Westminster will directly affect their own futures'.

SURF'S UP

Those who hope the general election will show that conventional politicians have been licked should consider the formative experience of the environmentalists. In 1989, the Green Party scored a thrilling 15 per cent in elections to the European Parliament and became the sudden sensation of British politics. It all ended in tears: David Icke, a top spokesman, quit spectacularly – surfacing in a turquoise track-suit to forecast imminent earthquakes and claim guidance by the spirit of a Chinese mandarin, Wang Yee Lee. Another leading light, Sara Parkin, left soon afterwards.

Meanwhile, proving themselves adept at spotting useful issues which conventional debate has left on the margins, the politicians had pounced on all things green. There were white papers and big speeches. Activists hate to admit it, but the main parties claim they managed to give average voters the impression that their environmental concerns were under control. The Green Party is now barely a blip on the radar.

So this election will fulfil a vital purpose in measuring the breadth and depth of the gaping hole in mainstream politics. Afterwards it will be up to the politicians to decide what to do. They can thumb their noses at the disaffected, or go charging in so fast to collect their votes that they bang foreheads with each other. To say it will not be easy to fuse the parallel universes of modern British politics would be the understatement of election year. But while Surfers Against Sewage, and many others, experience the exhilarating sensation of being on the crest of a wave – albeit a rather dirty one – they might bear in mind the fact that politicians specialise in being around when the tide goes out.

NIP AND TUCK

THE DAILY BATTLE WITH POLITICIANS
John Humphrys

John Humphrys has been a presenter of BBC Radio 4's 'Today' programme since January 1987 and the anchor of BBC-1's Sunday lunchtime political programme 'On the Record' since September 1993. He worked on the Western Mail before joining the BBC as a reporter based in Liverpool in 1966. A year later he became Northern Industrial Correspondent, moving to London in 1970. He became the BBC's first full-time television correspondent in the United States in 1971, and then moved on to Southern Africa in 1977 covering, among other things, the transformation of Rhodesia into Zimbabwe. He returned to London in 1980 and took up the post of BBC Diplomatic Correspondent. In 1981 John joined BBC-TV's 'Nine O'Clock News' as its main presenter. Since moving to the 'Today' programme, he has continued to stand in as presenter of the main BBC-TV news programmes.

There is one question that is asked almost as much as 'What time d'you have to get up to do the Today programme?', or 'What d'you say to each other at the end of the news?'. It is: 'What's the point of interviewing that pathetic bunch all the time when they never answer any of the questions?'

As Sherlock Holmes might have put it, the answer is elementary, and is linked to the mysterious business of the dog that did not bark. The silent dog gave Holmes the information he needed, and the uncommunicative politician frequently gives the inquiring voter the information he needs. At the very least it raises doubts in his mind.

Why is the politician ducking that particular question?

What's he got to hide?

What does his opposite number have to say on the subject?

So if the hapless politician gets into trouble when he does say something, and is dismissed as a wretched coward when he doesn't, you might wonder why he bothers at all. We are, after all, a relatively new phenomenon. Politics managed perfectly well without the 'Today' programme' or 'Newsnight' or 'On the Record' before they came barging into our living rooms and so did the politicians.

But you cannot put the genie back in the bottle and since he has emerged, flickering and muttering, the politicians have done their damndest to make him grant their wishes. In the early days he did. The genie was theirs to command.

HOW TIMES CHANGE...

How modern politicians must envy the respect accorded their forbears.

*'And have you anything else to say to a grateful nation, minister?'
is the stuff of interviewing folklore. Or: 'How shall we begin this
discussion, Prime Minister, at home ... or perhaps with foreign
matters?'*

By the time Harold Wilson arrived on the scene the questions were tougher, and the politicians were cannier. Wilson was probably the first political leader fully to appreciate and exploit the medium. He would time his speeches during a campaign to coincide with the main evening news, but much more than that. His handlers (yes, they did have spin doctors even in those far-off days) would liaise with the producer and when they gave him the signal, Harold would switch from whatever boring old rhetoric he was engaged on at the time to a scintillating sound-bite. Very puzzling for the audience in the town hall, but it made perfect sense to the rather larger audience watching the news on a few million television sets.

Wilson was, undoubtedly, the master of the medium and dealt just as effectively with interviewers. The tapping on the bowl of his pipe to give him thinking time (unkind friends said in truth he'd much prefer a good cigar but the pipe was a far more suitable prop for a Labour leader); the furrowed brow to indicate concern; the re-phrasing of the questions the better to suit his answers. It was all there, and the results speak for themselves. In electoral terms he was easily the most successful Labour politician of modern times.

True, he had a little help from his political enemies, who were not as media-smart. When Wilson won his first election it was against Alec Douglas Home. The battle could hardly have been less equal.

The clever grammar school boy who'd dragged himself up by his boot straps and talked about technology as if he understood it was up against an aristocrat who'd had to renounce his title to lead the Tories in the first place. Where Wilson made the television studio his second home, Sir Alec looked as if he couldn't wait to get back to the grouse moor.

If television has done nothing else, it has probably ensured that we shall never again see such an unequal match. The Tories did it with Home in the 1960s. Labour did it with Michael Foot in the 1980s: another intelligent, charming politician who simply did not - or could not - cope with the demands of the medium. Duffle coats in Whitehall on Armistice Day equalled double-barrelled shotguns in Scotland on the glorious twelfth.

You have only to try to imagine a modern leader allowing himself (or herself) to be filmed blasting our sweet little feathered friends out of the sky to see how far we have come in terms of media consciousness in such a relatively short time.

Now we have political leaders who make even the old pro Wilson look like an amateur, whether in image-building, interviewing or the black art of media manipulation.

True, Wilson did inveigh against the inequities of the BBC – but only after he'd become prime minister, please note; it's extraordinary how swiftly a political leader discovers that the organisation of which he'd so approved as opposition leader is in truth a bunch of anarchists determined to do down the splendid government. Wilson, however, was a model of restraint when it came to putting pressure on the broadcasters compared with his successors.

As election day nears, the pressure increases. So it was before the last election; so it has been before this one.

THE FIRING LINE

Imagine the scene in the production office of the 'Today' programme a few minutes after it has come off the air. The sense of relief is tangible, and that's the first thing you would notice. The great challenge is, simply, to do it. And then the phones start ringing. The cries go out:

'Tory Central Office on the line!'

They want to know why the Minister didn't get the last word after the discussion about whatever-it-was. He'd been promised it. No he hadn't, but never mind.

'Campbell's lot on the line!'

Alastair Campbell, who runs a tight ship in the Labour leader's office, has told someone to whinge about the prominence we gave to some criticism of whatever-it-was. Wildly exaggerated, they say. It wasn't, but never mind.

'Ashdown's furious about something-or-other!'

And so he is. Why didn't we include a Liberal-Democrat interview on whatever-it-was when we talked to everyone else. We're always ignoring them. We're not, but never mind.

And so it goes.

It's not so very different in the television newsroom, but the calls there are as likely to come in before the programme as after. The editor of the 'Six O'Clock News' picks up the phone and it's: 'You must be leading on the Minister's statement. Don't you realise how important this is?'

Or: 'Are you seriously telling me you're going to report that rubbish from the Tories?. No one takes it seriously and you'll be making a big mistake.'

All good knockabout stuff – most of the time. News selection, the content and order of a programme, matters to the politician and never more than during the election campaign itself.

What may matter even more is how the politician deals with the story once it's happened. The row over Jennifer's Ear or Labour's tax plans may cause immense and lasting damage or it may not. Which takes us back to the interviews.

FORGIVE ME FOR INTERRUPTING...

This is the age of 'media training'. I doubt whether Harold Wilson ever suffered the indignity of sitting before an earnest young woman with a clipboard and stopwatch while an earnest young man fired questions at him to test and improve his 'media skills'. If he were trying to get on a candidates' list for any of the main parties these days he'd have no choice.

An interviewer can usually spot the interviewee who's been trained. He'll invariably ask what the first question is going to be and then employ a variety of techniques to try to frustrate his questioner. Most of them can be spotted a mile off – by the interviewer and usually by the listener too. The old pros – the Heseltines and the Clarkes and the Prescotts – don't bother. They just do it – and the audience generally likes them the better because of it.

Not that some tricks don't work rather well. There is one senior politician who always preferred to appear on the 'Today' programme

at ten to eight – the last interview before the weather forecast.
Whatever else we do on 'Today', it's unforgivable to be 'late for the
weather'. So the canny old bird would spout a load of boring old
inconsequential nonsense and then, at about six minutes to eight,
he would launch into what he really wanted to say with a minute left.
Then he'd stop, look at the clock and look at you triumphantly,
knowing there was no way you could pick holes in what he'd just said
because you'd run out of time. It always worked.

Others will ignore the questions and tell you what you should be
asking them (Tony Benn: 'What the folk at home are really worried
about') and others will do their utmost to turn it into a monologue
rather than an interview. Some have developed the technique of
pausing for breath in the middle of the sentence with an upward
cadence and then sweeping on at the end of the next sentence so that
it's impossible to get a question in without seeming to interrupt.

Ah, interruptions.

Again, contrary to popular belief, many politicians are perfectly
happy to be interrupted. It gives them the excuse to appeal to the
audience ('if only this awful bully would let me get a word in
edgeways, I could tell you everything you want to know'). It might
also give them a bit of breathing space – like the long question with
half a dozen sub clauses.

The canny, experienced politician knows what the audience knows:
the best interview is a conversation in which both sides engage with
enthusiasm. It needs to be entertaining to listen to, as well as to treat
the audience like grown-ups.

Most politicians know a thing or two about stage management, too.
Where should the interview take place, for instance?

Mr Major was adamant, when he agreed to a 55-minute live
interview with me for 'On the Record' at the end of last year, that it
should take place at his home. Understandable, perhaps, because he
wanted a family lunch on that particular Sunday. But I suspect he was
not oblivious to the spin-off: the image of a relaxed family man at
home in his conservatory on a Sunday lunchtime. And he knew
precisely where he wanted the chairs placed ... and precisely where
the cameras should go, too.

Michael Heseltine much prefers to be interviewed for 'On the
Record' either at his home or a hotel nearby. On one occasion he
generously treated me to a guided tour of his magnificent arboretum
before the interview began. He is, rightly, hugely proud of it, and
instead of talking politics we talked trees for half an hour or so.

'Thanks for that', I said when we got back to the house and settled into our chairs for the interview, 'but I don't feel very combative after that bit of pastoral bliss.'

There was a little chuckle from the Deputy Prime Minister.

'Why d'you think I took you, eh?'

So how much affect does all this media jousting have on the voters when they step into the booth on the chosen Thursday?

The honest answer is, we just don't know.

ON STAGE

Roy Hattersley may well be right when he says that performance, the theatre of politics, is an essentially supplementary activity. It's obviously true that it is not an end in itself. As he says, politics should be primarily concerned with principles, policies and programmes. Incidentally he, like most other politicians, omits the other 'P' that most of us would include. Personalities. I wonder why. No one doubts that the personality of a chief executive or chairman is important in leading and motivating the company's work force. No one says the head teacher of a good school does it by organisational ability alone. Who could possibly doubt that Churchill's personality was a factor from 1939 to 1945 or, God forbid, Hitler's? And yet we are always having our wrist slapped for 'concentrating on personalities' as though leadership – which is surely an aspect of personality – counts for nothing.

However, it's hard to argue with Mr Hattersley when he says this:

A party's first democratic duty is to set out its manifesto. Its second is to oppose what it believes to be the shortcomings of its opponents' alternatives. Then, when the election is over, one of the manifestos becomes the mandate and its implementation the exercise of the popular will.

All undeniably true. But there is little point in setting out the manifesto and attacking the opposition's if the public is not listening. And, like it or not, in the broadcasting age we have become accustomed to being fed our politics over the airwaves. What's more, opinion polls tell us that BBC and ITV are trusted to tell the truth in a way that newspapers are not. That has nothing to do with our instrinsic moral superiority, but everything to do with the fact that newspapers are owned by proprietors (most of them, anyway) and most have a clear editorial line.

Newspapers report politics at great length and some of them in great depth, but newspapers are partisan. BBC and ITV are not, and that may be the explanation. Or it may simply be that many people have to see and hear a politician as he grapples live with a persistent interviewer before they feel competent to make an assessment of his worth.

IN TOUCH?

So, once again, back to the interview and its effect on the voter.

We are constantly told that real people (those who don't make their living, one way or another, from the business) are being turned off politics. There's something in that. Those of us who are directly involved often speak a language that borders on the unintelligible to those who aren't.

I winced to hear myself discussing a 'reasoned amendment' on 'Today'. A what? Hands up, class, if you can tell me what a reasoned amendment is. Why should the listener know?

Then there's the temptation for us all to talk in code. Oh, we clever dicks may know what the Labour front-bencher may be getting at, and why that comment by the junior minister was so devastating, but the airwaves don't exist to allow one politician to pass a coded message to another. Or at least, they shouldn't.

Where the interview does work – for the politicians – is when it is used, time and again, to hammer home one single and easily understood message. Labour equals tax rises. Conservatism equals fat cats. Liberal Democracy equals wasted votes.

Or so most politicians believe. That's why they do it. The politicians who rail against sound-bite journalism do it themselves all the time. They don't really expect their 40-minute speech to be broadcast in full on 'Newsnight' or 'On the Record'. They know precisely which bit (if any) is going to be used, and they know why. And they suspect that no election was lost by oversimplifying a complex issue or repeating too often the same charge against your opponent.

Every general election, we are told, is going to be the nastiest there has ever been. This one will certainly be the most highly managed and deftly spun. The Labour party under its new leader and with its experienced spin doctors is unlikely to repeat some of the mistakes it has made in the past.

That need not make it any more difficult for people like me. The calls will keep coming from party headquarters; the ritual protests will be made about this question or that interruption. And many in our audiences will say they let it all wash over them. In the end, though, for most voters, it comes down to a matter of trust. How they regard the credibility of political leaders is, of course, highly likely to influence where they'll place their cross on the ballot paper. So if exposing the politicians to raw live questioning occasionally reveals nothing more than a dog that isn't barking – or perhaps a dog whose only trick is to attack its neighbours – it is, at the very least, an opportunity for the voters to make their own judgement on the abilities, the integrity and the sincerity of those who'd like to govern us.

RETURN TO WESTMINSTER

THE POLITICAL OVERVIEW

RETURN TO WESTMINSTER

THE POLITICAL OVERVIEW
Robin Oakley

Robin Oakley is Political Editor for BBC News.
He joined the Liverpool Daily Post and Echo in
1964 and in 1967 became political correspondent
He has been a lobby correspondent ever since,
moving to Fleet Street in 1970, working on the
Sunday Express, Now! magazine, the Daily Mail
and, from 1986 to 1992, as Political Editor of The
Times. During this time he contributed to many TV
and radio programmes and was a regular presenter
of Radio 4's 'The Week in Westminster'. He
succeeded John Cole as the BBC's Political Editor in October 1992.

The inter-party battles of the 'phoney war' period have shown us what
this election will be about. Once more it is likely to boil down into a
battle cry of 'Time For A Change' from Labour against a Tory
counter-attack encapsulated in the slogan 'Don't Let Labour Ruin It'.
Labour has fought with a similar message before. But voters in 1992
appeared to conclude, narrowly, that the substitution of John Major
for Margaret Thatcher as leader of the governing Conservative party
was change enough. In an election dominated by Tory insistence that
a Labour victory would mean higher taxes, they returned the Tories
to power for a fourth successive term, although with a reduced
majority of just 21 seats.

The Parliament which ensued has seen the Tories still struggling to
come to terms with both the fact and the manner of Lady Thatcher's
departure. Their divisions over Europe have been painfully exposed
as their majority has been chipped away by deaths, by-election defeats
and defections. Their reputation for economic competence took a
savage blow when Britain was forced out of the Exchange Rate
Mechanism of the European Monetary System in September 1992.
Trust in their claims to be a tax-cutting party has been battered by

the huge tax increases brought about by that reversal and by a recession which lasted far longer than ministers had calculated.

With opinion poll evidence suggesting that the public regard privatisation as an idea whose time has come and gone, they have been accused of lacking any new 'Big Idea' or political vision at least until the pre-election flurry of new initiatives on pensions and residential care for the old. And a series of sexual or other scandals involving ministers and Tory MPs, bundled together by the media under the heading of the 'sleaze factor', have enabled the opposition to present a picture of a government which has been too long in office since it came to power in 1979, and in which standards have been slipping.

Only the belated turnaround in the economy has enabled the Tories to keep alive the hope that they can yet whittle back the huge opinion poll lead enjoyed for so long by Labour. They have been more unpopular and for longer than any government since polling began. But ministers kept hoping that rising living standards, lower interest and mortgage rates, tax cuts, maturing Tessas, privatised utility cash handbacks and falling unemployment would induce a restoration of the 'feelgood factor' in time for their political fortunes to recover.

Since the ERM debacle, they have struggled to establish a plateau of political calm sufficient to enable them to rebuild public confidence and party morale. What Harold Macmillan saw as the curse of governments – 'Events, dear boy, events' – have constantly thrown them off course. Even in the final days of the Parliament two gaffes by the normally sure-footed Stephen Dorrell, embarrassing disclosures on food safety involving the embattled Agriculture Minister Douglas Hogg, racist remarks by the backbencher David Evans and the defection of deselected MP Sir George Gardiner to the Referendum Party enabled opponents to depict the Government as a banana skin administration. Damage limitation and crisis management have become a way of life, taking attention away from what Mr Major would see as his central achievements of creating a deregulated, low-inflation economy, pursuing peace in Northern Ireland and pushing on with reforms in the NHS, education and the financing of the welfare state.

Soon after the ERM crisis came the problems over pit closures, when a rushed programme of winding down coal mines alarmed Tory MPs and forced ministers into a rethink. With the government at its most vulnerable the next shock was the collapse of the Matrix Churchill trial, which forced the Prime Minister to set up what became the marathon ordeal for ministers of the Scott inquiry into arms sales to Iraq, sapping governmental energies and raising further questions in the public mind about the government's moral standing.

The Prime Minister's attempt the next autumn to answer the question: 'What's the new Big Idea?' with his 'Back to Basics' programme then misfired as others built in their own moral interpretations and the media unearthed a series of financial and extra-marital affairs involving ministers or their close associates. The earlier resignation of David Mellor, the forced departure of Michael Mates over his relationship with the fugitive tycoon and Tory party benefactor Asil Nadir and the string of governmental departures linked in one way or another to 'Back to Basics' left the impression of an accident-prone administration always reacting to events rather than being in control of them.

The so-called 'sleaze factor' was compounded by opposition attacks on ex-ministers who moved rapidly to City boardrooms where their recent experience in government was likely to give their employers competitive advantage, by allegations about secret Tory party funding by overseas interests, and by claims and revelations that ministers and Tory MPs had failed to declare favours and benefits received from commercial interests.

Following public disquiet over the 'Cash for Questions' affair involving two Tory backbenchers who were censured for accepting money to raise points in Parliament, the Prime Minister set up another inquiry, under Lord Nolan, to examine standards in public life. The judge's recommendations, involving restrictions on parliamentary consultancies, further complicated the government's life by proving highly unpopular with many Tory MPs.

Yet another inquiry, the Greenbury committee's investigation into top people's pay, proved necessary when the government faced further political embarrassment over the generous pay, perks and share options which the directors and executives of the privatised public utilities had awarded themselves. It enabled the opposition parties to present themselves as champions of the consumer and to suggest that the Tories were the party of the privileged 'fat cats'. Labour and the Liberal Democrats did not miss their opportunities.

The government's authority and Mr Major's leadership suffered another blow when, having asked the independent Senior Salaries Review Board to make recommendations on MPs and ministers' pay, Mr Major called on MPs in July 1996 to reject their suggestion of a 26 per cent rise and settle for just 3 per cent, a call that was emphatically spurned.

The accident-prone nature of the Major administration, the desperate opinion poll ratings and the growing boldness of the Tory

Eurosceptics excited periodic bouts of speculation about a coup to unseat the prime minister. Although in 1995 he saw off the snipers by taking the supreme gamble of resigning and daring his critics to take him on, the attacks on Mr Major were a constant destabilising factor underlining Tory disunity. In latter days, manoeuvring for position by likely candidates in the Tory leadership contest which is likely to follow any election defeat has complicated Mr Major's efforts to sustain the Cabinet's 'wait and see' (they call it 'negotiate and decide') compromise position on the touchstone issue of the Single European Currency.

In what has been a comfortable period to be in opposition, Labour's travails have been of a different kind. They suffered the shock of losing a popular and respected leader with the death of John Smith. However, for them it has been a period of significant political recovery after the shattering blow of that fourth consecutive election defeat in 1992.

Neil Kinnock, Labour's leader at the last general election, had done much to modernise his party, but his past association with the Left meant there was perhaps too big a credibility gap to close with middle-class voters. They were suspicious that Labour remained at heart a union-dominated, tax-and-spend party. His replacement by John Smith and the ensuing 'one member, one vote' reforms of Labour's constitution gave Labour a more reassuring image and presented Mr Major with a formidable Parliamentary opponent.

Mr Smith's tragic death, the sympathy for Labour which it evoked, and the emergence in his turn of the younger Tony Blair then gave Labour's modernising image a huge further boost. His campaign to sweep away the old 'nationalisation' Clause IV of Labour's constitution epitomised the claim that what was on offer was a 'new Labour'. A party prepared to reform itself, he argued, was a party which could be trusted to reform the country.

Labour's carefully orchestrated move towards the centre ground of politics has seen some grumbles from the Left. Union chiefs have been annoyed by internal party reforms which have lessened union influence in Labour's affairs and distanced the party steadily from its industrial wing. But though the Left and the unions have occasionally made common cause, pressing for Labour to set specific levels for the minimum wage, to announce precise targets for reducing unemployment and to promise increased public expenditure, their criticism has been muted. Critics both inside and outside the party though have wondered if all the modernising has left Labour with a true core of belief. They argue that in reassuring middle class voters

Labour has moved ever closer to the policies of the Government whose record it so loudly condemns.

What Mr Blair likes to call 'new Labour' has been criticised for lacking policies. In fact it has a considerable list of commitments such as the minimum wage, signing up to Europe's Social Chapter, the creation of a Scottish Parliament and a Welsh Assembly, a Freedom of Information Act, a windfall tax on privatised utilities, a banking Ombudsman, and a green Budget. But what has been on offer has frequently been more themes and aims and values than precise policy detail.

Mr Blair and his associates argue that the Tories did not have many precise commitments when Mrs Thatcher came to power in 1979, although they had established a clear sense of the direction in which they would take the country. They intend to act in the same way. To the consternation of some Labour activists, Shadow Chancellor Gordon Brown has committed Labour for the first two years to the tight spending plans set by Chancellor Kenneth Clarke in his last Budget, targets which some economists and Tory MPs doubt can be met. And Mr Brown has also pledged that Labour would not increase the standard or top rates of income tax for the lifetime of the next Parliament, although opponents have noted he made no commitments on allowances or tax brackets.

Burned by the experience of having the Tories cost their policies in tax terms in 1992, Labour have been determined not to give them another chance to do so. That was why they produced their *Road to the Manifesto* document in the summer of 1996, to be endorsed first by the party conference and then by a referendum of nearly 400,000 party members. The idea was to bind in party activists to a precise programme, preventing policy 'freelancing' and to insulate Labour against a new Tory costing exercise by insisting that only items in that approved manifesto amounted to party policy. This has not stopped the Tories claiming that Labour has £30 billion worth of spending promises.

Labour's biggest problem, acknowledged privately by shadow ministers, is the expectations of their supporters, notably among public sector workers. Mr Blair has insisted that it will be 'fairness not favours' for the trade unions under a Labour government, and Gordon Brown has pledged that the party will not spend what it has not got, seeking to destroy Labour's old 'tax and spend' image. They will have to await the election outcome before they know if they have succeeded in changing public perceptions on that score, and there has been dissension in Labour's ranks over Mr Brown's insistence that no policy commitments can be made without identified savings to pay for them. Plans to redirect Child Benefit for 16-18-year-olds continuing in education caused a particular outcry.

The Labour leadership has been criticised by its potential allies in the Liberal Democrats for its 'safety first' attitude to policy-making, notably over Mr Blair's U-turn last June in promising a referendum on the question of the long-promised tax-raising Scottish Parliament after Tory attacks on the 'Tartan Tax'.

Under Paddy Ashdown's leadership the Liberal Democrats have prospered in this Parliament alongside Labour as Tory policies have attracted more opprobrium. They captured seats at Parliamentary by-elections with huge swings where they were perceived to be the best way of defeating the Tory candidate, and their consistent progress in local politics has seen them overtake the Tories in the town halls. With more than 5,000 councillors and control of 55 councils nationwide, they have become the second party of local government although they have lost ground in national opinion polls.

In 1994, they also won their first seats in the European Parliament, helping to weaken the old 'wasted vote' argument which plagues third parties. And in 1995 they scored a key by-election success at Littleborough and Saddleworth in a bitter contest with Labour. That, and the fact that they outdid Alan Howarth's defection from Tory ranks to Labour by winning over former Tory MPs Emma Nicholson and Peter Thurnham to join them, helped to keep them on the political map and to demonstrate to Labour that they were a force to be reckoned with.

The Liberal Democrats have become more adept at targeting seats. They have built up significant strength in the Southwest of England which makes it likely they will not suffer so badly at this election from the first-past-the-post electoral system. And Mr Ashdown has persuaded most of his party to adopt a strategic switch. Instead of claiming that they occupy a position 'equidistant' between the two major parties, they are now insisting that the first priority is to remove the Conservative government. Although this is causing problems in the party in areas where Labour is the traditional enemy, senior Liberal Democrats are convinced that it would have looked incredible to hold out any suggestion that they might help to restore to power a Conservative administration which had lost its majority after seventeen years.

Liberal Democrat and Labour spokesmen held a joint press conference to fight the government over the Scott inquiry. They united in outrage at 'Tory Cheating' in a key vote on Fisheries in

December. They worked together in the Scottish Constitutional
Convention, although that relationship came under strain after
Mr Blair's change of policy on a Scottish Parliament referendum.
And while the Liberal Democrats, seeking to establish their own
brand image as a party of the 'hard centre', have chided Labour for
failing to spell out more policy detail, they have many approaches in
common, notably on Europe and on constitutional reform.

Mr Blair has made overtures to the Liberal Democrats, offering
discussion on policy questions both before and after the election.
It has not escaped the notice of the Labour Left and the party's
Eurosceptics that if Mr Blair were to be elected with a small majority,
he might need the Liberal Democrats to help him take through parts
of his programme.

Recent years have seen a progressive cultural change in both major
parties. Labour suffered in the early 1980s from the Left-Right
divisions which led to the breakaway of the SDP. The resultant
fracturing of the anti-Conservative vote helped to boost Mrs
Thatcher's majorities. In this Parliament, with the aid to concentration
of having last won an election twenty-two years ago, Labour has for
the most part maintained its discipline, cloaked its divisions (although
they surfaced occasionally over Europe) and sustained a fierce level
of campaigning against the government, notably through Gordon
Brown's efforts on economic policy. The Tories, who used to be the
less ideological, more pragmatic party chiefly concerned with the
getting and holding of power, have become more ideological and less
easily whipped.

The troubles began under Margaret Thatcher. Her Home
Secretary, Douglas Hurd, lost the second reading of a Sunday trading
Bill. The government's majority dropped from 100 to 36 in one Poll
Tax vote. But the problems have intensified since, in a party deeply
divided over Europe. The precarious majority has forced the
government into painful climb-downs, as initially over pit closures and
in its dropping of Post Office privatisation.

It has seen Mr Major forced from his original (pragmatic rather
than romantic) 'Heart of Europe' position to an ever more
Eurosceptical tone, epitomised by his non-cooperation policy with the
European Union in the summer of 1996 over the BSE crisis. It saw the
withdrawal of the Conservative whip from eight backbenchers for
some months.

In the last 18 months of 'phoney war' election run-up the Tories
have constantly sought evidence that they have 'bottomed out'.
As economic circumstances improved, they hoped for a turning point,

first with John Major's leadership election victory, then with better party conferences and tax cutting Budgets. But opinion polls failed to provide evidence of any significant Tory lift-off. The announcement by large numbers of Tory MPs, some comparatively youthful, that they would stand down at the election has shown a lack of faith in the party's prospects.

Now it is down to manifestos and tactics. The Tories are likely to base their approach on the value of experience against a Labour team untried in office, highlighting the Prime Minister's record as a negotiator in Europe and in the slow, painful progress towards peace in Northern Ireland, although the resumption of the IRA's bombing campaign has made that prospect seem a remote one once again.

They will stress the improved economic indicators, low inflation, low interest and mortgage rates and falling unemployment. Their early advertising campaign centred on the theme that it may have hurt, but it had worked. They will point to the progress they have achieved on inward investment in making Britain a deregulated 'Enterprise Centre of Europe', their claims boosted by the huge £1.7 billion investment planned by the Korean firm LG. Labour and the Liberal Democrats will be depicted as 'soft on Europe', unready to fight battles with Brussels and happy to impose increased costs and job losses on British business by taking Britain into the Social Chapter.

But summer 1996 saw a significant strategy change by the Conservatives as they began to acknowledge that it was a 'new Labour' party they were facing under Mr Blair. Labour were no longer to be depicted as socialist wolves in moderates' clothing, nor attacked on the 'Coca Cola strategy', the suggestion that they have trimmed their policies so far that voters are better off voting Conservative for 'the real thing'. Instead, Mr Major has been insisting that while the Conservatives too are fighting on the middle ground of politics, there are sharp differences in approach on Europe, on education, on the unions and on Britain's constitution. The theme, and the advertisements, proclaim: 'New Labour, New Danger'.

The Tories will offer more workers shares schemes, a grammar school in every town which wants one, tougher sentencing policies and new plans to protect the family home and savings when old people have to be taken into expensive residential care. They will argue that in areas like education, the Harriet Harman case has illustrated that it is a case of 'Don't do as I do but do as I say' with Labour.

Labour will play heavily on job insecurity, so countering the government's claims about the economy. They will argue that a Blair administration will offer the country new energy in government and strong leadership with a sense of purpose both at home and in Europe. They will insist that they have the policies on education and training to equip Britain for the employment world of the 21st century, and that they will strip out bureaucracy from the health service.

They will offer more co-operation with Europe and a partnership with industry in place of the 'market rules' philosophy of the Conservatives, arguing that the BSE crisis is evidence of a misplaced faith in deregulation, weak leadership, and the divided Tories' lack of clout in Europe, and they will spell out the vision of a 'stakeholder society' in which workers will be more involved with the fortunes of their employers.

Harking back to the 'sleaze factor' and the question of standards in public life, Labour will too set out its stall on constitutional reform, including the Scottish Parliament, a Welsh Assembly, reform of the House of Lords and a Freedom of Information Act, saying that the way the country is governed has to be altered as well as the policies.

The preliminary *Road to the Manifesto* document set out five key pledges: cutting class sizes to 30 for 5, 6 and 7-year-olds, cutting NHS waiting lists by saving £100 million on red tape, fast-track punishment for persistent young offenders by halving the time from arrest to sentencing, getting 250,000 youngsters off benefits and into work with funds raised from a 'windfall tax' on privatised utilities, and keeping down inflation and interest rates with tough rules on government spending and borrowing.

The Liberal Democrats for their part will emphasise education and their willingness to raise extra funds for it by increasing income tax. Their leader insists that taxation is the price of a civilised society and that the other parties are being dishonest in presenting their programmes without clear enough price tags.

The final spat of the pre-campaign period put the Liberal Democrats in high dudgeon. Mr Major's offer of a TV debate with Tony Blair – a whole new dimension for a British general election – risked a legal and political minefield by suggesting that the Liberal Democrat and Nationalist party leaders should be excluded.

Two days before calling the election, during the Conservative Central Council Meeting in Bath on March 15th, Mr Major tackled head-on the 'Time for a Change' argument which Tory strategists acknowledge as their biggest handicap, saying that it would not be safe to change the country's economic management or to accept the changes in the constitution and in European policy proposed by his

opponents. He signalled strongly that he would reject the nostrums
of the right and fight on the centre ground of British politics, saying
that his kind of Conservatism was about helping those who did not
have a decent home or education or job – turning the 'have-nots
into haves'.

One final point as this campaign begins – all parties will insist that
they will not descend to muck-raking, personal attacks and 'negative
campaigning'. Almost certainly, by the end of the campaign, all of
them will. Whoever emerges the winner is likely to inherit a
comparatively healthy economy and a plateload of problems. There
are doubts about the achievability of the spending limits set out by
Kenneth Clarke and endorsed by Gordon Brown, which could force a
Government of any complexion to raise taxes, and which could prove
a severe test of a new administration under pressure to be seen
making a difference in fields like health and education and, in
Labour's case, sharply prodded by public sector unions.

Within weeks the new government will face crucial negotiations
on Europe's future as the Amsterdam Summit brings to a climax the
Inter-Governmental Conference on EU institutions, negotiations
which would restore to fever pitch the tensions within the party if it is
a Tory Government. And by the end of the year the new Government
will have to decide whether or not Britain should participate in the
first wave of a Single European Currency if it starts on time.
A Conservative Government, most observers agree would find it
politically impossible to take Britain in within the lifetime of the next
Parliament. But Labour's European splits would start to show too
were a Blair Government to make the attempt.

As for the party which loses the election, if it is the Conservatives
who go down, a leadership contest and a struggle for the soul of the
party seems inevitable. If it were to be Labour waking up to a fifth
election defeat after all the hopes invested in the 'new Labour' remake
of the party then the potential convulsions are almost unimaginable.

HOW YOUR VOTE COUNTS

THE GUIDE TO POLLING DAY AND RESULTS NIGHT

HOW YOUR VOTE COUNTS

BOUNDARIES, POLLS AND CHICKEN RUNS

Bill Bush

Bill Bush is Director of Research, BBC News. He has been Head of the BBC's Political Research Unit since 1989, and was formerly a local government officer.

Because people move around, some constituencies shrink, others grow. By 1992 the largest constituency in the UK was The Wrekin with 106,000 voters, while the smallest was Western Isles. The smallest mainland electorate was just over 31,000 in Caithness & Sutherland. Every ten years or so, therefore, the Parliamentary boundaries have to be changed, and 1997 sees a new political map of the UK being used for the new Parliament.

All sorts of things flow from the redrawing of the map. Apart from anything else, the next House of Commons will be bigger, growing from 651 to 659 MPs and over 400 of the seats fought in 1992 have new boundaries. Changed seats often get new names, but, more importantly, they often change their political nature. Usually the introduction of new boundaries helps the Conservative party. Expanding areas, often prosperous and often in the suburbs, are normally filled with Conservative voters. But this time the changes have not been as helpful as the Tory party initially hoped.

The language of politics also needs to change. To understand where the marginal seats are, to know which of the changed seats are safe and for which party, we have to re-run the 1992 election. So, two academics have helped us by producing 'notional' results for last time round which will give us a proper yardstick for this election*. How different would the result have been (Table 1)?

TABLE 1: HOW THE PARTIES STAND – NOTIONALLY AND ACTUALLY

	NOTIONAL	ACTUAL	DIFFERENCE
Conservative	343	336	+7
Labour	273	271	+2
Liberal Democrat	18	20	-2
Plaid Cymru	4	4	-
SNP	3	3	-
Democratic Unionist	4	3	+1
Ulster Unionist	9	9	-
SDLP	4	4	-
Independent Unionist	1	1	-
TOTAL SEATS	659	651	+8
Seats required for overall majority	330	326	
Conservative overall majority	27	21	+6
Conservative	70	65	+5

At the national level there does not seem to be that much difference. The Tory majority would have been a bit bigger, Labour's task is a bit harder. Under the old boundaries the Conservatives' lead over Labour was 7.5 per cent of the popular vote, but that gave them a majority of only 21 seats. A swing to Labour of only 0.5 per cent would have deprived the Tories of the 11 seats needed to stop them from having a majority. With the new boundaries their majority of 27 would disappear with a swing of 0.8 per cent and a loss of 14 seats. But that small change in the overall politics disguises the big changes on the ground. Of the existing 651 seats in Parliament, nearly two-thirds have been changed in a significant way. Some even look as if they would have been won by a different party – so watch out on election night for oddities (Table 2). This means that if the Conservatives win Ilford South on election day then we will regard this as a 'Conservative hold' even though the seat with the same name was won by Labour in 1992. Same seat name, different voters.

* A full analysis of the impact of the boundary changes is provided in the *Media Guide to the New Parliamentary Constituencies* (available from BBC Newsline on 0181 752 7942)

TABLE 2: NOTIONALLY DIFFERENT WINNING PARTY (SAME CONSTITUENCY NAME)

	1992 RESULTS	NOTIONAL RESULTS
Ayr	Conservative	Labour
Bolton North East	Conservative	Labour
Bristol North West	Conservative	Labour
Lincoln	Conservative	Labour
Slough	Conservative	Labour
Southampton Test	Conservative	Labour
Staffordshire Moorlands	Conservative	Labour
Ilford South	Labour	Conservative
Kingswood	Labour	Conservative
Warrington South	Labour	Conservative
Gordon	LibDem	Conservative

Adding to the confusion is the change in many of the constituency names that people have got used to. This can happen because an old name has been kept but the new seat looks very different. For example, there is an old seat called Arundel, and a new seat called Arundel and South Downs. Is it the same place? Not really, because most of old Arundel is now in a different new seat called Bognor Regis and Littlehampton, while most of the new Arundel comes from the old seat of Horsham. In Glasgow the old seat of Hillhead makes up 85 per cent of a new seat. Enough to keep the old name? No, it is now called Glasgow Kelvin.

In London there is one of the longest and perhaps most misleading new names. The old seat of Westminster North disappears. Most finds its way to the new seat of Regents Park and Kensington North. What makes this strange is that there are animals but few voters in Regents Park, and most of the voters in the new seat live in Paddington, which does not even get a mention!

Candidates now have to work hard to tell people about the changes. Many have worked hard for years to build local support, so they will want to make sure that no-one is confused if there has been a change. Of course, some MPs from the old Parliament have decided that the changes give them a chance to move, especially if their old seat looks less comfortable.

It's given their opponents the opportunity to deride them – sometimes unfairly – for having joined what's been dubbed 'the chicken run' of fleeing MPs seeking less competitive pastures.

The most politically significant mover is probably David Amess, who famously won Basildon in 1992. He's off now in search of safer Essex votes in Southend East. Also seeking safer territory are Peter Bottomley (Eltham) who will stand in Worthing West; Nick Hawkins

(Blackpool South) standing in Surrey Heath; and Nicholas Soames (Crawley) standing in Sussex Mid. All of the seats that these MPs will be contesting are notionally safer than and unconnected with the seats they were elected for in 1992.

A few Conservative MPs have seen the seats they won in 1992 become notionally Labour-held and have consequently decided to contest other seats unconnected with their original seats. John Watts (Slough) will be standing in Reading East, and Sir George Young (Ealing Acton) will be contesting Hampshire North West.

Some particularly high-profile MPs have left the seats they contested in 1992 to stand in safer places which have some connection with their old seats. Social Security Secretary Peter Lilley will be standing in Hitchen & Harpenden, 44 per cent of which used to be in his old St Albans seat. Conservative Party Chairman Brian Mawhinney has moved to Cambridgeshire North West, 42 per cent of which was in his Peterborough constituency. Health Secretary Stephen Dorrell will be standing in the new seat of Charnwood, under a third of which is made up of his old Loughborough seat. Elsewhere, David Evennett is to stand in Bexleyheath & Crayford, 39 per cent of which used to be in his old Erith & Crayford seat, Andrew Rowe is to contest Faversham & Kent Mid which includes less than a third of his old Kent Mid seat, and Peter Luff will be standing in Worcestershire Mid, which includes less than one-eighth of his old Worcester seat.

The reduction in the number of constituencies in some parts of the country has forced some MPs, who have failed to be selected for seats which succeeded their old ones, to move elsewhere. James Arbuthnot (Wanstead & Woodford) will stand in Hampshire North East, Eric Forth (Worcestershire Mid) will stand in Bromley & Chislehurst, and, after a long and public search for a seat, the former Chancellor, Norman Lamont (Kingston upon Thames) is contesting Harrogate & Knaresborough.

Five MPs have failed to be selected for any constituencies. One of them, Sir John Wheeler (Westminster North) is a minister; the others in this unfortunate predicament are Terry Dicks (Hayes & Harlington), Sir Winston Churchill (Daveyhulme), Michael Stephen (Shoreham) and Cyril Townsend (Bexleyheath).

'IF I WAS GOING TO DUBLIN, I WOULDN'T START FROM HERE'

The parties start this campaign in an odd circumstance: whoever wins will have to break a record to do so.

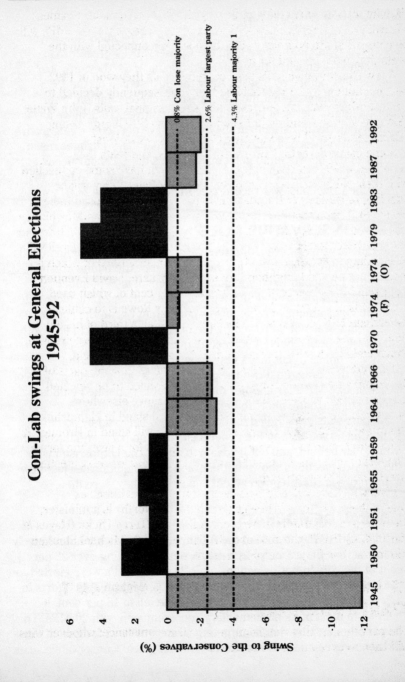

Con-Lab swings at General Elections 1945-92

Swing to the Conservatives (%)

0.8% Con lose majority
2.6% Labour largest party
4.3% Labour majority 1

1945 1950 1951 1955 1959 1964 1966 1970 1974 (F) 1974 (O) 1979 1983 1987 1992

LABOUR'S MOUNTAIN

In the long run of peacetime elections since 1945 Labour has never secured a swing in the vote from the Conservatives greater than 3 per cent – even when they managed that, in 1964, they only just squeaked to victory by 5 seats. After the dust settled on the 1992 results, it transpired that the Labour party had one million fewer votes, a huge 7 per cent behind the Conservatives. To achieve an overall majority in Parliament they would have needed a swing from the Conservatives of 4.1 per cent. And the boundary changes made things a little bit worse: to get a majority this time, Labour needs a swing of 4.3 per cent. So, to win outright they are going to have to break their own post-war record (see the chart on page 243).

THE CONSERVATIVE HOLE

The Conservatives have a different record to break. The opinion polls have been universally bleak for them ever since the pound crashed out of the European Exchange Rate Mechanism in September 1992. This single dramatic incident seems to have convinced the electorate that the government were no longer competent to run the economy. This feeling was not improved by the need to raise taxes to deal with the growing public debt; it seemed to many to be a breach of an election promise to cut taxes year on year. Nor was it just the economy that dragged down the government's ratings – allegations of sleaze as one MP after another ran into trouble generated endless tabloid stories, none likely to help them in the polls.

No party has ever trailed in the polls for so long and by so much. If the Conservatives win the general election, no party will have come from so far behind, and left it so late to do so. The comparison with the last two elections shown in the graph opposite indicates just how much more adrift the government is now than they were then.

LIBERAL DEMOCRATS

In 1983 and 1987, the vote of the Alliance parties was spread relatively evenly across the country. As a result, despite winning over 23 per cent of the vote in both elections, only 23 and 22 MPs were elected to the House of Commons. In 1992 the party concentrated its efforts in key seats, and although its share of the vote fell to 18 per cent, it held on to most of its parliamentary representation with 20 MPs. The party will be hoping that its targeting strategy will work again at the forthcoming election. There are 12 notionally held Conservative seats

Conservative opinion poll lead in run-up to elections

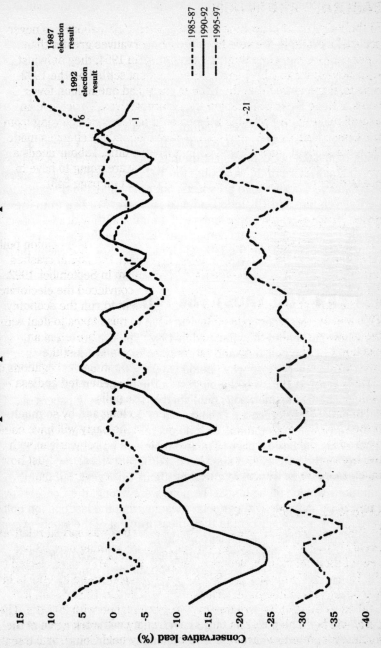

- - - - - 1985-87
——— 1990-92
—·—·— 1995-97

* 1987 election result
* 1992 election result

6
-1
-21

Conservative lead (%)

15
10
5
0
-5
-10
-15
-20
-25
-30
-35
-40

Source: MORI

the party is concentrating on which would be gained by them on a swing of less than 5 per cent.

OTHER PARTIES

This election will be the first general election to be contested by the Referendum Party and UK Independence Party. According to polls in the early part of 1997, the parties have the support of around 1 per cent of voters (Gallup/*Daily Telegraph*, 7 February), with one poll showing support for the Referendum Party rising to 2 per cent (ICM/*Guardian*, 4 March). Given that the Conservatives need a swing of just 0.8 per cent against them to lose their overall majority, even a small share of the vote (like the 1–2 per cent the polls suggest) may damage Conservative prospects, but only if most of the votes for the Referendum and UK Independence parties are drawn from the Tories. Their electoral importance will diminish if they draw support equally from all parties, and some analysts believe they will take many protest votes from the Liberal Democrats. For discussion on the position in Scotland and Wales, see pages 159-78.

BUT CAN YOU TRUST THE POLLS?

Labour's electoral mountain is measured in real votes – we really do know how far behind they finished in 1992. The Conservative hole is measured by the pollsters, and as every politician knows the pollsters 'got it wrong' in 1992, so why should we trust them now?

Their error in 1992 was the biggest in the history of British opinion polling. The five opinion polls published in the morning papers of election day 1992 forecast a Labour lead of 0.8 per cent, enough to ensure a House of Commons with no overall majority but where Labour was the largest party. The two main exit polls broadcast that evening as the polls closed suggested a different story, that it was the Conservatives who were ahead by about 4 per cent, but that the Commons would still be hung. The polls were wrong: the Conservative lead was actually over 7.5 per cent, meaning that the last opinion polls were out by over 8 per cent in their measurement of the gap between the two main parties (see chart opposite).

Why were the pollsters so wrong? The pollsters' own professional body, the Market Research Society (MRS), held an inquiry to see why the error happened. The inquiry came up with three likely causes of the problem:

1. Late Swing The polls can only report what people tell them at the time they were interviewed, so if some change their mind, or if the

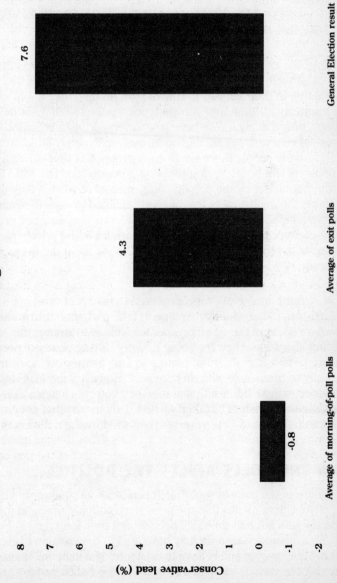

How Wrong Were the Polls?

Conservative lead (%)

8 7 6 5 4 3 2 1 0 -1 -2

-0.8 — Average of morning-of-poll polls

4.3 — Average of exit polls

7.6 — General Election result

Source: The Opinion Polls and the 1992 General Election (Market Research Society)

'don't knows' come down more for one party than another, then the
polls cannot be expected accurately to predict the future. It does seem
as if there was a bit of a shift in opinion between the hours of the
fieldwork (mainly Tuesday and Wednesday before polling day) and
the hours of voting (from 7 a.m. to 10 p.m. on Thursday 9 April).
However, this shift in opinion was only small, perhaps explaining
1 or 2 per cent of the error at most.

2. *Wrong Quotas* When pollsters send their interviewers into the field
they traditionally set quotas for each type of voter that they wanted
represented in their survey. If they did not do this, they might end up
with too many or too few of certain types – not enough trade unionists
perhaps, or too many low-income pensioners, or too few business
people. Of course, to work, this quota system depends on knowing
just how many people there are in each group. Get that wrong and
the pollsters will be surveying the wrong population. The MRS found
that the quotas set by the polling companies were wrong; they tended
to include too many voters from Labour-inclined groups (like council
tenants and manual workers) and too few from Tory-inclined groups
(like owner-occupiers and white-collar workers in the private sector).
This mistake probably explains another 2 per cent in the overall 8 per
cent error.

3. *The Refusal Rate* Not everyone asked to take part in an opinion
poll says 'yes'. Many politely decline to take part at all, and some who
do answer some of the questions politely refuse to answer the
question about how they are going to vote. Having plenty of people
refusing to take part does not matter so long as they are no different
politically to the people who do take part. However, the MRS Inquiry
found increasing evidence that some Tory voters are more likely to
be shy than supporters of other parties. This means that not enough
Tories were included in the figures published by the pollsters in 1992.

HOW THE POLLS AFFECT THE POLITICS...

The failure of the polls to spot that Tories were more likely to be shy
than other voters means that the polls were not only wrong at the time
of the election but had probably been wrong for a long time before as
well. This misunderstanding may have lead to the creation of election
myths. Many people still believe that Labour 'lost it' in the campaign.
They point to various campaign efforts like the Smith Budget (the tax

and spend plans launched right at the start), Jennifer's Ear (the health row about a young girl used in a Labour election broadcast) and the Sheffield rally (a big triumphal rally a week before polling day), and say that these were the events that Labour mishandled while John Major's use of the soapbox is quoted as the Tory master stroke.
As a result they say voters swung conclusively in the four weeks of the campaign and the Tories won the election. This theory is as wrong as can be. The polls were wrong on polling day, were wrong in the weeks and months before, and if they had been correct they would have shown the Tories consistently 5–9 per cent ahead of Labour for a year or more before the election took place.

There were clues that the polls might not have been telling an exact story. Buried away in the other questions were two findings that look odd in polls that put Labour ahead – the Tories had consistent leads before the 1992 election on which party would be the best to deal with the economy, and on which party leader would make the best Prime Minister (see the graphs on pages 250-1).

Perhaps we should have spent less time on the headline figure of voting intention and looked a bit more below the surface.

ADJUSTING THE POLLS

The poll companies have responded to their problems in 1992 by introducing adjustments to their methods. They have different approaches, but their objective is the same; to make sure that their sample accurately reflects opinion in the electorate.

Some companies are now using telephone polls where before they conducted polls at home or in the street. They argue that phone ownership is now so widespread that they are much more likely to be able to contact a proper cross-section of British society via the phone than if they try to hit quotas by trying face-to-face interviews. There is also an argument that voters might be less shy on the phone as they feel it gives them more anonymity than when confronted by a pollster with a clipboard.

There are technical adjustments too – for example, following detailed analysis of their post-1992 election recall survey, ICM assume that 60 per cent of those who say they 'don't know' which way they will vote, will return to the party they say they voted for in 1992; while NOP allocate the 'don't knows' according to which party they say they identify most closely with or which has the best policies on the economy.

Best party to manage the economy 1990-9

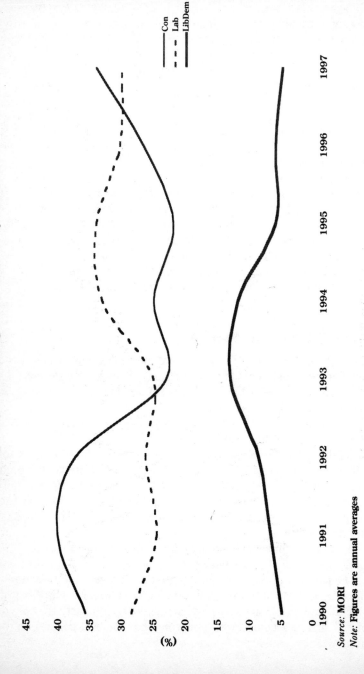

Con
Lab
LibDem

Source: MORI
Note: Figures are annual averages

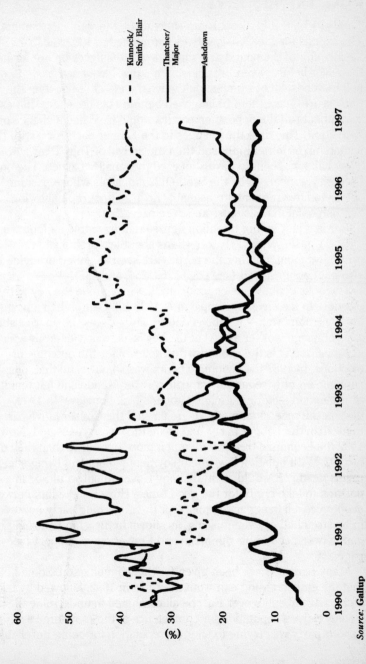

Best Prime Minister 1990-97

Kinnock/ Smith/ Blair

Thatcher/ Major

Ashdown

Source: Gallup

Note: Methodology changed in January 1997

POLL TRENDS 1992-1997

The polls have told a consistent story throughout this Parliament. The ratings for the Conservatives plummeted in 1992 with the devaluation of the pound and stayed lower than ever before for longer than ever before. Even the adjustments that have been made to the poll methods, all of which should have the effect of boosting the Tory score, leave them trailing well behind (see opposite). In past Parliaments all the opposition parties would have had a chance of benefiting. This time the changes to the Labour party, first with the leadership of John Smith, and then the arrival of Tony Blair and 'New Labour', seem to have squeezed the smaller parties. The one exception appears to be the Scottish Nationalists whose position seems to have remained reasonably firm, as the graph showing Scottish opinion polls illustrates (see page 254).

Nor is it just Voting Intention figures that have told a gloomy story for the Conservatives. The questions about leadership and the economy, about whether the parties are seen as united or divided, also put Labour ahead (see pages 250, 251, and 255).

The polls contain one conundrum that may prove the key to the election. In his election campaign in 1992 Bill Clinton had a poster on his 'war room' wall – 'it's the economy, stupid' – as the answer should any campaign worker ask what the key issue was. Generally speaking, in peacetime, it is the economy that determines the outcome of elections. In 1987 the economic boom was so powerful that, despite running a highly regarded campaign, Peter Mandelson felt that it was the 'feelgood factor' that made Labour's task hopeless. In 1992, despite the recession, many voters trusted the Conservative party more than the Labour party, and again they were re-elected. Now in 1997 the economic trends look much more optimistic than they did in 1992. With inflation low, unemployment falling, and living standards rising steadily it would seem that any Government would be in a position to take credit for the good times. However the link between economic well-being and support for the governing party now seems to be stretched or even missing, as shown in the graph showing the gap between economic optimism and Conservative support (see page 256).

Many reasons have been given for this phenomenon. Some believe that the embarrassing exit from the ERM in 1992, followed by tax increases and splits over Europe all combined to undermine the Conservatives' reputation for competence at the same time as the Labour party was trying to shed its reputation for being unreliable

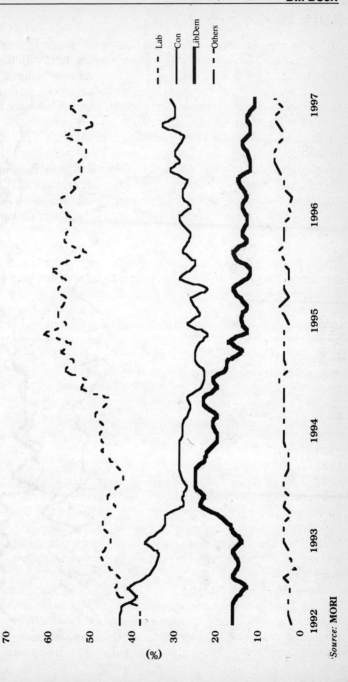

Voting Intention 1992-97

Lab
Con
LibDem
Others

Source: MORI

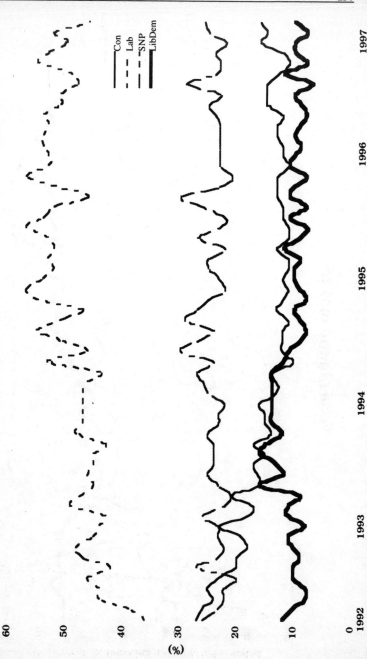

Opinion Polls 1992-97
Scotland

Con
Lab
SNP
LibDem

(%)

60
50
40
30
20
10
0

1992 1993 1994 1995 1996 1997

Source: System 3

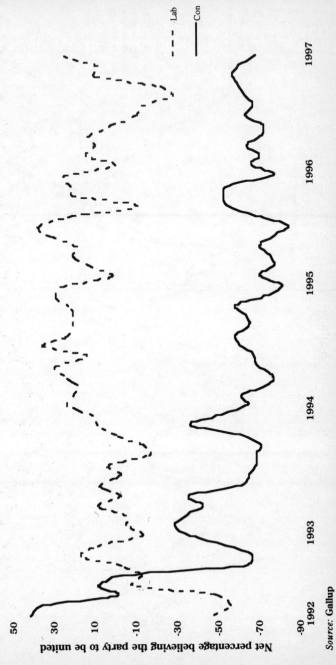

Party unity 1992-97

Lab

Con

Net percentage believing the party to be united

Source: Gallup

Question: 'Do you think that the Labour/Conservative Party is united or divided at the present time?'

The 'Feelgood Factor' and Conservative poll lead 1980 - 1997

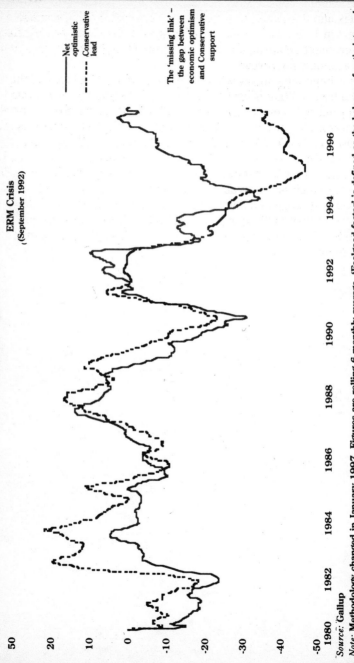

ERM Crisis
((September 1992)

— Net optimistic
--- Conservative lead

The 'missing link' – the gap between economic optimism and Conservative support

Source: Gallup

Note: Methodology changed in January 1997. Figures are rolling 6-monthly average. 'Feelgood factor' is defined as the balance of optimists and pessimists in hopes for the immediate financial future of individuals on tax and the economy. It may be, others add, that in persuading voters in 1992 that the recession was caused by forces beyond the government's control, it has proved difficult to get the credit when the economy improves.

It is impossible to say what the causes are for this break in the usual trends. What is certain is that the Conservatives will strain every nerve to convince voters that they deserve the credit for the recovery. They will hope that buried away in the polling figures are millions of 'Don't Knows' waiting to make their minds up: Don't Knows, who, when reminded of the strengthening economy – and constantly warned that even 'new' Labour would jeopardise it – will return to their previous allegiance. What is equally certain is that Labour's strategy of doing nothing which could 'frighten the horses' will mean their tactics pin-point the 'soft' voters – people the parties believe, whatever the polls say, will be 'persuadable' during the rough and tumble of a bare-knuckle campaign.

HOW YOUR VOTE COUNTS

SWINGS AND ROUNDABOUTS

Peter Snow

Peter Snow is a presenter for BBC 2's 'Newsnight' programme. From 1962 to 1979 he worked for ITN as a newscaster, followed by appointments as Diplomatic Correspondent and Defence Correspondent. He joined the BBC as a 'Newsnight' presenter in 1979 and has also worked on General Election and By-Election programmes, where his presentation of election swings have become an institution.

I make no apology for being an enthusiast for election nights. In the space of just a few hours we have revealed to us, minute by minute, the sharpening contours of the political landscape we will be faced with for the next few years. And this election will do more than make history. It is likely to make records too. If John Major wins, he will have equalled the achievement of the Tory government that won five successive elections between 1807 and 1828. And, as Bill Bush points out in the previous chapter, if Mr Blair wins outright, he will almost certainly have achieved a Labour swing greater than any since Clement Attlee's huge 12 per cent swing in 1945. Some believe he may even better that. But we are not just looking for electoral records this time: we are hoping to break records of our own for speed, colour and clarity of analysis too.

The computer which calculates the ups and downs of the vote and generates our graphic designs will have a brain that will work 20 times faster than the one used for the last election. So this time, for example, we will actually be flying over the 'battleground' to witness the opposition's attack on the Tories, and our swingometer will display the swing in each seat within a split second of the returning officer's announcement of the outcome.

THE BATTLEGROUND

Our main focus will be on the seats where the opposition believe they
are within reach of victory – the marginal seats where every British
election is decided. We have selected 115 seats won – or estimated
on the new boundaries to have been won – by the Conservatives in
April 1992 (see pages 260-1). This great wall of blue seats will be the
Government's defensive rampart – the territory they *have* to hold if
they are to survive, and it is the changing colour of this battleground
that will provide us with the sharpest measure of the Tories' success
or failure in holding off their opponents. We will rank these
Conservative outposts, their key marginals, as if they were a great
staircase of higher and higher blue steps – beginning with the lowest
of all, the Vale of Glamorgan with its tiny majority of 19. That first step
will be the easiest of all for the opposition to mount: it will turn red if
Labour win it, yellow if the victor is Liberal Democrat. Up and up will
go the range of Conservative seats until we reach Salisbury, the
115th most vulnerable seat with a Liberal Democrat in second place
last time. In most of them Labour are the closest challengers to the
Tories; in about a quarter of them the Liberal Democrats, Plaid Cymru
or the Scottish Nationalists were second last time. John Major can
afford to lose no more than 13 of these 115 seats if he is to survive
with an overall majority in the new Parliament.

LABOUR'S TARGETS

But if the battleground is the best measure of the Conservative
defence – the *targets* will show us how effective the opposition's
attack turns out to be. We have selected the 100 best chances for
Labour – in which Tony Blair's bid to end more than a decade and a
half of Conservative rule will be decided (see pages 263-4). Of these,
96 are defended by the Conservatives, three of them by Liberal
Democrats (Inverness East, Nairn and Lochaber, where Sir Russell
Johnston, the Liberal Democrat who has staved off attacks from all
comers for three decades, is now retiring; Rochdale, where Liz
Lynne's 1,839 majority has been slimmed down by the boundary
changes, we estimate, to 128; and Southwark North and Bermondsey,
where the Liberal Democrat Simon Hughes has a far more comfortable
7,269) and one – Ceredigion – held by Plaid Cymru, the Welsh
Nationalist party.

The map of Britain that viewers will see on election night will rank
these 100 Labour target seats by the scale of the challenge each of
them presents to Labour. The higher the pile of votes that separated

CONSERVATIVE SEATS BEING DEFENDED

NUMBER	CONSTITUENCY	NOTIONAL MAJORITY	SWING TO GAIN	2ND PLACED PARTY
1	Vale of Glamorgan	19	0.03	Labour
2	Hayes & Harlington	44	0.10	Labour
3	Halesowen & Rowley Regis	125	0.23	Labour
4	Croydon North	160	0.28	Labour
5	Brecon & Radnorshire	130	0.29	Liberal Democrat
6	Portsmouth South	242	0.45	Liberal Democrat
7	Stirling	236	0.56	Labour
8	Corby	342	0.60	Labour
9	Blackpool South	394	0.67	Labour
10	Oldham East & Saddleworth	559	0.98	Liberal Democrat
11	Luton South	532	1.03	Labour
12	Edmonton	593	1.24	Labour
13	Bury South	728	1.34	Labour
14	Preseli Pembrokeshire	603	1.38	Labour
15	Dover	860	1.49	Labour
16	Leicestershire North West	866	1.59	Labour
17	Batley & Spen	845	1.66	Labour
18	Hazel Grove	929	1.70	Liberal Democrat
19	Plymouth Sutton	1060	2.01	Labour
20	Amber Valley	1283	2.10	Labour
21	Isle of Wight	1827	2.29	Liberal Democrat
22	Conwy	995	2.36	Liberal Democrat
23	Middlesbrough South & Cleveland East	1401	2.49	Labour
24	Brentford & Isleworth	1675	2.83	Labour
25	St Ives	1645	2.88	Liberal Democrat
26	Derbyshire South	1947	3.08	Labour
27	Harlow	1687	3.16	Labour
28	Mitcham & Morden	1734	3.39	Labour
29	Crawley	1890	3.65	Labour
30	Eltham	1780	3.84	Labour
31	Norwich North	2270	3.92	Labour
32	Chester, City of	2360	4.12	Labour
33	Chorley	2524	4.16	Labour
34	Basildon	2646	4.37	Labour
35	Ilford South	2530	4.81	Labour
36	Warrington South	2753	4.89	Labour
37	Exeter	3064	4.91	Labour
38	Vale of Clwyd	2177	4.98	Labour
39	Brighton Pavilion	2530	5.06	Labour
40	Coventry South	2904	5.10	Labour
41	Kingswood	3340	5.17	Labour
42	Taunton	3336	5.19	Liberal Democrat
43	Stevenage	2919	5.32	Labour
44	Devon West & Torridge	3271	5.42	Liberal Democrat
45	Southport	3063	5.52	Liberal Democrat
46	Galloway & Upper Nithsdale	2400	5.55	Scottish National Party
47	Worcester	2947	5.59	Labour
48	Elmet	3261	5.60	Labour
49	Hereford	3154	5.65	Liberal Democrate
50	Falmouth & Camborne	3267	5.70	Liberal Democrat
51	Perth	2726	6.07	Scottish National Party
52	Cardiff North	2969	6.22	Labour
53	Monmouth	3204	6.29	Labour
54	Tynemouth	3529	6.34	Labour
55	Keighley	3596	6.56	Labour
56	Redditch	3287	6.75	Labour
57	Loughborough	3492	6.98	Labour

CONSERVATIVE SEATS BEING DEFENDED

NUMBER	CONSTITUENCY	NOTIONAL MAJORITY	SWING TO GAIN	2ND PLACED PARTY
58	Burton	4127	6.99	Labour
59	Somerton & Frome	4251	7.12	Liberal Democrat
60	Northampton North	4067	7.17	Labour
61	Waveney	4376	7.25	Labour
62	Derby North	4453	7.55	Labour
63	Tayside North	3439	7.58	SNP
64	Birmingham Hall Green	3665	7.80	Labour
65	Calder Valley	4878	7.98	Labour
66	High Peak	4818	8.04	Labour
67	Bury North	4764	8.08	Labour
68	Bolton West	4281	8.23	Labour
69	Edinburgh West	4291	8.32	Liberal Democrat
70	Leeds North East	4244	8.57	Labour
71	Gloucester	5407	8.71	Labour
72	Erewash	5723	9.01	Labour
73	Bedford	4545	9.03	Labour
74	Edinburgh Pentlands	4148	9.03	Labour
75	Battersea	4781	9.12	Labour
76	Milton Keynes South West	4687	9.16	Labour
77	Gravesham	5368	9.17	Labour
78	Colchester	5268	9.35	Liberal Democrat
79	Wolverhampton South West	4966	9.43	Labour
80	Stockton South	4896	9.44	Labour
81	Weston-Super-Mare	5372	9.54	Liberal Democrat
82	Birmingham Edgbaston	5056	9.94	Labour
83	Great Yarmouth	5309	9.98	Labour
84	Torbay	5787	10.08	Liberal Democrat
85	Tamworth	5405	10.18	Labour
86	Twickenham	6121	10.23	Liberal Democrat
87	Oxford West & Abingdon	6222	10.41	Liberal Democrat
88	Aberdeenshire West & Kincardine	4437	10.48	Liberal Democrat
89	Stourbridge	5388	10.56	Labour
90	Aberdeen South	4725	10.71	Liberal Democrat
91	Wells	6649	11.51	Liberal Democrat
92	Welwyn Hatfield	6583	11.53	Labour
93	Peterborough	6254	11.70	Labour
94	Eastbourne	6809	11.82	Liberal Democrat
95	Cleethorpes	6413	12.02	Labour
96	Dorset Mid & Poole North	6054	12.13	Liberal Democrat
97	Blackpool North & Fleetwood	7276	12.14	Labour
98	Lewes	6337	12.21	Liberal Democrat
99	Colne Valley	7225	12.23	Labour
100	Hastings & Rye	6634	12.34	Liberal Democrat
101	Cornwall South East	7704	12.84	Liberal Democrat
102	Hammersmith & Fulham	7174	13.00	Labour
103	Stafford	7235	13.14	Labour
104	Dumfries	6766	13.50	Labour
105	Luton North	7357	14.04	Labour
106	Watford	8263	14.12	Labour
107	Brigg & Goole	7241	14.15	Labour
108	Richmond Park	8384	14.20	Liberal Democrat
109	Ribble Valley	8629	14.34	Liberal Democrat
110	Newark	8229	14.56	Labour
111	Pudsey	8372	14.59	Labour
112	Dorset West	8011	14.67	Liberal Democrat
113	Dartford	8314	14.68	Labour
114	Winchester	9318	14.77	Liberal Democrat
115	Salisbury	8973	14.79	Liberal Democrat

Labour from victory last time, the higher the pillar representing each seat on the map. So, in Stirling for example, Michael Forsyth the Conservative Secretary of State for Scotland, has a tiny pile of only 236 votes separating him from Labour; even smaller, of course, is the Vale of Glamorgan – seat Number 1 in our Battleground – the most vulnerable of all the Tory heights for Labour to conquer. Those two should be easy targets for Mr Blair's Labour party. Malcolm Rifkind's Edinburgh Pentlands seat (majority 4,148) will be more difficult. And if Portsmouth North, the tallest of the 100 pillars of blue on the map, where the Tories are estimated to have been 8,758 votes ahead last time, flares red for Labour, then Mr Blair will be comfortably home.

Just as important, notice the way Labour's targets are concentrated mainly into three groups; 26 of them are clustered around Manchester, Bradford and Leeds in the North. Labour's vote has held up pretty well in the North throughout the long Tory reign – except in the year of Labour's disastrous collapse in 1983, when their vote slipped below the Conservatives for the first time in recent memory. But now cast your eye down to the Midlands, London and the Southeast, where no fewer than 56 of those 100 Labour seats are – all but Simon Hughes' seat held by the Tories. This is where Labour has to break through if it is to win, in seats where the Tories' successful wooing of the middle class and skilled working class in the 1980s built up an enduring set of strongholds in the city suburbs and county towns. Most of these survived Labour's assault even in the economic gloom year of 1992. If the Conservatives can hold these clusters of seats in a semi-circle around Derby in the East Midlands and the fringes of Birmingham and Wolverhampton in the West Midlands, around Bedford, Luton and Hertford in the Home Counties, and in west and southwest London, then they could deny Labour victory for the fifth time in succession.

Watch one seat, Gravesham, on the eastern edge of London, in particular. It and its predecessor seat, Gravesend, has been a bellwether ever since 1951, falling to the party that has formed the government each time. If the Conservatives hold Gravesham and it broadly reflects the national position, Mr Major should not need the removal van in Downing Street next day.

Although Labour's attack fell short of victory in the south and Midlands in 1992, this was where the party bounced back better than anywhere else in the country. And if the opinion polls are anywhere near right, that trend has continued since 1992 – reflecting the sense of job insecurity that has now spread right across the country and all the income brackets as well. On election night we will see each seat

LABOUR TARGET SEATS

TARGET NUMBER	CONSTITUENCY	HELD BY	SWING TO GAIN
1	Vale of Glamorgan	Conservative	0.02
2	Hayes & Harlington	Conservative	0.05
3	Halesowen & Rowley Regis	Conservative	0.12
4	Rochdale	Liberal Democrat	0.12
5	Croydon North	Conservative	0.13
6	Stirling	Conservative	0.28
7	Corby	Conservative	0.31
8	Blackpool South	Conservative	0.34
9	Luton South	Conservative	0.52
10	Edmonton	Conservative	0.63
11	Bury South	Conservative	0.67
12	Preseli Pembrokeshire	Conservative	0.69
13	Dover	Conservative	0.75
14	Leicestershire North West	Conservative	0.79
15	Batley & Spen	Conservative	0.83
16	Plymouth Sutton	Conservative	1.01
17	Amber Valley	Conservative	1.06
18	Middlesbrough South & Cleveland East	Conservative	1.25
19	Brentford & Isleworth	Conservative	1.42
20	Derbyshire South	Conservative	1.54
21	Harlow	Conservative	1.58
22	Mitcham & Morden	Conservative	1.70
23	Crawley	Conservative	1.83
24	Eltham	Conservative	1.92
25	Inverness East, Nairn & Lochaber	Liberal Democrat	1.92
26	Norwich North	Conservative	1.96
27	Chester, City of	Conservative	2.06
28	Chorley	Conservative	2.08
29	Basildon	Conservative	2.19
30	Ilford South	Conservative	2.41
31	Warrington South	Conservative	2.45
32	Exeter	Conservative	2.46
33	Vale of Clwyd	Conservative	2.49
34	Brighton Pavilion	Conservative	2.53
35	Coventry South	Conservative	2.55
36	Kingswood	Conservative	2.59
37	Stevenage	Conservative	2.66
38	Elmet	Conservative	2.80
39	Worcester	Conservative	2.80
40	Cardiff North	Conservative	3.11
41	Monmouth	Conservative	3.15
42	Tynemouth	Conservative	3.17
43	Keighley	Conservative	3.28
44	Redditch	Conservative	3.38
45	Loughborough	Conservative	3.49
46	Burton	Conservative	3.50
47	Northampton North	Conservative	3.58
48	Waveney	Conservative	3.63
49	Derby North	Conservative	3.77
50	Falmouth & Camborne	Conservative	3.85

LABOUR TARGET SEATS

TARGET NUMBER	CONSTITUENCY	HELD BY	SWING TO GAIN
51	Birmingham Hall Green	Conservative	3.91
52	Calder Valley	Conservative	4.00
53	High Peak	Conservative	4.02
54	Bury North	Conservative	4.04
55	Bolton West	Conservative	4.12
56	Oldham East & Saddleworth	Conservative	4.21
57	Leeds North East	Conservative	4.29
58	Gloucester	Conservative	4.36
59	Erewash	Conservative	4.51
60	Edinburgh Pentlands	Conservative	4.52
61	Bedford	Conservative	4.52
62	Battersea	Conservative	4.56
63	Milton Keynes South West	Conservative	4.58
64	Gravesham	Conservative	4.59
65	Wolverhampton South West	Conservative	4.72
66	Stockton South	Conservative	4.72
67	Birmingham Edgbaston	Conservative	4.97
68	Great Yarmouth	Conservative	4.99
69	Tamworth	Conservative	5.09
70	Stourbridge	Conservative	5.28
71	Conwy	Conservative	5.62
72	Welwyn Hatfield	Conservative	5.77
73	Peterborough	Conservative	5.85
74	Cleethorpes	Conservative	6.01
75	Blackpool North & Fleetwood	Conservative	6.07
76	Colne Valley	Conservative	6.12
77	Hammersmith & Fulham	Conservative	6.50
78	Stafford	Conservative	6.58
79	Aberdeen South	Conservative	6.73
80	Dumfries	Conservative	6.75
81	Luton North	Conservative	7.02
82	Watford	Conservative	7.06
83	Brigg & Goole	Conservative	7.08
84	Newark	Conservative	7.28
85	Pudsey	Conservative	7.30
86	Dartford	Conservative	7.34
87	Ribble South	Conservative	7.51
88	Selby	Conservative	7.74
89	Ealing North	Conservative	7.80
90	Putney	Conservative	7.80
91	Leeds North West	Conservative	7.88
92	Ceredigion	Plaid Cymru	7.92
93	Wrekin, The	Conservative	7.93
94	Broxtowe	Conservative	8.11
95	Wirral South	Conservative	8.13
96	Wyre Forest	Conservative	8.13
97	Stroud	Conservative	8.43
98	Southwark North & Bermondsey	Liberal Democrat	8.43
99	Hemel Hempstead	Conservative	8.66
100	Portsmouth North	Conservative	8.76

flare in its new party colour as we fly over it – red for Labour, blue
for Conservative, yellow for Liberal Democrat, and green for Plaid
Cymru if they fight off Mr Blair's challenge in Ceredigion. If he wins
20 of these 100 seats, Mr Blair will leave Mr Major clinging on by his
fingernails: if he wins 57 and does not lose any other seats, he will
have an overall majority.

THE LIBERAL DEMOCRAT TARGETS

The outcome of the election will be decided not just by the Tories'
struggle with Labour but with the Liberal Democrats too. There are a
handful of three-way marginals like Conwy in North Wales, Seb Coe's
seat in Falmouth and Camborne, and Colne Valley in West Yorkshire,
where it is hard to distinguish which of the opposition parties can
mount the strongest challenge to the Conservatives. But most of the
Liberal Democrats' top 50 target seats are straight fights with the
Tories. Brecon and Radnor is their best chance: only 130 votes
separated them from the Tories in 1992; 35th on the list of Liberal
Democrat targets is Jeremy Hanley's seat in Richmond, now called
Richmond Park, 44th is William Waldegrave's Bristol West and
Michael Howard, the Home Secretary had a majority of just under
9,000 in Folkestone and Hythe which puts him 47th on their target list.

Unluckily for Paddy Ashdown, his targets seats are only half the
number of Labour's. The Conservatives hold twice as many marginal
seats from Labour as they do from the Liberal Democrats. The
distribution of the vote means Mr Ashdown has to make double the
effort Mr Blair has to to gain the same number of seats. Indeed the
most vulnerable seats of all will fall three times more quickly to
Mr Blair than to Mr Ashdown.

But there is another striking feature of the Liberal Democrats' best
chances. The single most fertile region for them – the Southwest –
is one of the least promising for Labour. If Paddy Ashdown can attract
largely useless Labour votes in the Southwest (outside of the cities
of Bristol, Exeter and Plymouth where it is Labour that threatens
the Tories), he could double his parliamentary representation in one
sweep. And if Labour can attract useless Liberal Democrat votes in
some of its toughest battles with the Conservatives, it will do
disproportionately well at the expense of the Conservatives. If the
opposition could concentrate the anti-Tory vote behind the Labour
or Liberal Democrat candidate best placed to win in each seat, they
could devastate Mr Major and his party. Labour *did* attract some of
those tactical votes in key marginal seats last time – enough to make
a difference between defeat and victory in about ten seats, but we

LIBERAL DEMOCRAT TARGET SEATS

TARGET NUMBER	CONSTITUENCY	HELD BY	SWING TO GAIN
1	Brecon & Radnorshire	Conservative	0.15
2	Portsmouth South	Conservative	0.23
3	Oldham East & Saddleworth	Conservative	0.49
4	Hazel Grove	Conservative	0.85
5	Isle of Wight	Conservative	1.15
6	Conwy	Conservative	1.18
7	St Ives	Conservative	1.44
8	Ceredigion	Plaid Cymru	2.23
9	Taunton	Conservative	2.60
10	Devon West & Torridge	Conservative	2.71
11	Southport	Conservative	2.76
12	Hereford	Conservative	2.83
13	Falmouth & Camborne	Conservative	2.85
14	Liverpool Wavertree	Labour	3.29
15	Somerton & Frome	Conservative	3.56
16	Edinburgh West	Conservative	4.16
17	Birmingham Yardley	Labour	4.27
18	Colchester	Conservative	4.68
19	Greenwich & Woolwich	Labour	4.76
20	Weston-Super-Mare	Conservative	4.78
21	Torbay	Conservative	5.05
22	Twickenham	Conservative	5.12
23	Oxford West & Abingdon	Conservative	5.21
24	Aberdeenshire West & Kincardine	Conservative	5.24
25	Aberdeen South	Conservative	5.36
26	Aberdeen North	Labour	5.64
27	Chesterfield	Labour	5.73
28	Wells	Conservative	5.76
29	Eastbourne	Conservative	5.91
30	Sheffield Hillsborough	Labour	5.92
31	Dorset Mid & Poole North	Conservative	6.07
32	Lewes	Conservative	6.11
33	Hastings & Rye	Conservative	6.17
34	Cornwall South East	Conservative	6.42
35	Richmond Park	Conservative	7.10
36	Ribble Valley	Conservative	7.17
37	Dorset West	Conservative	7.34
38	Winchester	Conservative	7.39
39	Salisbury	Conservative	7.40
40	Colne Valley	Conservative	7.50
41	Teignbridge	Conservative	7.56
42	Leeds North West	Conservative	7.59
43	Totnes	Conservative	7.63
44	Bristol West	Conservative	7.98
45	Blyth Valley	Labour	8.18
46	Congleton	Conservative	8.39
47	Folkestone & Hythe	Conservative	8.49
48	Bridgwater	Conservative	8.54
49	Pudsey	Conservative	8.64
50	Northavon	Conservative	8.67

have yet to see a really effective tactical assault by any opposition in a British election.

SNP AND PLAID CYMRU TARGETS

Both the Nationalist parties are – rhetorically at least – scaling down the level of expectations about the number of seats they might capture. Indeed Plaid Cymru are looking to increase their overall share of the vote rather than targeting an ambitiously large number of seats. Like the SNP, their expectations of a Labour government means their best hope is beyond this election – anticipating the future beneficial effects of a reaction against a Labour government.

SCOTTISH NATIONAL PARTY TARGET SEATS

TARGET NUMBER	CONSTITUENCY	HELD BY	SWING TO GAIN
1	Inverness East, Nairn & Lochaber	Liberal Democrat	0.8
2	Galloway & Upper Nithsdale	Conservative	2.77
3	Perth	Conservative	3.04
4	Tayside North	Conservative	3.79
5	Western Isles	Labour	5.31
6	Argyll & Bute	Liberal Democrat	5.55
7	Dundee East	Labour	6.13
8	Aberdeen North	Labour	6.32
9	Kilmarnock & Loudoun	Labour	7.04
10	Edinburgh North & Leith	Labour	7.29
11	Glasgow Govan	Labour	7.71
12	Falkirk East	Labour	7.89
13	Ochil	Labour	8.5
14	Linlithgow	Labour	9.53
15	Ross, Skye & Inverness West	Liberal Democrat	9.93
16	Livingston	Labour	9.95
17	Clydesdale	Labour	10.76
18	Dunfermline West	Labour	10.85
19	Renfrewshire West	Labour	11.13
20	Kirkcaldy	Labour	11.48

PLAID CYMRU TARGET SEATS

TARGET NUMBER	CONSTITUENCY	HELD BY	SWING TO GAIN
1	Carmarthen East & Dinefwr	Labour	6.23
2	Llanelli	Labour	19.38
3	Carmarthen West & Pembrokeshire South	Labour	20.4
4	Clwyd South	Labour	22.29
5	Conwy	Conservative	24.02
6	Pontypridd	Labour	25.85
7	Clwyd West	Conservative	26.27
8	Caerphilly	Labour	26.99
9	Swansea West	Labour	27.58
10	Montgomeryshire	Liberal Democrat	27.96

THE SWINGOMETER

Seats are the hard currency of elections. Whoever wins 330 or more seats in the election will win no matter what happens to other indicators like the ups and downs of the share of the vote. But the best single measure of the relative performance of the parties in their various contests with each other will be swing. Once again the BBC's swingometer will be our earliest guide to the likely outcome. From the moment the very first seat is declared, its pendulum will instantly and automatically swing to the party that has gained the advantage over the other since the last election.

Things can, of course, go wrong: during one of the rehearsals in the last few months we practised a scenario in which Mr Major's majority in his safe seat of Huntingdon dropped a little. This should have registered a swing of 5 per cent on our swingometer. But – to my horror – the pendulum went past 5 per cent, travelling on smoothly through 10 per cent, then 20 per cent and finally off the swingometer altogether! It was embarrassing enough in rehearsal; it will be a lot more embarrassing if it happens on the night, but that is what rehearsals are for. For some reason in 1987 I did not rehearse in the brown suede shoes I wore on election night. If I had, and had noticed how much they stood out, I would have been spared the embarrassment of thousands of viewers calling in and remarking on them.

Swing sums up in one figure and in one very vivid display the net movement in the share of the vote between any two parties since the last election. Thus, if the net effect of all the switching around from the last election is that one person in every hundred who voted Conservative last time votes Labour this time, there will be a 1 per cent swing to Labour. In order to gain the 57 seats that would give Mr Blair an overall majority, his Labour party needs a swing of just over 4 per cent from the last election. If the swing is less than 1 per cent to Labour, Mr Major may just be able to hang on. And so a swing of anything between 1 per cent and 4 per cent would point to a hung parliament, in which neither of the main parties would have an overall majority, and they would have to look for support to the Liberal Democrats and other parties.

By its very nature, of course, a swingometer operates as a pendulum, which can swing either way. The experts, the opinion polls – even the body language of many Conservatives – all suggest that the swingometer will be trundling across the currently blue battleground. It's worth remembering, though, that many of the red piles on the Labour side of the pendulum, were during the 80s, blue. The Conservatives,

CONSERVATIVE TARGET SEATS

TARGET NUMBER	CONSTITUENCY	HELD BY	SWING TO GAIN
1	Slough	Labour	0.03
2	Rossendale & Darwen	Labour	0.04
3	Birmingham Yardley	Labour	0.19
4	Ipswich	Labour	0.31
5	Halifax	Labour	0.41
6	Angus	Scottish National Party	0.53
7	Cambridge	Labour	0.57
8	Devon North	Liberal Democrat	0.69
9	Forest of Dean	Labour	0.71
10	Dudley North	Labour	0.88
11	Swindon North	Labour	0.89
12	Southampton Itchen	Labour	0.92
13	Lincoln	Labour	0.93
14	Thurrock	Labour	1.09
15	Staffordshire Moorlands	Labour	1.10
16	Warwickshire North	Labour	1.22
17	Ynys Mon	Plaid Cymru	1.29
18	Lewisham East	Labour	1.30
19	Feltham & Heston	Labour	1.31
20	Nuneaton	Labour	1.37
21	Carmarthen West & Pembrokeshire S	Labour	1.53
22	Cornwall North	Liberal Democrat	1.54
23	Inverness East, Nairn & Lochaber	Liberal Democrat	1.61
24	Birmingham Northfield	Labour	1.70
25	Bath	Liberal Democrat	1.73
26	Cheltenham	Liberal Democrat	1.73
27	Dulwich & West Norwood	Labour	1.77
28	Hyndburn	Labour	1.83
29	Birmingham Selly Oak	Labour	1.87
30	Pendle	Labour	1.99
31	Carlisle	Labour	2.01
32	Lewisham West	Labour	2.09
33	Ayr	Labour	2.09
34	Tweeddale, Ettrick & Lauderdale	Liberal Democrat	2.18
35	Sherwood	Labour	2.32
36	Southampton Test	Labour	2.52
37	Darlington	Labour	2.53
38	Dudley South	Labour	2.57
39	Copeland	Labour	2.66
40	Bolton North East	Labour	2.70
41	Hampstead & Highgate	Labour	2.72
42	Ellesmere Port & Neston	Labour	2.89
43	Nottingham South	Labour	2.95
44	Walsall South	Labour	3.18
45	Barrow & Furness	Labour	3.22
46	Bristol North West	Labour	3.24
47	Cunninghame North	Labour	3.43
48	Ceredigion	Plaid Cymru	3.49
49	Ealing Acton & Shepherd's Bush	Labour	3.50
50	Wallasey	Labour	3.52

too, in their more optimistic moments, will be picturing target seats where, if the campaign were to be exceptionally successful, they could gleefully confound the pollsters once more (see page 269).

What seems a more likely scenario on the electoral map, however, is just how far a prevailing wind can carry Tony Blair into Tory territory. And in this, Labour have a big advantage in the distribution of votes. Their supporters, interestingly, it seems, are more efficiently dispersed.

So, a 4 per cent swing would put Labour at just over 39 per cent (35 per cent in 1992 + 4 per cent) and Conservatives on just under 39 per cent (43 per cent in 1992 −4 per cent) and yet see Labour with 40 seats more than the Tories. Indeed, Labour could win as many seats as the Conservatives with 2 per cent less vote share. Put another way the Tories need to be some 4 per cent ahead of Labour to win the election outright, whereas Labour need be only 1 per cent ahead to win.

We estimate the boundary changes have presented the Tories with a net gain of five seats, but the fact that the vote is now distributed so cost effectively for Labour gives them a valuable step-up.

That's reinforced by the largely complementary relationship – at least in the way support is placed geographically – between Labour and the Liberal Democrats.

So, large though the challenge is for Labour to break Harold Wilson's record, the Tories, too, face an enormous task – and not just politically. If they are to extend the run from 1979 which, at times to the despair of the opposition parties during the 80s, almost made them appear the only party of government, then the Conservatives will have to confound their critics to an extent which would make their 1992 comeback seem barely an effort.

RESULTS TO LOOK OUT FOR ON THE NIGHT

Basildon	Former world light-welterweight boxing champion, Terry Marsh, is standing for the Liberal Democrats in this likely early declaring seat which provided the most famous result of the 92 election.
Belfast West	Sinn Fein Leader, Gerry Adams, is contesting the seat he held 1983-92
Birmingham Yardley	Three-way marginal. Labour have a majority of just 162 votes. All three parties are within 2,000 votes.
Blackburn	Seat of the Labour Home Affairs Spokesman, Jack Straw.
Brecon & Radnorshire	Three-way marginal with a Conservative majority of just 130 over the Liberal Democrats. All three parties are within 4,400 votes.
Bristol East or South	Likely early declaring seat.
Cambridgeshire South	Robin Page, presenter of the BBC series *One Man and His Dog,* will stand for the Referendum Party.
Cambridgeshire North West	Conservative Party Chairman, Brian Mawhinney, is standing in this seat; he has been accused by Labour of 'chicken-running' from his old seat of Peterborough.
Canterbury	Cheryl Hall, who played the girlfriend of Tooting Popular Front leader Wolfie in BBC sitcom *Citizen Smith* is standing for Labour.
Cheltenham	Likely early declaring seat won by Liberal Democrat MP Nigel Jones in 1992.
Cities of London & Westminster	Sir Alan Walters, the former Economic Adviser to Mrs Thatcher will stand for the Referendum Party.
Conwy	Three-way marginal with a Conservative majority of just 995 over the Liberal Democrats. All three parties are within 3,400 votes.
Derbyshire South	Former Health Minister, Edwina Currie, has a majority of under 2,000 over Labour.
Dunfermline East	Seat of the Shadow Chancellor, Gordon Brown.
Edinburgh Pentlands	Malcolm Rifkind, Foreign Secretary, has a majority of 4,150 over Labour.

Falmouth & Camborne	Three-way marginal held by former Olympic athlete Seb Coe with a majority over the Liberal Democrats of under 3,300 votes. All three parties are within 4,500 votes. Peter de Savary, the entrepreneur, will stand for the Referendum Party.
Folkestone & Hythe	Seat of the Home Secretary, Michael Howard, who is to be challenged by zoo owner John Aspinall, standing for the Referendum Party.
Galloway & Upper Nithsdale	President of the Board of Trade, Ian Lang, has a majority of 2,400 over the SNP.
Gravesham	In every General Election since 1945 this seat has been won by the party that forms the new government. It is 64th on Labour's list of targets.
Guildford	Likely early declaring seat.
Hamilton South	Likely early declaring seat held by Shadow Scottish Secretary George Robertson.
Hartlepool	Seat of Labour's Election co-ordinator, Peter Mandelson.
Henley	Seat of the Deputy Prime Minister, Michael Heseltine.
Hull East	Seat of the Labour Deputy Leader, John Prescott.
Huntingdon	Seat of the Prime Minister, John Major, the safest Conservative seat after the 1992 election. Environmentalist David Bellamy is to stand for the Referendum Party.
Inverness East, Nairn & Lochaber	Four-way marginal; Liberal Democrats have a majority of just 736 votes. All four parties are within 1,650 votes.
Kensington & Chelsea	Former MP and diarist, Alan Clark, is standing in notionally the safest Conservative seat in this election.
Livingston	Seat of the Labour Foreign Affairs Spokesman, Robin Cook.
Manchester Blackley or Central	Likely early declaring seat.
Northampton North or South	Likely early declaring seat.
Old Bexley & Sidcup	Seat of the former Prime Minister and Father of the House, Sir Edward Heath, who is standing again, aged 80.
Oldham East & Saddleworth	Three-way marginal won by Chris Davies for the Liberal Democrats in 1995 by-election. Notionally Conservative-held, all three parties are within 3,000 votes.

Portsmouth South	Conservative MP David Martin has a notional majority of 2,423 over Liberal Democrat candidate, Mike Hancock, the former MP for the seat.
Putney	Former Cabinet Minister, David Mellor, facing a challenge from the Leader of the Referendum Party, Sir James Goldsmith.
Rochdale	The Liberal Democrat MP Liz Lynne has a notional majority of just 128 over the Labour candidate, Lorna Fitzsimmons, a former president of the National Union of Students.
Romsey	UK Independence Party Leader, Dr Alan Sked, is to contest the seat.
Ross, Skye and Inverness West	Donnie Munro, the lead singer with the Scottish rock/folk band Runrig is standing for Labour against the Liberal Democrat Charles Kennedy.
Rushcliffe	Seat of Kenneth Clarke, the Chancellor of the Exchequer.
Sedgefield	Seat of the Labour Leader, Tony Blair.
Stirling	Secretary of State for Scotland, Michael Forsyth, has a majority of just 236 votes over Labour.
Sunderland North or South	Likely early declaring seat.
Torbay	Likely early declarer, seat of spy-writer Rupert Allason (a.k.a. Nigel West).
Upper Bann	Seat of the Ulster Unionist Party Leader, David Trimble.
Vale of Glamorgan	The most vulnerable Conservative-held seat; sitting MP Walter Sweeney has a majority of just 19 votes over Labour.
West Bromwich West	Seat of the Speaker, Betty Boothroyd.
Western Isles	Anne Lorne Gillies, the Scottish writer, singer and television entertainer, is to contest the seat for the SNP.
Wokingham	Seat of the Tory leadership challenger, John Redwood.
Yeovil	Seat of the Liberal Democrat Leader, Paddy Ashdown.

COMPLETE LIST OF CONSTITUENCIES

The majority for each constituency shown in this table gives a notional majority that there would have been in the 1992 election if that election had been held on the basis of the 1997 constituency boundaries (see pages 239-240 for a fuller explanation).

ENGLAND

CONSTITUENCY	HELD BY	NOTIONAL MAJORITY	2ND PLACED
Aldershot	Conservative	18,716	Liberal Democrat
Aldridge-Brownhills	Conservative	11,024	Labour
Altrincham & Sale West	Conservative	15,616	Labour
Amber Valley	Conservative	1,283	Labour
Arundel & South Downs	Conservative	20,016	Liberal Democrat
Ashfield	Labour	12,963	Conservative
Ashford	Conservative	17,359	Liberal Democrat
Ashton under Lyne	Labour	15,432	Conservative
Aylesbury	Conservative	18,040	Liberal Democrat
Banbury	Conservative	15,731	Labour
Barking	Labour	7,180	Conservative
Barnsley Central	Labour	23,504	Conservative
Barnsley East & Mexborough	Labour	27,721	Conservative
Barnsley West & Penistone	Labour	14,504	Conservative
Barrow & Furness	Labour	3,578	Conservative
Basildon	Conservative	2,646	Labour
Basingstoke	Conservative	17,886	Labour
Bassetlaw	Labour	9,995	Conservative
Bath	Liberal Democrat	2,009	Conservative
Batley & Spen	Conservative	845	Labour
Battersea	Conservative	4,781	Labour
Beaconsfield	Conservative	23,864	Liberal Democrat
Beckenham	Conservative	22,813	Labour
Bedford	Conservative	4,545	Labour
Bedfordshire Mid	Conservative	21,545	Labour
Bedfordshire North East	Conservative	20,603	Labour
Bedfordshire South West	Conservative	17,340	Labour
Berwick-upon-Tweed	Liberal Democrat	5,043	Conservative
Bethnal Green & Bow	Labour	12,365	Liberal Democrat
Beverley & Holderness	Conservative	15,957	Liberal Democrat
Bexhill & Battle	Conservative	16,340	Liberal Democrat
Bexleyheath & Crayford	Conservative	12,003	Labour
Billericay	Conservative	20,998	Liberal Democrat
Birkenhead	Labour	17,613	Conservative
Birmingham Edgbaston	Conservative	5,056	Labour
Birmingham Erdington	Labour	8,523	Conservative
Birmingham Hall Green	Conservative	3,665	Labour
Birmingham Hodge Hill	Labour	7,068	Conservative
Birmingham Ladywood	Labour	21,469	Conservative
Birmingham Northfield	Labour	1,379	Conservative

ENGLAND

CONSTITUENCY	HELD BY	NOTIONAL MAJORITY	2ND PLACED
Birmingham Perry Barr	Labour	7,729	Conservative
Birmingham Selly Oak	Labour	2,060	Conservative
Birmingham Sparkbrook & Small Heath	Labour	18,448	Conservative
Birmingham Yardley	Labour	162	Conservative
Bishop Auckland	Labour	7,716	Conservative
Blaby	Conservative	19,669	Labour
Blackburn	Labour	6,027	Conservative
Blackpool North & Fleetwood	Conservative	7,276	Labour
Blackpool South	Conservative	394	Labour
Blaydon	Labour	13,343	Conservative
Blyth Valley	Labour	8,044	Liberal Democrat
Bognor Regis & Littlehampton	Conservative	15,007	Liberal Democrat
Bolsover	Labour	20,679	Conservative
Bolton North East	Labour	3,017	Conservative
Bolton South East	Labour	12,671	Conservative
Bolton West	Conservative	4,281	Labour
Bootle	Labour	27,120	Conservative
Boston & Skegness	Conservative	11,422	Labour
Bosworth	Conservative	14,131	Labour
Bournemouth East	Conservative	11,243	Liberal Democrat
Bournemouth West	Conservative	11,717	Liberal Democrat
Bracknell	Conservative	23,880	Labour
Bradford North	Labour	7,664	Conservative
Bradford South	Labour	4,902	Conservative
Bradford West	Labour	9,502	Conservative
Braintree	Conservative	13,388	Labour
Brent East	Labour	5,949	Conservative
Brent North	Conservative	10,230	Labour
Brent South	Labour	9,917	Conservative
Brentford & Isleworth	Conservative	1,675	Labour
Brentwood & Ongar	Conservative	15,175	Liberal Democrat
Bridgwater	Conservative	9,716	Liberal Democrat
Brigg & Goole	Conservative	7,241	Labour
Brighton Kemptown	Conservative	10,257	Labour
Brighton Pavilion	Conservative	2,530	Labour
Bristol East	Labour	5,282	Conservative
Bristol North West	Labour	3,871	Conservative
Bristol South	Labour	8,115	Conservative
Bristol West	Conservative	9,494	Liberal Democrat
Bromley & Chislehurst	Conservative	25,658	Liberal Democrat
Bromsgrove	Conservative	13,752	Labour
Broxbourne	Conservative	21,350	Labour
Broxtowe	Conservative	9,871	Labour
Buckingham	Conservative	20,644	Liberal Democrat
Burnley	Labour	11,491	Conservative
Burton	Conservative	4,127	Labour
Bury North	Conservative	4,764	Labour
Bury South	Conservative	728	Labour
Bury St Edmunds	Conservative	10,645	Liberal Democrat
Calder Valley	Conservative	4,878	Labour
Camberwell & Peckham	Labour	12,050	Conservative

ENGLAND

CONSTITUENCY	HELD BY	NOTIONAL MAJORITY	2ND PLACED
Cambridge	Labour	580	Conservative
Cambridgeshire North East	Conservative	13,161	Liberal Democrat
Cambridgeshire North West	Conservative	18,809	Labour
Cambridgeshire South	Conservative	18,938	Liberal Democrat
Cambridgeshire South East	Conservative	20,863	Liberal Democrat
Cannock Chase	Labour	6,469	Conservative
Canterbury	Conservative	9,997	Liberal Democrat
Carlisle	Labour	1,921	Conservative
Carshalton & Wallington	Conservative	9,943	Liberal Democrat
Castle Point	Conservative	16,830	Labour
Charnwood	Conservative	22,600	Labour
Chatham & Aylesford	Conservative	13,423	Labour
Cheadle	Conservative	15,976	Liberal Democrat
Chelmsford West	Conservative	16,186	Liberal Democrat
Cheltenham	Liberal Democrat	1,947	Conservative
Chesham & Amersham	Conservative	21,601	Liberal Democrat
Chester, City of	Conservative	2,360	Labour
Chesterfield	Labour	6,414	Liberal Democrat
Chichester	Conservative	19,281	Liberal Democrat
Chingford & Woodford Green	Conservative	20,201	Labour
Chipping Barnet	Conservative	16,213	Labour
Chorley	Conservative	2,524	Labour
Christchurch	Conservative	22,324	Liberal Democrat
Cities of London & Westminster	Conservative	15,144	Labour
Cleethorpes	Conservative	6,413	Labour
Colchester	Conservative	5,268	Liberal Democrat
Colne Valley	Conservative	7,225	Labour
Congleton	Conservative	9,350	Liberal Democrat
Copeland	Labour	2,439	Conservative
Corby	Conservative	342	Labour
Cornwall North	Liberal Democrat	1,921	Conservative
Cornwall South East	Conservative	7,704	Liberal Democrat
Cotswold	Conservative	11,017	Liberal Democrat
Coventry North East	Labour	12,229	Conservative
Coventry North West	Labour	8,658	Conservative
Coventry South	Conservative	2,904	Labour
Crawley	Conservative	1,890	Labour
Crewe & Nantwich	Labour	4,871	Conservative
Crosby	Conservative	9,591	Labour
Croydon Central	Conservative	14,661	Labour
Croydon North	Conservative	160	Labour
Croydon South	Conservative	23,338	Liberal Democrat
Dagenham	Labour	6,447	Conservative
Darlington	Labour	2,798	Conservative
Dartford	Conservative	8,314	Labour
Daventry	Conservative	21,011	Labour
Denton & Reddish	Labour	10,154	Conservative
Derby North	Conservative	4,453	Labour
Derby South	Labour	4,227	Conservative
Derbyshire North East	Labour	6,270	Conservative
Derbyshire South	Conservative	1,947	Labour

ENGLAND

CONSTITUENCY	HELD BY	NOTIONAL MAJORITY	2ND PLACED
Derbyshire West	Conservative	18,120	Liberal Democrat
Devizes	Conservative	13,019	Liberal Democrat
Devon East	Conservative	13,993	Liberal Democrat
Devon North	Liberal Democrat	793	Conservative
Devon South West	Conservative	17,130	Liberal Democrat
Devon West & Torridge	Conservative	3,271	Liberal Democrat
Dewsbury	Labour	3,549	Conservative
Don Valley	Labour	7,119	Conservative
Doncaster Central	Labour	10,682	Conservative
Doncaster North	Labour	19,141	Conservative
Dorset Mid & Poole North	Conservative	6,054	Liberal Democrat
Dorset North	Conservative	10,071	Liberal Democrat
Dorset South	Conservative	12,617	Liberal Democrat
Dorset West	Conservative	8,011	Liberal Democrat
Dover	Conservative	860	Labour
Dudley North	Labour	954	Conservative
Dudley South	Labour	2,729	Conservative
Dulwich & West Norwood	Labour	1,803	Conservative
Durham North	Labour	17,764	Conservative
Durham North West	Labour	15,666	Conservative
Durham, City of	Labour	15,058	Conservative
Ealing Acton & Shepherd's Bush	Labour	3,471	Conservative
Ealing North	Conservative	9,075	Labour
Ealing Southall	Labour	5,031	Conservative
Easington	Labour	26,390	Conservative
East Ham	Labour	9,461	Conservative
Eastbourne	Conservative	6,809	Liberal Democrat
Eastleigh	Conservative	11,912	Liberal Democrat
Eccles	Labour	14,230	Conservative
Eddisbury	Conservative	10,996	Labour
Edmonton	Conservative	593	Labour
Ellesmere Port & Neston	Labour	3,233	Conservative
Elmet	Conservative	3,261	Labour
Eltham	Conservative	1,780	Labour
Enfield North	Conservative	9,430	Labour
Enfield Southgate	Conservative	15,545	Labour
Epping Forest	Conservative	21,183	Labour
Epsom & Ewell	Conservative	22,060	Liberal Democrat
Erewash	Conservative	5,723	Labour
Erith & Thamesmead	Labour	5,630	Conservative
Esher & Walton	Conservative	21,224	Liberal Democrat
Essex North	Conservative	19,250	Liberal Democrat
Exeter	Conservative	3,064	Labour
Falmouth & Camborne	Conservative	3,267	Liberal Democrat
Fareham	Conservative	20,099	Liberal Democrat
Faversham & Kent Mid	Conservative	19,599	Labour
Feltham & Heston	Labour	1,400	Conservative
Finchley & Golders Green	Conservative	12,474	Labour
Folkestone & Hythe	Conservative	8,911	Liberal Democrat
Forest of Dean	Labour	732	Conservative
Fylde	Conservative	20,912	Liberal Democrat

ENGLAND

CONSTITUENCY	HELD BY	NOTIONAL MAJORITY	2ND PLACED
Gainsborough	Conservative	13,926	Liberal Democrat
Gateshead East & Washington W	Labour	14,700	Conservative
Gedling	Conservative	10,637	Labour
Gillingham	Conservative	15,760	Labour
Gloucester	Conservative	5,407	Labour
Gosport	Conservative	16,318	Liberal Democrat
Grantham & Stamford	Conservative	17,158	Labour
Gravesham	Conservative	5,368	Labour
Grimsby	Labour	7,506	Conservative
Great Yarmouth	Conservative	5,309	Labour
Greenwich & Woolwich	Labour	4,473	Liberal Democrat
Guildford	Conservative	13,342	Liberal Democrat
Hackney North & Stoke Newington	Labour	10,727	Conservative
Hackney South & Shoreditch	Labour	9,003	Conservative
Halesowen & Rowley Regis	Conservative	125	Labour
Halifax	Labour	478	Conservative
Haltemprice & Howden	Conservative	17,313	Liberal Democrat
Halton	Labour	14,937	Conservative
Hammersmith & Fulham	Conservative	7,174	Labour
Hampshire East	Conservative	19,657	Liberal Democrat
Hampshire North East	Conservative	20,540	Liberal Democrat
Hampshire North West	Conservative	17,164	Liberal Democrat
Hampstead & Highgate	Labour	2,477	Conservative
Harborough	Conservative	10,152	Liberal Democrat
Harlow	Conservative	1,687	Labour
Harrogate & Knaresborough	Conservative	9,211	Liberal Democrat
Harrow East	Conservative	11,405	Labour
Harrow West	Conservative	17,890	Labour
Hartlepool	Labour	8,782	Conservative
Harwich	Conservative	15,325	Labour
Hastings & Rye	Conservative	6,634	Liberal Democrat
Havant	Conservative	14,169	Liberal Democrat
Hayes & Harlington	Conservative	44	Labour
Hazel Grove	Conservative	929	Liberal Democrat
Hemel Hempstead	Conservative	10,158	Labour
Hemsworth	Labour	19,801	Conservative
Hendon	Conservative	10,848	Labour
Henley	Conservative	19,043	Liberal Democrat
Hereford	Conservative	3,154	Liberal Democrat
Hertford & Stortford	Conservative	17,534	Liberal Democrat
Hertfordshire North East	Conservative	14,136	Liberal Democrat
Hertfordshire South West	Conservative	21,155	Liberal Democrat
Hertsmere	Conservative	18,966	Labour
Hexham	Conservative	13,438	Labour
Heywood & Middleton	Labour	8,294	Conservative
High Peak	Conservative	4,818	Labour
Hitchin & Harpenden	Conservative	22,636	Liberal Democrat
Holborn & St Pancras	Labour	9,787	Conservative
Hornchurch	Conservative	9,165	Labour
Hornsey & Wood Green	Labour	5,177	Conservative
Horsham	Conservative	22,691	Liberal Democrat

ENGLAND

CONSTITUENCY	HELD BY	NOTIONAL MAJORITY	2ND PLACED
Houghton & Washington East	Labour	20,949	Conservative
Hove	Conservative	12,268	Labour
Huddersfield	Labour	7,258	Conservative
Hull East	Labour	18,723	Conservative
Hull North	Labour	15384	Conservative
Hull West & Hessle	Labour	9,617	Conservative
Huntingdon	Conservative	21,971	Liberal Democrat
Hyndburn	Labour	2,031	Conservative
Ilford North	Conservative	14,049	Labour
Ilford South	Conservative	2,530	Labour
Ipswich	Labour	335	Conservative
Isle of Wight	Conservative	1,827	Liberal Democrat
Islington North	Labour	12,784	Conservative
Islington South & Finsbury	Labour	10,551	Conservative
Jarrow	Labour	18,735	Conservative
Keighley	Conservative	3,596	Labour
Kensington & Chelsea	Conservative	21,899	Labour
Kettering	Conservative	12,187	Labour
Kingston & Surbiton	Conservative	15,164	Liberal Democrat
Kingswood	Conservative	3,340	Labour
Knowsley North & Sefton East	Labour	15,386	Conservative
Knowsley South	Labour	26,135	Conservative
Lancashire West	Labour	4,227	Conservative
Lancaster & Wyre	Conservative	11,284	Labour
Leeds Central	Labour	18,992	Conservative
Leeds East	Labour	12,697	Conservative
Leeds North East	Conservative	4,244	Labour
Leeds North West	Conservative	7,671	Liberal Democrat
Leeds West	Labour	13,828	Conservative
Leicester East	Labour	11,316	Conservative
Leicester South	Labour	9,440	Conservative
Leicester West	Labour	3,978	Conservative
Leicestershire North West	Conservative	866	Labour
Leigh	Labour	16,855	Conservative
Leominster	Conservative	14,601	Liberal Democrat
Lewes	Conservative	6,337	Liberal Democrat
Lewisham Deptford	Labour	12,421	Conservative
Lewisham East	Labour	1,123	Conservative
Lewisham West	Labour	1,809	Conservative
Leyton & Wanstead	Labour	6,769	Conservative
Lichfield	Conservative	10,590	Labour
Lincoln	Labour	964	Conservative
Liverpool Garston	Labour	12,874	Conservative
Liverpool Riverside	Labour	21,016	Liberal Democrat
Liverpool Walton	Labour	28,299	Conservative
Liverpool Wavertree	Labour	3,380	Liberal Democrat
Liverpool West Derby	Labour	23,533	Liberal Democrat
Loughborough	Conservative	3,492	Labour
Louth & Horncastle	Conservative	10,970	Liberal Democrat
Ludlow	Conservative	12,307	Liberal Democrat
Luton North	Conservative	7,357	Labour

ENGLAND

CONSTITUENCY	HELD BY	NOTIONAL MAJORITY	2ND PLACED
Luton South	Conservative	532	Labour
Macclesfield	Conservative	19,130	Labour
Maidenhead	Conservative	17,496	Liberal Democrat
Maidstone & The Weald	Conservative	14,714	Liberal Democrat
Makerfield	Labour	20,147	Conservative
Maldon & Chelmsford East	Conservative	21,585	Liberal Democrat
Manchester Blackley	Labour	15,692	Conservative
Manchester Central	Labour	19,428	Conservative
Manchester Gorton	Labour	16,270	Conservative
Manchester Withington	Labour	9,714	Conservative
Mansfield	Labour	11,724	Conservative
Medway	Conservative	8,787	Labour
Meriden	Conservative	14,699	Labour
Middlesbrough	Labour	17,119	Conservative
Middlesbrough South & Cleveland East	Conservative	1,401	Labour
Milton Keynes North East	Conservative	14,176	Labour
Milton Keynes South West	Conservative	4,687	Labour
Mitcham & Morden	Conservative	17,34	Labour
Mole Valley	Conservative	18,827	Liberal Democrat
Morecambe & Lunesdale	Conservative	10,572	Labour
Morley & Rothwell	Labour	6,320	Conservative
New Forest East	Conservative	10,348	Liberal Democrat
New Forest West	Conservative	15,399	Liberal Democrat
Newark	Conservative	8,229	Labour
Newbury	Conservative	11,057	Liberal Democrat
Newcastle-under-Lyme	Labour	9,839	Conservative
Newcastle upon Tyne Central	Labour	7,888	Conservative
Newcastle upon Tyne East & Wallsend	Labour	16,045	Conservative
Newcastle upon Tyne North	Labour	8,946	Conservative
Norfolk Mid	Conservative	16,944	Labour
Norfolk North	Conservative	12,445	Liberal Democrat
Norfolk North West	Conservative	11,564	Labour
Norfolk South	Conservative	16,364	Liberal Democrat
Norfolk South West	Conservative	17,250	Labour
Normanton	Labour	7,192	Conservative
Northampton North	Conservative	4,067	Labour
Northampton South	Conservative	15,044	Labour
Northavon	Conservative	10,941	Liberal Democrat
Norwich North	Conservative	2,270	Labour
Norwich South	Labour	4,350	Conservative
Nottingham East	Labour	7,680	Conservative
Nottingham North	Labour	10,743	Conservative
Nottingham South	Labour	3,181	Conservative
Nuneaton	Labour	1,631	Conservative
Old Bexley & Sidcup	Conservative	19,572	Labour
Oldham East & Saddleworth	Conservative	559	Liberal Democrat
Oldham West & Royton	Labour	5,794	Conservative
Orpington	Conservative	17,930	Liberal Democrat
Oxford East	Labour	8,313	Conservative
Oxford West & Abingdon	Conservative	6,222	Liberal Democrat
Pendle	Labour	2,113	Conservative

ENGLAND

CONSTITUENCY	HELD BY	NOTIONAL MAJORITY	2ND PLACED
Penrith & The Border	Conservative	15,182	Liberal Democrat
Peterborough	Conservative	6,254	Labour
Plymouth Devonport	Labour	6,766	Conservative
Plymouth Sutton	Conservative	1,060	Labour
Pontefract & Castleford	Labour	23,495	Conservative
Poole	Conservative	12,981	Liberal Democrat
Poplar & Canning Town	Labour	10,418	Conservative
Portsmouth North	Conservative	8,758	Labour
Portsmouth South	Conservative	242	Liberal Democrat
Preston	Labour	11,466	Conservative
Pudsey	Conservative	8,372	Labour
Putney	Conservative	7,526	Labour
Rayleigh	Conservative	21,197	Liberal Democrat
Reading East	Conservative	10,584	Labour
Reading West	Conservative	12,632	Labour
Redcar	Labour	11,414	Conservative
Redditch	Conservative	3,287	Labour
Regent's Park & Kensington North	Labour	3,814	Conservative
Reigate	Conservative	16,940	Liberal Democrat
Ribble South	Conservative	8,840	Labour
Ribble Valley	Conservative	8,629	Liberal Democrat
Richmond (Yorks)	Conservative	16,707	Liberal Democrat
Richmond Park	Conservative	8,384	Liberal Democrat
Rochdale	Liberal Democrat	128	Labour
Rochford & Southend East	Conservative	16,077	Labour
Romford	Conservative	14,064	Labour
Romsey	Conservative	21,722	Liberal Democrat
Rossendale & Darwen	Labour	49	Conservative
Rother Valley	Labour	17,222	Conservative
Rotherham	Labour	17,561	Conservative
Rugby & Kenilworth	Conservative	13,324	Labour
Ruislip Northwood	Conservative	20,609	Labour
Runnymede & Weybridge	Conservative	22,740	Liberal Democrat
Rushcliffe	Conservative	19,766	Labour
Rutland & Melton	Conservative	22,581	Liberal Democrat
Ryedale	Conservative	12,998	Liberal Democrat
Saffron Walden	Conservative	16,493	Liberal Democrat
St Albans	Conservative	9,134	Liberal Democrat
St Helens North	Labour	16,244	Conservative
St Helens South	Labour	18,309	Conservative
St Ives	Conservative	1,645	Liberal Democrat
Salford	Labour	12,987	Conservative
Salisbury	Conservative	8,973	Liberal Democrat
Scarborough & Whitby	Conservative	11,734	Labour
Scunthorpe	Labour	8,903	Conservative
Sedgefield	Labour	17,230	Conservative
Selby	Conservative	8,987	Labour
Sevenoaks	Conservative	17,687	Liberal Democrat
Sheffield Attercliffe	Labour	15,480	Conservative
Sheffield Brightside	Labour	22,681	Conservative
Sheffield Central	Labour	17,380	Liberal Democrat

ENGLAND

CONSTITUENCY	HELD BY	NOTIONAL MAJORITY	2ND PLACED
Sheffield Hallam	Conservative	8,440	Liberal Democrat
Sheffield Heeley	Labour	14,954	Conservative
Sheffield Hillsborough	Labour	7,063	Liberal Democrat
Sherwood	Labour	2,910	Conservative
Shipley	Conservative	12,382	Labour
Shrewsbury & Atcham	Conservative	10,965	Liberal Democrat
Shropshire North	Conservative	13,181	Labour
Sittingbourne & Sheppey	Conservative	11,128	Liberal Democrat
Skipton & Ripon	Conservative	17,397	Liberal Democrat
Sleaford & North Hykeham	Conservative	19,482	Labour
Slough	Labour	36	Conservative
Solihull	Conservative	25,075	Liberal Democrat
Somerton & Frome	Conservative	4,251	Liberal Democrat
South Holland & The Deepings	Conservative	16,763	Labour
South Shields	Labour	15,821	Conservative
Southampton Itchen	Labour	1,053	Conservative
Southampton Test	Labour	2,722	Conservative
Southend West	Conservative	11,902	Liberal Democrat
Southport	Conservative	3,063	Liberal Democrat
Southwark North & Bermondsey	Liberal Democrat	7,269	Labour
Spelthorne	Conservative	19,843	Labour
Stafford	Conservative	7,235	Labour
Staffordshire Moorlands	Labour	1,185	Conservative
Staffordshire South	Conservative	18,615	Labour
Stalybridge & Hyde	Labour	7,727	Conservative
Stevenage	Conservative	2,919	Labour
Stockport	Labour	5,468	Conservative
Stockton North	Labour	10,666	Conservative
Stockton South	Conservative	4,896	Labour
Stoke-on-Trent Central	Labour	13,420	Conservative
Stoke-on-Trent North	Labour	9,504	Conservative
Stoke-on-Trent South	Labour	6,909	Conservative
Stone	Conservative	15,079	Labour
Stourbridge	Conservative	5,388	Labour
Stratford-on-Avon	Conservative	21,005	Liberal Democrat
Streatham	Labour	5,471	Conservative
Stretford & Urmston	Labour	4,482	Conservative
Stroud	Conservative	10,581	Labour
Suffolk Central & Ipswich North	Conservative	18,006	Liberal Democrat
Suffolk Coastal	Conservative	16,705	Labour
Suffolk South	Conservative	13,208	Liberal Democrat
Suffolk West	Conservative	15,763	Labour
Sunderland North	Labour	14,226	Conservative
Sunderland South	Labour	14,123	Conservative
Surrey East	Conservative	19,972	Liberal Democrat
Surrey Heath	Conservative	22,754	Liberal Democrat
Surrey South West	Conservative	14,975	Liberal Democrat
Sussex Mid	Conservative	17,407	Liberal Democrat
Sutton & Cheam	Conservative	10,756	Liberal Democrat
Sutton Coldfield	Conservative	26,036	Liberal Democrat
Swindon North	Labour	882	Conservative

ENGLAND

CONSTITUENCY	HELD BY	NOTIONAL MAJORITY	2ND PLACED
Swindon South	Conservative	10,103	Labour
Tamworth	Conservative	5,405	Labour
Tatton	Conservative	22,365	Labour
Taunton	Conservative	3,336	Liberal Democrat
Teignbridge	Conservative	9,548	Liberal Democrat
Telford	Labour	7,927	Conservative
Tewkesbury	Conservative	9,797	Liberal Democrat
Thanet North	Conservative	18,210	Labour
Thanet South	Conservative	11,499	Labour
Thurrock	Labour	1,172	Conservative
Tiverton & Honiton	Conservative	11,664	Liberal Democrat
Tonbridge & Malling	Conservative	20,741	Liberal Democrat
Tooting	Labour	4,107	Conservative
Torbay	Conservative	5,787	Liberal Democrat
Totnes	Conservative	8,626	Liberal Democrat
Tottenham	Labour	11,968	Conservative
Truro & St Austell	Liberal Democrat	7,570	Conservative
Tunbridge Wells	Conservative	13,146	Liberal Democrat
Twickenham	Conservative	6,121	Liberal Democrat
Tyne Bridge	Labour	19,077	Conservative
Tynemouth	Conservative	3,529	Labour
Tyneside North	Labour	17,634	Conservative
Upminster	Conservative	11,157	Labour
Uxbridge	Conservative	12,368	Labour
Vale of York	Conservative	17,228	Liberal Democrat
Vauxhall	Labour	12,761	Conservative
Wakefield	Labour	4,224	Conservative
Wallasey	Labour	3,809	Conservative
Walsall North	Labour	3,824	Conservative
Walsall South	Labour	3,178	Conservative
Walthamstow	Labour	3,351	Conservative
Wansbeck	Labour	18,174	Conservative
Wansdyke	Conservative	11,770	Labour
Wantage	Conservative	16,473	Liberal Democrat
Warley	Labour	8,409	Conservative
Warrington North	Labour	10,206	Conservative
Warrington South	Conservative	2,753	Labour
Warwick & Leamington	Conservative	11,464	Labour
Warwickshire North	Labour	1,453	Conservative
Watford	Conservative	8,263	Labour
Waveney	Conservative	4,376	Labour
Wealden	Conservative	20,928	Liberal Democrat
Weaver Vale	Labour	6,750	Conservative
Wellingborough	Conservative	11,816	Labour
Wells	Conservative	6,649	Liberal Democrat
Welwyn Hatfield	Conservative	6,583	Labour
Wentworth	Labour	22,449	Conservative
West Bromwich East	Labour	4,985	Conservative
West Bromwich West	Labour	6,174	Conservative
West Ham	Labour	10,488	Conservative
Westbury	Conservative	11,153	Liberal Democrat

ENGLAND/NORTHERN IRELAND

CONSTITUENCY	HELD BY	NOTIONAL MAJORITY	2ND PLACED
Westmorland & Lonsdale	Conservative	15,394	Liberal Democrat
Weston-Super-Mare	Conservative	5,372	Liberal Democrat
Wigan	Labour	17,490	Conservative
Wiltshire North	Conservative	14,760	Liberal Democrat
Wimbledon	Conservative	14,761	Labour
Winchester	Conservative	9,318	Liberal Democrat
Windsor	Conservative	14,551	Liberal Democrat
Wirral South	Conservative	8,168	Labour
Wirral West	Conservative	11,064	Labour
Witney	Conservative	20,593	Liberal Democrat
Woking	Conservative	17,731	Liberal Democrat
Wokingham	Conservative	19,117	Liberal Democrat
Wolverhampton North East	Labour	3,747	Conservative
Wolverhampton South East	Labour	10,240	Conservative
Wolverhampton South West	Conservative	4,966	Labour
Woodspring	Conservative	12,006	Liberal Democrat
Worcester	Conservative	2,947	Labour
Worcestershire Mid	Conservative	14,454	Liberal Democrat
Worcestershire West	Conservative	12,869	Liberal Democrat
Workington	Labour	9,600	Conservative
Worsley	Labour	11,403	Conservative
Worthing East & Shoreham	Conservative	9,905	Liberal Democrat
Worthing West	Conservative	19,279	Liberal Democrat
Wrekin, The	Conservative	7,720	Labour
Wycombe	Conservative	17,058	Liberal Democrat
Wyre Forest	Conservative	9,585	Labour
Wythenshawe & Sale East	Labour	7,958	Conservative
Yeovil	Liberal Democrat	8,744	Conservative
York, City of	Labour	6,342	Conservative
Yorkshire East	Conservative	12,272	Labour

NORTHERN IRELAND

Antrim East	UUP	6,546	APNI
Antrim North	DUP	14,936	UUP
Antrim South	UUP	23,050	SDLP
Belfast East	DUP	11,298	APNI
Belfast North	UUP	14,392	SDLP
Belfast South	UUP	16,337	APNI
Belfast West	SDLP	1,018	SF
Down North	UPUP	2,265	Conservative
Down South	SDLP	10,877	UUP
Fermanagh & South Tyrone	UUP	14,089	SDLP
Foyle	SDLP	12,482	DUP
Lagan Valley	UUP	25,504	APNI
Londonderry East	UUP	16,153	SDLP
Newry & Armagh	SDLP	6,810	UUP
Strangford	UUP	12,178	DUP
Tyrone West	DUP	3,148	SDLP
Ulster Mid	DUP	4,914	SDLP
Upper Bann	UUP	16,163	SDLP

SCOTLAND

CONSTITUENCY	HELD BY	NOTIONAL MAJORITY	2ND PLACED
Aberdeen Central	Labour	5,397	Conservative
Aberdeen North	Labour	4,237	Liberal Democrat
Aberdeen South	Conservative	4,725	Liberal Democrat
Aberdeenshire West & Kincardine	Conservative	4,437	Liberal Democrat
Airdrie & Shotts	Labour	19655	SNP
Angus	SNP	473	Conservative
Argyll & Bute	Liberal Democrat	2,622	Conservative
Ayr	Labour	1,895	Conservative
Banff & Buchan	SNP	6,568	Conservative
Caithness, Sutherland & Easter Ross	Liberal Democrat	6,759	Conservative
Carrick, Cumnock & Doon Valley	Labour	14,686	Conservative
Clydebank & Milngavie	Labour	11,420	Conservative
Clydesdale	Labour	10,187	Conservative
Coatbridge & Chryston	Labour	18,100	SNP
Cumbernauld & Kilsyth	Labour	9,215	SNP
Cunninghame North	Labour	2,939	Conservative
Cunninghame South	Labour	10,680	SNP
Dumbarton	Labour	6,129	Conservative
Dumfries	Conservative	6,766	Labour
Dundee East	Labour	5,517	SNP
Dundee West	Labour	9,464	SNP
Dunfermline East	Labour	17,755	Conservative
Dunfermline West	Labour	7,184	Conservative
East Kilbride	Labour	11,940	SNP
East Lothian	Labour	7,099	Conservative
Eastwood	Conservative	11,838	Labour
Edinburgh Central	Labour	3,757	Conservative
Edinburgh East & Musselburgh	Labour	9,101	Conservative
Edinburgh North & Leith	Labour	4,334	Conservative
Edinburgh Pentlands	Conservative	4,148	Labour
Edinburgh South	Labour	4,156	Conservative
Edinburgh West	Conservative	4,291	Liberal Democrat
Falkirk East	Labour	6,856	SNP
Falkirk West	Labour	11,430	SNP
Fife Central	Labour	10,991	SNP
Fife North East	Liberal Democrat	3,303	Conservative
Galloway & Upper Nithsdale	Conservative	2,400	SNP
Glasgow Anniesland	Labour	13,589	SNP
Glasgow Baillieston	Labour	14,165	SNP
Glasgow Cathcart	Labour	10,552	Conservative
Glasgow Govan	Labour	5,609	SNP
Glasgow Kelvin	Labour	9,989	SNP
Glasgow Maryhill	Labour	14,512	SNP
Glasgow Pollok	Labour	9,453	SNP
Glasgow Rutherglen	Labour	13,299	Conservative
Glasgow Shettleston	Labour	15,644	SNP
Glasgow Springburn	Labour	16,197	SNP
Gordon	Conservative	8,486	Liberal Democrat
Greenock & Inverclyde	Labour	10,238	Conservative
Hamilton North & Bellshill	Labour	15,490	SNP
Hamilton South	Labour	12,742	SNP

SCOTLAND

CONSTITUENCY	HELD BY	NOTIONAL MAJORITY	2ND PLACED
Inverness East, Nairn & Lochaber	Liberal Democrat	736	SNP
Kilmarnock & Loudoun	Labour	6,979	SNP
Kirkcaldy	Labour	8,685	SNP
Linlithgow	Labour	7,797	SNP
Livingston	Labour	8,448	SNP
Midlothian	Labour	8,864	SNP
Moray	SNP	2,927	Conservative
Motherwell & Wishaw	Labour	14,090	SNP
Ochil	Labour	7,350	SNP
Orkney & Shetland	Liberal Democrat	5,033	Conservative
Paisley North	Labour	10,414	SNP
Paisley South	Labour	10,469	SNP
Perth	Conservative	2,726	SNP
Renfrewshire West	Labour	6,046	Conservative
Ross, Skye & Inverness West	Liberal Democrat	6,505	Conservative
Roxburgh & Berwickshire	Liberal Democrat	4,453	Conservative
Stirling	Conservative	236	Labour
Strathkelvin & Bearsden	Labour	6,948	Conservative
Tayside North	Conservative	3,439	SNP
Tweeddale, Ettrick & Lauderdale	Liberal Democrat	1,735	Conservative
Western Isles	Labour	1,703	SNP

WALES

CONSTITUENCY	HELD BY	NOTIONAL MAJORITY	2ND PLACED
Aberavon	Labour	21,310	Conservative
Alyn & Deeside	Labour	6,387	Conservative
Blaenau Gwent	Labour	30,067	Conservative
Brecon & Radnorshire	Conservative	130	Liberal Democrat
Bridgend	Labour	7,326	Conservative
Caernarfon	PC	14,476	Conservative
Caerphilly	Labour	22,672	Conservative
Cardiff Central	Labour	3,465	Conservative
Cardiff North	Conservative	2,969	Labour
Cardiff South & Penarth	Labour	10,425	Conservative
Cardiff West	Labour	9,291	Conservative
Carmarthen East & Dinefwr	Labour	5,490	PC
Carmarthen West & Pembrokeshire S	Labour	1,310	Conservative
Ceredigion	PC	1,893	Liberal Democrat
Clwyd South	Labour	8,332	Conservative
Clwyd West	Conservative	7,313	Labour
Conwy	Conservative	995	Liberal Democrat
Cynon Valley	Labour	21,364	Conservative
Delyn	Labour	3,178	Conservative
Gower	Labour	7,048	Conservative
Islwyn	Labour	2,4728	Conservative
Llanelli	Labour	17,271	Conservative
Meirionnydd Nant Conwy	PC	4,613	Conservative
Merthyr Tydfil & Rhymney	Labour	26,713	Liberal Democrat
Monmouth	Conservative	3,204	Labour
Montgomeryshire	Liberal Democrat	5,209	Conservative
Neath	Labour	23,975	Conservative
Newport East	Labour	9,899	Conservative
Newport West	Labour	7,779	Conservative
Ogmore	Labour	23,827	Conservative
Pontypridd	Labour	19,797	Conservative
Preseli Pembrokeshire	Conservative	603	Labour
Rhondda	Labour	28,816	PC
Swansea East	Labour	23,482	Conservative
Swansea West	Labour	9,478	Conservative
Torfaen	Labour	20,754	Conservative
Vale of Clwyd	Conservative	2,177	Labour
Vale of Glamorgan	Conservative	19	Labour
Wrexham	Labour	7,090	Conservative
Ynys Mon	PC	1,106	Con